Translating Law

PEFC/16-33-111
CATG-PEFC-052
www.pefc.org

TOPICS IN TRANSLATION
Series Editors: Susan Bassnett, *University of Warwick, UK*
Edwin Gentzler, *University of Massachusetts, Amherst, USA*
Editor for Translation in the Commercial Environment:
Geoffrey Samuelsson-Brown, University of Surrey, UK

For more details of these or any other of our publications, please contact:
Multilingual Matters, Frankfurt Lodge, Clevedon Hall,
Victoria Road, Clevedon, BS21 7HH, England
http://www.multilingual-matters.com

TOPICS IN TRANSLATION 33
Series Editors: Susan Bassnett, *University of Warwick* and
Edwin Gentzler, *University of Massachusetts, Amherst*

Translating Law

Deborah Cao

MULTILINGUAL MATTERS LTD
Clevedon • Buffalo • Toronto

Library of Congress Cataloging in Publication Data
Cao, Deborah
Translating Law/Deborah Cao.
Topics in Translation: 33
Includes bibliographical references and index.
1. Law–Translating. 2. Law–Language. 3. Law–Interpretation and construction.
I. Title.
K213.C365 2007
340–dc22   2006022563

British Library Cataloguing in Publication Data
A catalogue entry for this book is available from the British Library.

ISBN-13: 978-1-85359-954-5 (hbk)

Multilingual Matters Ltd
UK: Frankfurt Lodge, Clevedon Hall, Victoria Road, Clevedon BS21 7HH.
USA: UTP, 2250 Military Road, Tonawanda, NY 14150, USA.
Canada: UTP, 5201 Dufferin Street, North York, Ontario M3H 5T8, Canada.

The policy of Multilingual Matters/Channel View Publications is to use papers that are natural, renewable and recyclable products, made from wood grown in sustainable forests. In the manufacturing process of our books, and to further support our policy, preference is given to printers that have FSC and PEFC Chain of Custody certification. The FSC and/or PEFC logos will appear on those books where full certification has been granted to the printer concerned.

Typeset by Florence Production Ltd.
Printed and bound in Great Britain by MPG Books Ltd.

Contents

Foreword

THE HON. JUSTICE MICHAEL KIRBY AC CMG

Like most judges and lawyers, I spend my life puzzling over the meaning of words. The words may exist in a national or sub-national constitution. They may appear in local legislation. Or they may emerge from judicial reasons, written over the centuries, in the exposition of the common law.

Finding the meaning of these texts is often quite difficult, even when one is working entirely within a familiar legal paradigm, with a language learned at one's mother's knee and with concepts that are known and accepted.

We should not be surprised about such difficulties. There is such a variety of languages – there are hundreds of dialects in Papua New-Guinea alone. The sources to which language adapts are so diverse and their needs so different. Individual and group varieties are inescapable. So it is something of a miracle that human minds can ever convey meaning to each other. It is astonishing really that extremely complex concepts of morality, ethics, science and technology can somehow be put into verbal sounds and then cut up into little pieces known as words, sentences, paragraphs and chapters. It is also amazing that groups (sometimes intercontinental groups such as those who speak the English or Spanish languages) can communicate with a fair degree of ease and at least get the general drift of what they are on about – linking brain synapses to those of others through the vehicle of language.

This miracle, known as communication, would probably go unremarked (and just be taken for granted from the experiences learned in infant school) were it not for the uncomfortable discovery, relatively early life, that other people speak languages different from one's own. To watch children try to communicate across the language barrier – to look at the expressions of puzzlement and the blank stares of incomprehension – is an eye-opener. How can it be that other human beings cannot understand perfectly simple things that we are saying to them? How is it that others do not speak the English language?

We should not laugh about these questions. I am old enough to remember a time when learned judges and bewigged advocates thought that it was sufficient to get their meaning across to the variety of people who had come to Australia from different lands, with different languages and cultures, simply by shouting at them. If we spoke loudly enough, they believed, these people would understand the English language, like everyone else who was civilised. Only slowly did Australians come to realise that more people speak languages other than English; indeed that English is not even the most commonly spoken language in the world – simply the most intercontinental and universal of them.

Gradually, in about the 1960s in Australia, the fog began to lift. Judges and lawyers began to realise the necessities of translation. And also the perils. Those perils, and the difficulties and dangers, form the subjects of this book. As we learn, with growing experience of translation, the transfer of words, sentences and ideas from one language to another is no mechanical task. Language, not least the English language, is full of idioms and peasant expressions, figures of speech and brilliant metaphors that are difficult to translate exactly into other languages. To the demand of the trial judge or counsel 'just translate what the witness says' comes back the baleful stare of the translator. Occasionally, he or she would stand up to this insistence and point out that, without further questions and clarification, the exact nuance and refinement of meaning, necessary to accurate translation, could not be procured.

Just when we were congratulating ourselves on having understood the added peril of translating words in a legal context, we began to realise the additional complications that Dr Cao has collected in this excellent book. The last fifty years have seen a huge increase in international travel and communication, to a degree that would have seemed astonishing in 1950. In part, this was because of the rapid expansion of international physical travel following the development of civilian jet aircraft. But, in part, it also arose out of the remarkable growth of telecommunications, the invention of the Internet, the expansion of cyberspace and the electronic interconnection of human minds in every part of the world and far out into space.

So that this interconnection would not simply be a jabbering roar of incomprehensible static, it is necessary to bridge the gulf of linguistic differences. And so, the need for translating words in a legal context expanded far beyond the humble courtroom into the global economy, the international world of treaties and agreements and the dealings of different communities living in ever closer association with each other.

As Dr Cao points out, Canada, from the time of confederation and even before, had to accommodate its basically bilingual character with its law and practice. Its statutes were written, accurately and succinctly, in English and French. The need to express words in the different languages was hard enough. But it was harder still when those words were addressed to a whole culture of legal assumptions compacted into a single sound bite. There is a good illustration in this book of the use in one Canadian federal statute of the English word 'court'. Did this connote a 'cour' or a 'tribunal' in the French language? Did it embrace the Human Rights Commission, which Anglophones might not think of as a 'court' but which Francophones might view as a 'tribunal', having regard to certain of its decision-making functions?

Dr Cao points out that other bilingual or multilingual societies are now treading the same path that Canada has done for more than a century. In Hong Kong, for example, statutes are now expressed both in English and Chinese, with each text having equivalent authenticity. Inevitably, differences emerge over meaning. The reconciliation of the texts is an important legal function. On Canadian experience, the problem will rarely be so trivial as a dispute over the meaning of a particular word, as such. In the legal context, the disputes will commonly arise because many words have specialised meanings.

Even within the comfortable confines of the English language, we can see illustrations of this in court decisions. Recently, in the High Court of Australia, the question arose as to the meaning of the word 'pawn' when appearing in a State statute. Was the word to be given its popular meaning, so as to address the mischief of unregulated pawnshops to which Parliament seemed to be addressing itself? Or was the word to be given a different, specialised and 'technical' meaning, because it was used by the lawmaker in a legal context? The majority took the latter view. I took the former view. See *Palgo Holdings Pty Ltd v Gowans* (2005) 221 CLR 249 at 264-266 [35]-[41]. Parliament promptly amended the act to overcome the majority opinion. But how much more difficult are issues of this kind when a translator is seeking to comprehend meaning from the standpoint of an entire legal culture, looking from the outside at expressions used by another?

Dr Cao, who has personal reasons to have grown up with these issues in her own family, is an excellent expositor of the complexities and challenges that are involved in translating legal notions. In fact, she has spent a lifetime thinking about this problem. We are most fortunate that she has now collected and explained her analysis of it. She has offered countless intriguing illustrations of the difficulties of translation of legal texts. She has done so by reference to private legal documents, domestic legislation and international legal instruments. Because the world of regional and global commerce and culture will continue to expand, the need for bridges of language will necessarily proliferate. Those bridges will be needed in and outside the legal sphere. Unless the bridges can be built, a culture of peace, understanding and mutual respect will be difficult to secure.

Law has a vital part to play in reinforcing communication between nations and peoples. Building the international rule of law is a mighty challenge for the 21st century. We cannot achieve this goal by simply talking away to ourselves, confined within our own legal jurisdictions and linguistic groups. We must cross the barriers of language. For this we need expert translators of language. And, as Dr Cao points out, we must also be ready to cross the barriers erected by history, culture and institutions. We must hope that when the bridges of understanding are built, there will yet be sufficient commonality to bind humanity together. Law has a part to play in the achievement of this goal. That is why this book addresses a problem of great importance for the future of law and life on this planet.

I therefore welcome Dr Cao's text. There must be no more judicial shouting at translators. We must look at them with appreciation and awe for theirs is a subtle and challenging role as the pages of this book reveal and illustrate.

Michael Kirby
High Court of Australia
Canberra
7 February 2007

Preface

Is translation art or science? This question has been asked over the years and there is still no answer. We may never have a definitive answer to it, but that hardly matters as translators around the world and over the centuries have carried out the tasks of translation in an artful and scientific manner. Perhaps translation is both art and science. It may defy a strict delineation as translation involves so many facets and both artistic and scientific efforts. Of translation work, translating law, I believe, is the most intriguing and challenging, the focus of this book.

The book reflects part of the directions of my research in the past ten years or so. In this work, I hope to make use of my training and background in linguistics and law and my experience as a legal translator and court interpreter to look at legal translation from an interdisciplinary perspective, exploring the linguistic and legal aspects of translating law, and examining the interpretive interaction between various languages and legal cultures.

This book is also a tribute to all the legal translators and court interpreters working in different corners of the globe, tirelessly and admirably, whose work is vital but often unappreciated or under-appreciated. It pays tribute too to the linguistic and cultural diversity that constitutes our world and so much of our contemporary lives. On a personal note, I am Chinese by birth and a naturalised Australian. Some years ago I married into a Jewish Italian family from New York whose family name is Tedesco (which in Italian means 'German'). So, it is only fitting that I make occasional reference to all of these languages and laws in this book – Jewish/Hebrew, Italian, American/Australian/English and German, plus French and Chinese. Before I left China, life had always involved Chinese and Chinese only, even though I was trained and qualified as a United Nations interpreter. But since then, my personal and professional life has taught me much about the diversity of human as well as non-human lives, the life of the Other, and of many. So, in a way, the book is a tribute to the Tedescos and Fuchs of my extended family that is a miniature reflection of our civilised society today.

Acknowledgements

First of all, my sincere thanks go to Justice Kirby for kindly writing the Foreword despite his busy schedule.

I would like to thank my colleagues at Griffith University for their kind encouragement, advice and support in the last few years and during the course of writing this book: Rosemary Hunter, Richard Johnstone, Wayne Hudson, William Macneil, Shaun McVeigh, James Sneddon, Michael Levy, David Schak, Andrew Munro, A.J. Brown, Steven White, Roshan de Silver, Afshin A-Khavari and others at the Griffith Law School and the Socio-Legal Research Centre that provided me with a research grant in 2006 to enable me to complete this book.

I would also like to thank Zhao Xingmin at the Chinese Translation Section, Languages Service, United Nations Office in Geneva, and William Robinson at the Legal Service of the European Commission for their assistance and input during the preparation of the book. Thanks go to Professor Dragan Milovanovic, Editor of the International Journal for the Semiotics of Law, Professor Jean Delisle, Director of the School of Translation and Interpretation, Ottawa University, and Professor Randall Peerenboom of the UCLA Law School, for their generous encouragement and advice in my research in the last few years. I also thank Anne Wagner, Teresa Chataway, Christian Morris and Dr Nick Sawyer. I must thank Mr Tommi Grover, Ken Hall, the editors and editorial staff at Multilingual Matters.

My ultimate indebtedness goes to my parents, to Larry and other family members, and my beloved Mimi, Maomao, Mia, Mingming, Genghis and Lanlan.

Chapter 1
Introduction

Yan Fu (1854–1921), one of the most influential Chinese modern thinkers and a leading translator, in his Chinese translation of Montesquieu's *De l'esprit des lois* published in 1913, warned his readers about the difference between the Chinese *fa* (law) and Western 'law' this way:

In the Chinese language, objects exist or do not exist, and this is called *li* [order in nature, things as they are, or the law of nature]. The prohibitions and decrees that a country has are called *fa* [human-made laws]. However, Western people call both of these 'law'. Westerners accordingly see order in nature and human-made laws as if they were the same. But, by definition, human affairs are not a matter of natural order in terms of existence or non-existence, so the use of the word 'law' for what is permitted and what is prohibited as a matter of law of nature is a case in which several ideas are conveyed by one word. The Chinese language has the most instances in which several ideas are expressed by one word, but in this particular case the Chinese language has an advantage over Western languages. The word 'law' in Western languages has four different interpretations in Chinese as in *li* [order], *li* [rites, rules of propriety], *fa* [human-made laws] and *zhi* [control]. Scholars should take careful note.[1]

Yan Fu was not the only person who saw the linguistic difficulty and complication in translating legal terminology between English and Chinese. For more than the past century, both translators and legal scholars have been pondering over the question of whether *fa* is indeed the equivalent of 'law'. Furthermore, Chinese is certainly not the only language that presents a dilemma and challenge in translation. Examples of similar difficulties abound in the translation of basic legal concepts between most languages. For instance, one may ask: are the English 'Rule of Law', the French *État de droit* and the German *Rechtsstaat* equivalent? Or can the English 'law' reflect

1

the German words *Gesetz* (concrete-specific law) and *Recht* (general-abstract law)? Is the French *droit* conceptually the same as 'law'? Similarly, in Hebrew, *hazakah* in Jewish law has at least four meanings when translated into English: a form of acquisition, a *praesumptio juris*, possession, and a rule of procedure and evidence in real property (Elon 1985: 242). Conversely, the English term 'contract' is translated into modern legal Hebrew as *hozeh* (agreement), but it also has various corresponding or related terms in Jewish law including *hiyuv* (non-contractual obligation) and *shetar* (an evidentiary document) (Elon 1985: 242).

It is a fact that translating law between any languages is not a straightforward affair. Notwithstanding, the translation of law has played a very important part in the contact between different peoples and different cultures in history, and is playing an even more important role in our increasingly globalised world. This fact, unfortunately, is not often acknowledged, in particular in the development of law and legal studies. A good illustration of the increasing role that legal translation plays is found in the European Union (EU). Multilingualism and linguistic equality among its Member States has been one of the foundational principles and practices since the inception of the EU. Linguistic and cultural diversity is what gives the EU its specific character (Wilson 2003: 2). The European Parliament, as the legislature, makes laws that become national laws and have direct binding force on the citizens of the Member States. EU laws are translated and published in its Member States' official languages. Thus, translation is indispensable for the functioning of the European Parliament. As pointed out, EU laws are inconceivable without translation (Correia 2003: 40).

At another level, the demand for legal translation is on the increase around the world owing to globalisation and the increased contact and exchange between peoples and states. For example, the EU now has twenty official languages and the demand for translation in the EU is growing with the addition of new Member States and with the preparation for accession (see Wagner *et al.* 2002). In the national arena, in bilingual and multilingual jurisdictions such as Canada and Switzerland, there is the constant demand and legal requirement for bilingual or multilingual drafting and translation. In the more recent past, Hong Kong, following the change of sovereignty in 1997, became a bilingual jurisdiction where bilingual legislative drafting and bilingual laws have now become the norm heavily involving translation. There are new challenges and demands that have not been experienced before in other traditional bilingual or multilingual jurisdictions. Separately, in monolingual countries, the demand for translation of legal texts has also risen in recent years. For instance, in China, with the flood of legislation came a multitude of English and other European language translations of Chinese laws. Apart from the traditional printed translations with a limited audience of academics and lawyers, a large number of Internet sites now offer English translations of Chinese laws, accessible to a worldwide audience for anyone with an interest in China. Most of the foreign law firms in China employ translators, and translating legal documents such as contracts is a substantial workload of these firms. However, currently the quality of many translations leaves much room for improvement. For instance, at the time of China's accession to the World Trade Organisation (WTO) in 2001, the Chinese government had to declare some Chinese translations of the WTO legal instruments unacceptable due to translation errors. It has since published officially sanctioned Chinese translation, although only the WTO legal instruments in its official languages (English, French and Spanish), not their Chinese translation, have legal force.

It is obvious that translation is integral to the interaction in law and other spheres between different peoples and cultures. Given its important role in the intellectual and institutional development in different countries and its pragmatic value in economic arenas, legal translation deserves close scrutiny. This study attempts to make modest contributions in this regard. It has the major objective of studying legal translation as an intellectual pursuit and a profession in our increasingly interconnected world.

It is commonly acknowledged that legal translation is complex, and it requires special skills, knowledge and experience on the part of the translator to produce such translation. As has been pointed out, bold claims have been made about legal translation (Harvey 2002: 177). It has been described as a category in its own right, and as 'the ultimate linguistic challenge', combining the inventiveness of literary translation with the terminological precision of technical translation (Cairns and McKeon 1995, Gémar 1995, Pelage 2000, all cited in Harvey 2002). Then, what is so special about legal translation? Or is it just an excuse or exaggeration that legal translation is seen as being special, and more complex, requiring more time and skills than other types of translation so that legal translators would be better remunerated (Harvey 2002)? So, for practising legal translators, aspiring legal translators and translation researchers and teachers of both the general and legal kind, it is necessary to understand legal translation as a linguistic and translation phenomenon, if indeed it is special. At the same time, we also need to demystify legal translation without oversimplifying the complex and interdisciplinary nature of the problems involved.

Then, what are the major sources of difficulty in legal translation? What makes legal translation special and challenging? What is required of the legal translator? What are the linguistic features of different legal text types and the challenges they pose to the translator and why are legal texts written the way they are? These are some of the issues that this book attempts to address.

The examination of legal translation in this book is not language specific in the sense that it is not exclusively or predominantly targeted at one specific language pair. English is cited in most instances. This is because the English language is now the dominant language in many translations of law, as in the case of multilingual international instruments such as those formulated under the auspices of the United Nations (UN) and also in bilateral agreements. In the latter case, even when the official languages of the two countries concerned do not include English, in many bilateral agreements, the English text is often included as an authentic text. English is also the language used in most international trade documents. Besides, English is the language of the Common Law. Legislative drafting in English has also had a major influence over the drafting of multilateral instruments today.

This book explores the important aspects of legal translation, and provides a theoretical and practical guidance for the study and practice of legal translation. It adopts an interdisciplinary approach combining linguistic and legal theories with translation practice. The first part of the book presents the theoretical aspects related to legal translation, such as the nature of legal language, the relationships between law and language and their implications for legal translation, and the perennial question of equivalence and the possibility and impossibility of legal translation. It defines and characterises legal translation competence. The second part of the book is practice oriented, focusing on the practical aspects of legal translation, particularly the different types of legal texts. Whenever possible, case law related to language issues and linguistic disputes from various jurisdictions are cited and discussed, prominently the bilingual jurisdictions of Canada and Hong Kong and the multilingual jurisdiction of the European Court of Justice (ECJ). It is important for us to see the different effects and consequences that translation can have on the working and development of law. The choice of words and different methods of translation of law can have a long-lasting impact on law. It also shows that translation enriches the law, cultures and human experience as a whole.

This book can be used by both general translators to be trained to become legal translators, and lawyers or people with legal training intending to become legal translators. It is important to bear in mind that legal trans-lators are not lawyers. Likewise, bilingual lawyers are not automatically translators. The legal translator's job is not to provide legal advice and solve legal problems, but to translate and facilitate communication across linguistic, cultural and legal barriers through the medium of language. The legal translator's skills and tasks are very different from the lawyer's. The legal translator does not read and interpret the law the way a lawyer does. The legal translator does not write the law either. However, the legal translator needs to know how lawyers, including judges and lawmakers, think and write and why they write the way they do, and at the same time, to be sensitive to the intricacy, diversity and creativity of language, as well as its limits and power.

In short, in this book, legal translation is analysed and discussed in terms of cross-cultural and interlingual communicative act and as a complex human and social behaviour. On the one hand, legal translation is constrained by the nature of law and legal language, of the source language (SL) and the target language (TL). On the other hand, legal translation is a product of a human process with the translator working in particular situations and contexts under an array of legal and other constraints. Thus, the different variables involved in the act of translation, linguistic and legal, need to be properly understood for the performance of the task. An underlying argument of the book is that law is translatable despite the various inherent difficulties, and despite the often-heard claims to the contrary. Furthermore, translating law is a challenging interdisciplinary endeavour, the skills of which can be learned and developed. It is nevertheless special, different from other types of translation.

Chapter 2 presents the different views and arguments on law and language. It addresses the relationships between language and law and the nature of legal language. It attempts to answer the often-asked question of why legal translation is difficult, and identifies the sources of such difficulty. It also touches on the question of equivalence and the possibility and impossibility of legal translation. The chapter provides a comparative analysis of the two most important legal systems in the world, the Common Law and the Civil Law.

Chapter 3 investigates translation competence of the legal translator. It proposes that translation competence is identifiable and describable, and that there exists an underlying general competence that applies to all translators including specialist translators such as the legal translator. The chapter proceeds to identify and describe translation competence and its componential variables, including translational language competence, translational knowledge structures and translational strategic competence. It argues that translation is the product of a total act of interlingual and intercultural mediation involving the interactions of different variables in situational contexts.

Chapter 4 examines legal terminological issues. It discusses the major lexical features and difficulties in translation, with illustrations from various languages and jurisdictions. The focus is on the lexical characteristics of legal language in general covering legal conceptual issues, system-bound legal terms and the issue of linguistic uncertainty.

Chapter 5 explores the translation of private legal documents. Private legal documents mainly refer to contracts, agreements, wills and other legal documents. The translation of these documents constitutes the bulk of actual work in real life for many legal translation practitioners. In this chapter, the legal and linguistic features of major private legal documents in English are examined.

Chapter 6 addresses the translation of domestic legislation. It begins with an outline of the two types of translated statutes. This is followed by a comparative description of the various linguistic features of statutes. It proceeds to examine the pragmatic features of statutes in English and their relevance to translation. It lastly discusses the case law on linguistic uncertainty in bilingual legislation in Canada and Hong Kong, and examines how the courts deal with such uncertainties and the relevant rules developed for such a purpose.

Chapter 7 focuses on the translation of international legal instruments, both bilateral and multilateral, and the various legal and translational aspects involved. It explains the basic concepts of international law and international legal instruments, and describes the legal and linguistic features of such instruments. The chapter proceeds to outline the process of bilateral treaty negotiation involving translation as an example for an insight into the treaty making process involving two languages. It then explores the various aspects associated with translating multilingual instruments and the judicial interpretive rules for construing multilingual legal texts in the ECJ. It lastly touches on the use of computer aided or assisted translation (CAT) technology at the UN and the EU.

Note

1. From Yan Fu's translation of Montesquieu's *De l'esprit des lois*, and the English translation of Yan Fu's words is my own.

Chapter 2
Law, Language and Translation

Legal translation is a special and specialised area of translational activity. This is due to the fact that legal translation involves law, and such translation can and often does produce not just linguistic but also legal impact and consequence, and because of the special nature of law and legal language. Moreover, as is noted, the translation of legal texts of any kind, from statute laws to contracts to courtroom testimony, is a practice that stands at the crossroads of legal theory, language theory and translation theory (Joseph 1995: 14). Therefore, it is essential that the legal translator have a basic understanding of the nature of law and legal language and the impact it has on legal translation.

This chapter begins with a classification of legal translation. This is followed by an analysis of the nature of legal language in terms of its normative, performative and technical character and the tension between legal certainty and linguistic indeterminacy. A characterisation of legal language is also proposed in terms of legal lexicon, syntax, pragmatics and style. Then, the chapter elaborates on the three major sources of difficulty in legal translation, that is, the legal, linguistic and cultural complications. In particular, it offers a comparative analysis of the two major legal systems: the Common Law and the Civil Law. Lastly, the chapter contemplates the possibility and impossibility of legal translational equivalence and whether it is indeed achievable.

Legal Translation Typology

Translation is classifiable into various categories. It can be divided into two general categories of literary and non-literary translation or the categories of ideational (technical and non-technical) and interpersonal (non-fictional and fictional) translation (House 1977), and the translation of pragmatic texts and literary or artistic texts (Delisle 1988). Translation can

7

also be classified according to the division of natural and artificial language based on language use, and on the types of translation activities, literary or industrial (Sager 1993).[1] A commonly used typology is the classification of translation into general, literary and specialist or technical translation.

Relevant to translation typology is how we view the differences and similarities among the different types of translation. In this connection, the prototypology proposed by Snell-Hornby (1988: 27–36) is particularly constructive.[2] This is the so-called 'natural categorisation', that is, in the form of prototypes that have a hard core and blurred edges (Snell-Hornby 1988: 27). The prototypology is a dynamic, gestalt-like system of relationships that covers various types of translation ranging from literary to technical (Snell-Hornby 1988: 31). In the classification of general, specialist and literary translation, we need to recognise that these categories of translation involve different language uses that have their own peculiarities, but they also share common grounds. As Vermeer (1986: 35, cited in Snell-Hornby 1988: 51) points out, for instance, the differences between general and literary translation are one of degree, not of kind. It is not a polarised dichotomy, but a spectrum that admits blends and overlapping, a question of quality and intensity, not one of fundamental difference (Snell-Hornby 1988: 51). As Harvey (2002: 177) puts it, literary and scientific translations are not watertight and they may be in a hybrid form.

For our purpose, if we follow the general, literary and specialist classification of translation, legal translation falls under the specialist category, or technical translation. It is a type of the translational activity involving special language use, that is, language for special purpose (LSP) in the context of law, or language for legal purpose (LLP). Legal translation has the characteristics of technical translation and also shares some of the features of general translation.

Legal translation can be further classified according to different criteria. For instance, legal translation has been classified according to the subject matter of the SL texts into the following categories: (1) translating domestic statutes and international treaties; (2) translating private legal documents; (3) translating legal scholarly works; and (4) translating case law. Legal translation can also be divided according to the status of the original texts: (1) translating enforceable law, e.g. statutes; and (2) translating non-enforceable law, e.g. legal scholarly works.

According to Sarcevic (1997), legal translation can be classified according to the functions of the legal texts in the SL into the following categories: (1) primarily prescriptive, e.g. laws, regulations, codes, contracts, treaties and conventions. These are regulatory instruments containing rules of conduct or norms. They are normative texts; (2) primarily descriptive and also prescriptive, e.g. judicial decisions and legal instruments that are used to carry on judicial and administrative proceedings such as actions, pleadings, briefs, appeals, requests, petitions etc.; and (3) purely descriptive, e.g. scholarly works written by legal scholars such as legal opinions, law textbooks, articles etc. They belong to legal scholarship, the authority of which varies in different legal systems (Sarcevic 1997: 11). Sarcevic (1997: 9) defines legal translation as special-purpose communication between specialists, excluding communication between lawyers and non-lawyers.

One major problem with the existing classifications of legal translation is that they are based on the function or use of the original legal texts in the SL, without due regard to the various TL factors, such as the functions or status of the translated texts. However, there is a need to distinguish the functions of the SL text from those of the TL text (cf. Roberts 1992). It is necessary to consider the TL variables, in addition to those of the SL. Another problem of the existing classifications is that many documents that are used in the legal process and translated as such are excluded from the classifications, e.g. documents used in court proceedings. A third major problem is that some of the classifications such as Sarcevic's exclude communications between lawyers and non-lawyers (clients). The restriction in Sarcevic's 'legal texts for specialists only' disqualifies some text types that make up a large part of the legal translator's workload in real life: private agreements and correspondence between lawyers and clients, for instance (see Harvey 2000).

Given these reasons, before we offer another classification of legal translation, let us first examine how legal texts may be classified.

In this study, legal language refers to the language of and related to law and legal process. This includes language of the law, language about law, and language used in other legal communicative situations (cf. Kurzon 1998, who distinguishes language of the law from legal language, i.e. language about law). Legal language is a type of register, that is, a variety of language appropriate to different occasions and situations of use, and in this case, a variety of language appropriate to the legal situations of use. Legal texts refer to the texts produced or used for legal purposes in legal settings.

We may distinguish four major variants or sub-varieties of legal texts in the written form: (1) legislative texts, e.g. domestic statutes and subordinate laws, international treaties and multilingual laws, and other laws produced by lawmaking authorities; (2) judicial texts produced in the judicial process by judicial officers and other legal authorities; (3) legal scholarly texts produced by academic lawyers or legal scholars in scholarly works and commentaries whose legal status depends on the legal systems in different jurisdictions; and (4) private legal texts that include texts written by lawyers, e.g. contracts, leases, wills and litigation documents, and also texts written by non-lawyers, e.g. private agreements, witness statements and other documents produced by non-lawyers and used in litigation and other legal situations.[3] These different sub-text types have their own peculiarities. As noted, legal language is not homogeneous, not just one legal discourse, but 'a set of related legal discourses' (Maley 1994: 13). Legal language does not just cover language of law alone, but all communications in legal settings.

Legal texts may have various communicative purposes. They can be for normative purpose as in the case of bilingual and multilingual statutes and other laws and documents that establish legal facts or create rights and obligations. These are mostly prescriptive. Legal texts can also be for informative purpose as in some legal scholarly works and commentaries, legal advice, correspondence between lawyers, between lawyers and clients, and documents used in court proceedings. These are mostly descriptive. For the translator, it is necessary to ascertain the legal status and communicative purpose of the original texts and the target texts as these may impact on translation. Also importantly for our purpose, the legal status and communicative purposes in the SL texts are not automatically transferred or carried over to the TL texts. They can be different.

Given the foregoing description of legal language and legal texts, legal translation refers to the rendering of legal texts from the SL into the TL. Legal translation can be classified into three categories in the light of the purposes of the TL texts.[4]

Firstly, there is legal translation for normative purpose. It refers to the production of equally authentic legal texts in bilingual and multilingual jurisdictions of domestic laws and international legal instruments and other laws. They are the translation of the law. Often such bilingual or multilingual texts are first drafted in one language and then translated into another language or languages. They may also be drafted simultaneously in both or all languages. In either case, the different language texts have equal legal force and one is not superior to another irrespective of their original status. Such legal texts in different languages are regarded as authoritative once they go through the authentication process in the manner prescribed by law. By virtue of this process, such texts are not mere translations of law, but the law itself (Sarcevic 1997: 20). Examples of these are the legislation in the bilingual jurisdictions of Canada and Hong Kong, the multilingual legal instruments of the UN, and the multilingual laws of the EU. In the case of the EU, the authentic language versions of EU laws, now twenty languages, are equivalent since they have the same legal force and value and can be invoked indiscriminately in appeals to the ECJ by EU citizens or businesses, irrespective of their Member State of origin or that country's official language or languages (Correia 2003: 41). They are usually drafted in English or French first to be translated into the other official languages. Nevertheless, they all have equal legal force.

This category of legal translation may also include private documents such as contracts, the bilingual texts of which are equally authentic in a bilingual or monolingual jurisdiction. For instance, in a non-English speaking country, contracts sometimes may stipulate that the versions of the contract in the official language of the country and English are both authentic, even though the language of the court and the country does not include English. In this first category of legal translation, the communicative purposes of the SL and TL texts are identical.

Secondly, there is legal translation for informative purpose, with constative or descriptive functions. This includes the translation of statutes, court decisions, scholarly works and other types of legal documents if the translation is intended to provide information to the target readers. This is most often found in monolingual jurisdictions. Such translations are different from the first category where the translated law is legally binding. In this second category, the SL is the only legally enforceable language while the TL is not. For instance, a statute written in French from France translated into English for informative purpose for the benefit of foreign lawyers or other English readers is not legally enforceable. This is different from the first category where, for instance, a statute written in French in the bilingual jurisdiction of Canada is translated into English or vice versa and where both the French and English versions are equally authentic. Sometimes, publishers of translations of laws in the second category include a disclaimer to the effect that the translation of such and such a law is for reference only, and that in legal proceedings, the original language text of the law shall prevail. Another example is the translation of the legal instruments of the WTO, which has English, French and Spanish as its official languages. Here only the texts written in the official languages have legal force while their translations into other languages are not binding, but for information only. In this category, the SL and TL texts may have different communicative purposes.

Thirdly, there is legal translation for general legal or judicial purpose. Such translations are primarily for information, and are mostly descriptive. This type of translated document may be used in court proceedings as part of documentary evidence. Original SL texts of this type may include legal documents such as statements of claims or pleadings, contracts and agreements, and ordinary texts such as business or personal correspondence, records and certificates, witness statements and expert reports, among many others. The translations of such documents are used by clients who do not speak the language of the court, e.g. statements of claims, or by lawyers and courts who otherwise may not be able to access the originals such as contracts, correspondence or other records and documents. Such translated texts have legal consequences attached to them due to their use in the legal process. In practice, for instance, in Australian courts, a sworn affidavit from the translator is normally required as to the quality of the translation and the competency of the translator. Sometimes, the translator is also called upon as a witness in court regarding the translation. For some of these, the otherwise ordinary non-legal documents written by non-lawyers are elevated to legal status because of the special use of the original and the translation. This is similar to court interpreting. Court interpreters in most cases interpret oral evidence of witnesses who may be retelling ordinary events and answering ordinary personal questions. These witnesses could say the same or similar things outside the courtroom in non-legal settings. The main difference is that interpreting the same story in a non-legal setting is ordinary interpreting while interpreting the same in court is legal interpreting as the interpreted words are used for a legal purpose under special circumstances and conditions. In these situations, the language use or translation use is contingent upon the existence of a legal order, which must be considered to be part of the communicative situation. The law's institutional character plays a major part in language use in legal settings (Madsen 1997b), thus, should be given prominent consideration in our classifications of legal texts and legal translation. Many parts of the court or litigation documents are the closest to resemble everyday language use in all the sub-types of legal texts.

The third type of translation is different from the second category described above in that the third category may include ordinary texts that are not written in legal language by legal professionals, but by the layperson. This type of legal translation is often left out in the discussion and classification of legal translation. However, in fact, in the practice of legal translation, it constitutes a major part of the translation work of the legal translator in real life, the 'bread and butter' activities (Harvey 2002: 178).

Thus, we can say that legal translation refers to the translation of texts used in law and legal settings. Legal translation is used as a general term to cover both the translation of law and other communications in the legal setting. For the legal translator, it is important to ascertain the status and communicative purposes of both the original text and the translation.

The Nature of Legal Language

As is commonly acknowledged, legal translation is complex and difficult. There are many reasons why this is the case. In general, the complexity and difficulty of legal translation is attributable to the nature of law and the language that law uses, and the associated differences found in intercultural and interlingual communication in translating legal texts. Prominently, legal language is identified and linked with the normative, performative and technical nature of language use, and the inherent indeterminate nature of language in general.

The normative nature of legal language

Legal philosophers agree that legal language is a normative language. It is related to norm creation, norm production and norm expression (Jori 1994). This means that the language used from law or legal sources is largely prescriptive.

The normative language of law derives from the fact that law has the basic function in society of guiding human behaviour and regulating human relations. Law is distinguished from most other types of human institutions. Law embodies the ideals and standards people have and seek to realise in such concepts as equity, justice, rights, liberty, equal protection and the general welfare that enter the body of law (Jenkins 1980: 98). In other words, law has a normative existence that is embodied in the ideals and principles that people cherish, the purposes and aspirations they pursue, and the notions they hold (Jenkins 1980: 103). These constitute the existential goals of law. Thus, law exists as a set of prescriptions having the form of imperatives, defining and enforcing the arrangements, relationships, procedures and patterns of behaviour that are to be followed in a society (Jenkins 1980: 98).

Consequently, the language used in law to achieve its purpose is predominantly prescriptive, directive and imperative. Laws are written in language the function of which is not just to express or convey knowledge and information, but also to direct, influence or modify people's behaviour, whether it be a legal enactment, judicial pronouncement or a contract. As is noted by Maley (1994: 11):

> In all societies, law is formulated, interpreted and enforced . . . and the greater part of these different legal processes is realised primarily through language. Language is the medium, process and product in the various arenas of the law where legal texts, spoken or written, are generated in the service of regulating social behaviour.

In the words of Olivecrona (1962: 177, quoted by Jackson 1985: 315),

> . . . the purpose of all legal enactments, judicial pronouncements, contracts, and other legal acts is to influence men's behaviour and direct them in certain ways, thus, the legal language must be viewed primarily as a means to this end.

In short, the language of the law is a normative language. Its predominant function is to direct people's behaviour in society. It authoritatively posits legal norms.

The performative nature of legal language

Closely related to the normative nature of law and legal language is the notion that language is performative. Law depends upon language, in particular the normative and performative nature of language. In speech act theory as first proposed by J.L. Austin (1962, 1979, see also Searle 1969, 1976, 1979), speech is not just words, as people normally associate it with, but also actions. Words are not only something we use to say things, we also use them to do things. The performative use of language is not exclusive to law, but law relies heavily on performative utterances. Legal effects and legal consequences are commonly obtained by merely uttering certain words, for instance, 'You are guilty', or 'You are fined $1000' as regularly pronounced in court. Language used in law can perform such acts as conferring rights, prescribing prohibition and granting permission. By merely uttering words, people accept public and private legal responsibilities, assume legal roles and qualities, transfer legal rights and impose or discharge obligations (Jori 1994: 2092). Thus, legal speech acts are said to be constitutive of their effects.

In relation to legal discourse, Danet (1980) classifies legal language use into different types of speech acts, based on Searle's (1976) general classification of speech acts. Thus, legal speech acts are said to consist of the following categories (Danet 1980: 457–461):

(1) Representatives, which are utterances that commit the speaker to something being the case or assert the truth of a proposition, including testifying, swearing, asserting, claiming and stating.

(2) Commissives, which commit the speaker to do something in the future, such as in contracts, marriage ceremonies and wills.

(3) Expressives, which express the speakers' psychological state about or attitude to a proposition, including apologising, excusing, condemning, deploring, forgiving and blaming.

(4) Declaratives, whose successful performance brings about a correspondence between their propositional content and reality, including marriage ceremonies, bills of sale, receipts, appointments, and nominations; and the legislative stipulation of rights and of definitions of concepts; lawyers' objections, sentences, and appellate opinions, indictments, confessions, pleas of guilty/not guilty, and verdicts. There is a sub-category of representative declarations for certain institutional situations, e.g. a judge making factual claims, requiring claims to be issued with the force of declaration, and this would requires the speaker to have certain authority. This would cover marriage ceremony, bills of sale, appointment or nominations, legislative stipulation of rights and definition of concepts, indictments, confessions, pleas of guilty/not guilty, and verdicts.

(5) Directives, which are future-oriented speech acts, seeking to change the world, to get someone to do something, most prominent in legislation that imposes obligations.

Hence, the performative nature of language is indispensable to law in achieving its purpose of regulating human behaviour and society and setting out obligation, prohibition and permission.

The technical nature of legal language

Legal language is a technical language and legal translation is technical translation involving special language texts, that is, texts written in LLP. But in fact, there have been debates as to the nature of legal language, whether legal language actually exists and whether it is a technical language.

There are two main positions regarding the nature of legal language. One view holds that legal language is a technical language while the opposite view is that there is no legal language, and, even if it exists, it is part of the ordinary language. For the latter view, some question whether it is scientifically correct to speak of the language of law. In this view, there is no law language. Legal language is no more than a specialised form of the ordinary language. It is a use of the ordinary language for particular purposes, and in this case, legal purpose. On the other hand, many believe that legal language is an identifiable technical language. They accept the validity of the designation 'legal language'. Some even argue that it is a separate language, a sub-language or a social dialect.[5]

If we accept, as has been mostly accepted now, that there is such a linguistic phenomenon as legal language, and that it is a technical language, then, what kind of language is legal language? What makes it different from other types of language use?

Diverse views have been expressed over the years on the nature of legal language as a technical language. For instance, Charles Caton (1963), a linguistic philosopher, believes that legal language is a technical language, but 'technical language is always an adjunct of ordinary language' (Caton 1963: viii), whether ordinary English, ordinary French or ordinary Swahili. He argues that technical languages have the same syntax as ordinary language, and speech acts performable in ordinary discourse are performable in technical contexts, but only differ in vocabulary (Caton 1963). Caton counts languages of physics, mathematics, farming, chess and the law as among technical languages (see also Morrison 1989). Similarly, according to Schauer (1987: 571), a legal philosopher, legal language as a technical language often operates in a context that makes legal terms have meanings different from those they bear in non-legal contexts of use. Legal language is thus parasitic on ordinary language.

In contrast, others argue that legal language as a technical language differs from ordinary language. For instance, legal philosopher, H.L.A. Hart (1954, 1961/1994) argues that owing to the distinctive characteristics of legal language, 'legal language is *sui generis*', 'unique onto itself'. Fundamental to Hart's view is that legal language is distinctive because it presupposes the existence of a legal system and presupposes particular rules of law, against the background of which legal language obtains its meaningfulness and particular meaning, and because of the distinctive feature of rules of law as rules (see also Morrison 1989). Hart argues that technical terms affect the meaning of each other word used in connection with the technical word and that legal terms have meanings only in the context of the existence of a legal system and only through particular rules of law (Hart 1954).

Another important view is that of Bernard Jackson (1985), legal philosopher and legal semiotician, viewing legal language from a semiotic perspective. His theory has implications in particular for legal translation. For Jackson, legal language is a technical language. Legal lexicon and its structure display some of the characteristics of this technical language. He further argues that legal language is autonomous of the natural language. This can be seen in two aspects. Firstly, in Greimasian semiotics, the legal lexicon is autonomously constituted in the sense that legal institutions determine which semiotic objects enter the legal lexicon (Jackson 1985: 46). Secondly, the autonomy of legal language resides in the semantic relations of the lexicon as proposed by Carcaterra (Jackson 1985: 46). Once constituted as a system, the language of law represents an entire universe of legal meanings, the choice of any one of which reflects the exclusion or absence of the other available legal meanings (Carcaterra 1972, cited in Jackson 1985: 46). Thus, the specificity of legal language resides in the legal system. Legal language, 'having a lexicon constituted in a manner different from that of the ordinary language, and involving terms related to each other in ways different from those of the ordinary language, must be autonomous of the ordinary language', although this does not exclude the possibility of historical influence from ordinary to legal language or of considerable factual correspondence (Jackson 1985: 47).

According to Jackson, it is true that legal language needs to draw upon the whole resources of the natural language for its intelligibility, but legal language may only, to the extent that it resembles ordinary language, appear to be intelligible to the layperson (Jackson 1985: 47). The layperson may read legal language as if it were natural language; he or she may be quite oblivious to those systematic differences that give the same words a different meaning to the lawyer (Jackson 1985: 47). Equally, we have to account for the occurrence of incomprehension of legal language even amongst those who have a sophisticated knowledge of the natural language concerned (Jackson 1985: 47). It is 'lack of knowledge of the system, rather than lack of knowledge of individual lexical items, which produces this effect' (Jackson 1985: 48). Although legal language depends upon the semantics of ordinary language as judges frequently invoke the ordinary meaning of language in legal interpretation, yet, according to Jackson, if ordinary language meanings are admitted, 'it is solely by virtue of the choice made within the legal system to admit such meanings' (Jackson 1985: 48). The 'non-legal sense of a word adopted into the legal lexicon provides the jurist with the source of one possible choice as to its particular meaning in law', but the choice can only be made from within the legal system, and 'does not occur automatically as a result of the semantic pull of the non-legal meaning' (Jackson 1985: 50). Thus, according to Jackson, the legal system is critical to understanding. The words make sense only within the context of the legal system itself. Understanding an item of the legal lexicon requires knowing the legal system. This is an important reminder for the legal translator.

Regarding the discussion above, as we know, language and language use, including legal language, consist of more than just the lexicon. Therefore, we can benefit the study of legal language and its nature by looking at legal language as a register. This will give an additional perspective to the foregoing discussion.

Register is a language variety according to use (Halliday and Hasan 1985: 41). Register is 'what you are speaking at the time, depending on what you are doing and the nature of the activity in which the language is functioning' and it 'reflects the social order, the types of social activity' (Halliday and Hasan 1985: 41). Register is a functional language variation, a contextual category correlating groups of linguistic features with recurrent situational features (see Halliday *et al.* 1964).[6] It is a variety of language use. Register comprises an open-ended set of varieties of language typical of occupational fields such as the language of religion, legal language and medical language. Furthermore, registers are differentiated from one another in their meaning, and therefore they differ in the vocabularies that express that meaning and in grammatical structure. Thus, register markers are firstly lexical, e.g. technical terms, and secondarily, structural, e.g. particular use of grammatical features (Halliday and Hasan 1985: 41).

If we consider legal language as a register, firstly, it spans a continuum from almost normal formal usage to highly complex varieties that differ substantially from normal formal usage (Danet 1980: 472).[7] Secondly, even though legal register differs from other language use, different registers are not entirely discrete. Rather there is a common core that extends, not necessarily evenly, across all registers together with variations in each register (Ingram and Wylie 1991: 9). According to Ingram and Wylie:

> A special purpose register is not so much a special language as one language used in special contexts, for special purposes, with numerous but potentially identifiably features emerging more or less frequently in each situation and differentiating the register as a sub-system of the language by the frequency of occurrence of the syntactic, lexical, semantic, functional, cohesive and other features. (Ingram and Wylie 1991: 9)

If such a view is adopted, then language should be perceived as 'a systematic whole which responds to situational requirements', with different language forms occurring more or less frequently in different situations, and registers are 'different manifestations of a total system' (Ingram and Wylie 1991: 9). For our purpose, this means that legal register shares common features with ordinary language. Thus, one may say that the relation between legal language as a special purpose register and the rest of the language is that of a part to the whole, a part in which the general features of the language occur even if in different frequencies of occurrence (Ingram and Wylie 1991: 11).

To sum up, we may say that legal language as a register is a variety of language use of the technical nature. It shares the common core of general language but is not identical to ordinary language. There are lexical, syntactical, textual and pragmatic features that are singular to legal language as a technical language.

The indeterminate nature of language

Language is inherently indeterminate.[8] This linguistic nature is not often realised or appreciated. People are often guided by an ideal conception of language as precise, determinate, literal and univocal.[9] As is often quoted, people tend to think that anything that can be said can be said clearly, and anything that can be thought can be thought clearly. Perhaps not! In actual use, language falls far short of such an ideal conception. Moreover and importantly, the universe and human behaviour are inherently uncertain and indeterminate, law included. Ambiguity, vagueness, generality and other such features are often pervasive as well as important. They are not the shortcomings of language use or a deficiency in the system of natural language, not 'the common cold of the pathology of language' (Kaplan 1950, cited in Kooij 1971: 1).[10] Linguistic uncertainty should not be overrated as an insurmountable obstacle in communication because linguistic and pragmatic strategies often, although not always, overcome such obstacles to achieve effective or successful communication (see Kooij 1971: 3–4).

Relevant to law, language used in law as in other areas is characterised by indeterminacy, or 'open textureness' as Hart (1961/1994) calls it, 'with a core of settled meaning' and 'a penumbra of uncertainty'.[11] The English legal language is full of imprecise and ambiguous expressions. English legal terms such as 'fair and reasonable' and 'due process of law' are vague and elusive. So are abstract legal expressions such as 'justice', 'due diligence' and 'reasonable endeavours'. As said before, linguistic uncertainty is inherent in language, and cannot be eliminated, thus is ineliminable from a legal system (Endicott 2000: 190). However, law demands exactness and precision. Ambiguity and imprecision of any kind are likely to lead to disagreement. Ambiguity in language, arising from the 'penumbra of uncertainty' is often points of legal contentions and disputes (see Chapter 4 for further discussion). As Schauer (1993: xi) says, legal systems are expected to resolve disputes that are sometimes created by the indeterminacies of language.

Linguistic uncertainty, whether it is ambiguity, generality or vagueness includes both intralingual uncertainty, that is, uncertainty found within a language, and interlingual uncertainty, that is, uncertainty arises when two languages are compared or when one language is translated into another language. In such cases, words, phrases and sentences in one language may or may not be uncertain, but additional ambiguity or other uncertainty may arise when they are considered across two languages. More complications may emerge as a result. The bilingual and multilingual jurisdictions of Canada and the EU have produced sufficient case law for illustrations in this respect (see Chapters 4, 6 and 7 and also Cao 2007).

Characterising Legal Language

If we say that legal language is a recognisable linguistic phenomenon, we must demonstrate and determine what we mean by it. Are there any common characteristics found in legal language? Is legal language definable in terms of identifiable linguistic traits?

It is plainly clear that people find legal documents difficult to comprehend as compared with other professional expositions. There have been efforts in English speaking countries in the legal profession to simplify the language that law uses to make law more accessible to the average person. It is undeniable that certain idiosyncrasies are associated with the way lawyers speak and write. As discussed previously, law as a body of rules regulating the conduct of people, delineating the accepted social norms and human behaviour, is closely tied to the language that it uses and is constrained by language. Because of the nature and function of law, the language of the law has developed particular linguistic features, lexical, syntactical and pragmatic, to fulfil the demands of the law and accommodate the idiosyncrasies of law and its applications. Such linguistic characteristics of legal language have profound implications for legal translation.

If we examine legal language as a whole, common and singular linguistic features can be identified across different legal languages. They are manifested with respect to lexicon, syntax, pragmatics, and style.

Lexicon

In terms of legal lexicon, a distinctive feature of legal language is the complex and unique legal vocabulary found in different legal languages. This is a universal feature of legal language but different legal languages have their own unique legal vocabulary. It is the most visible and striking linguistic feature of legal language as a technical language. The legal vocabulary in each language is often extensive. It results from and reflects the law of the particular legal system concerned. In translation, due to the differences in legal systems, many of the legal terms in one language do not correspond to terms in another, the problem of non-equivalence, a major source of difficulty in translation.

Furthermore, within each legal lexicon, there are also peculiarities, and they do not always correspond in different legal languages. For instance, studies have identified specific linguistic characteristics of the English legal language. The English legal lexicon is full of archaic words, formal and ritualistic usage, word strings, common words with uncommon meanings and words of over-precision, among others (see Mellinkoff 1963, Danet 1980, Bowers 1989, Tiersma 1999). In legal German, the terminology is often highly abstract, with a high frequency of the use of nouns (Smith 1995). In contrast, the language used in Chinese law is often ordinary, using the common vocabulary but with legal meanings. The Chinese legal language is replete with general, vague and ambiguous usage (see Cao 2004).

Syntax

A common feature of the syntax of legal language is the formal and impersonal written style coupled with considerable complexity and length. Generally speaking, sentences in legal texts are longer than in other text types (Salmi-Tolonen 2004: 1173), and they may serve various purposes. In statutes, often long and complex sentences are necessary due to the complexity of the subject matters and the prospective nature of legislative law. This is the case with most legal languages. Extensive use of conditions, qualifications and exceptions are the additional linguistic features of legislative language, commonly employed to express complex contingencies. These peculiar linguistic features, according to Bhatia (1997), often create barriers to the effective understanding of such writing for the ordinary reader including the translator. Thus, to be able to understand and translate legislative provisions, one is inevitably required to take into account the typical difficulties imposed by some of these factors (Bhatia 1997: 208).

Apart from long and complex sentence structures found in most legal languages, there are also syntactical peculiarities to each legal language. For instance, German legal texts commonly employ multiple attributive adjectives. In legal English, complex structures, passive voice, multiple negations, and prepositional phrases are extensively used.

Pragmatics

As stated earlier, law depends upon the performative nature of language. Legal utterances perform acts, creating facts, rights and institutions. Typically, legislation is a prime example of 'saying as doing'. A statute is a master speech act with each provision constituting individual speech acts. As pointed out, 'performativity and modality are the linguistic means which express the institutional ideology of the role relationships involved in legislative rule-making' (Maley 1994: 21). Contracts and wills are other examples of legal speech acts in action. Words in legal language differ in meaning, import and effect depending on who utters them, where and when (Hart 1954). Of these speech acts, a prominent linguistic feature is the frequent use of performative markers. For instance, in English legal documents, 'may' and 'shall' are extensively employed. Performative verbs such as 'declare', 'announce', 'promise', 'undertake', 'enact', 'confer' and 'amend' are also common. Another pragmatic consideration in legal texts is ambiguity, vagueness and other uncertainties found in statutes and contracts, which are often points of legal contention. The courts often have to deal with such linguistic problems in the search for uniform interpretation and legal certainty.

Style

Legal style refers to the linguistic aspects of the written legal language and also the way in which legal problems are approached, managed and solved (Smith 1995: 190). Legal style results from legal traditions, thought and culture (Smith 1995). Generally speaking, legal writing is characterised by an impersonal style, with the extensive use of declarative sentences pronouncing rights and obligations. But different legal languages also have their own styles. For instance, the style of German legal texts is distinct. German law has been developed in a systematic, logical, abstract and conceptual manner over the centuries, and German law thinks in terms of general principles rather than in pragmatic terms, conceptualising problems rather than working from case to case (de Cruz 1999: 91). The German legal terminology and central method of lawmaking distinguishes it from the Common Law approach (de Cruz 1999: 91). As a result, the German Civil Code, the *Bergerliches Gesetzbuch* (BGB), is not written for the layperson but the legal profession (de Cruz 1999: 86). It 'deliberately eschews easy comprehensibility and waives all claims to educate its reader', and it adopts an abstract conceptual language that the layperson and the foreign lawyer find largely 'incomprehensible', but for the trained legal experts, after many years of familiarity, they cannot help but admire 'for its precision and rigour of thought' (Zweigert and Kötz 1992: 150). It is written in a special format and structure with a peculiar judicial style. Its language is abstract and complex (de Cruz 1999: 88). To understand it, one needs to be familiar with the various concepts as interpreted by the courts and in practice, and with the technical legal German language. It is characterised by deference to accuracy, clarity, completeness and complex syntax (de Cruz 1999: 88). It has been described as 'the legal calculating machine par excellence', a 'legal filigree work of extraordinary precision' and 'perhaps the code of private law with the most precise and logical legal language of all time' (Zweigert and Kötz 1992: 151). In short, in language, method, structure and concepts, the BGB is the child of the deep, exact and abstract learning of the German Pandectist School (Zweigert and Kötz 1992: 150). It forms a contrast to another legislative style of writing in the Civil Law as embodied in the French Code. The latter was deliberately written in a manner designed to be easily comprehensible to the layperson. So, there are peculiar legal styles in different legal languages.[12]

To sum up, the foregoing characterisation of legal language is a general description of the linguistic markers believed to be common in most if not all legal languages in varying degrees. However, it is important to bear in mind that major differences also exist in different legal languages and such variations constitute a source of difficulty in legal translation.

Sources of Difficulty in Legal Translation

The nature of law and legal language contributes to the complexity and difficulty in legal translation. This is compounded by further complications arising from crossing two languages and legal systems in translation. Specifically, the sources of legal translation difficulty include the systemic differences in law, linguistic differences and cultural differences. All these are closely related.

Different legal systems and laws

Legal language is a technical language. Furthermore and importantly, legal language is not a universal technical language but one that is tied to a national legal system (Weisflog 1987: 203), very different from the language used in pure science, say mathematics or physics. Law and legal language are system-bound, that is, they reflect the history, evolution and culture of a specific legal system. As Justice Oliver Wendell Holmes famously said a long time ago:

> The life of the law has not been logic: it has been experience. The felt necessities of the time, the prevalent moral and political theories, intuitions of public policy, avowed or unconscious, even the prejudices which judges share with their fellow-men, have had a good deal more to do than the syllogism in determining the rules by which men should be governed. The law embodies the story of a nation's development through many centuries, and it cannot be dealt with as if it contained

only the axioms and corollaries of a book of mathematics. (Holmes 1881/1990: 1)

Law as an abstract concept is universal as it is reflected in written laws and customary norms of conduct in different countries. However, legal systems are peculiar to the societies in which they have been formulated. Each society has different cultural, social and linguistic structures developed separately according to its own conditioning. Legal concepts, legal norms and application of laws differ in each individual society reflecting the differences in that society. Legal translation involves translation from one legal system into another. Unlike pure science, law remains a national phenomenon. Each national law constitutes an independent legal system with its own terminological apparatus, underlying conceptual structure, rules of classification, sources of law, methodological approaches and socio-economic principles (Sarcevic 1997: 13). This has major implications for legal translation when communication is channelled across different languages, cultures and legal systems.

Firstly, law is culturally and jurisdictionally specific. In the study of comparative law, the major legal systems of the world have been classified into various categories. Here 'legal system' refers to the nature and content of the law generally, and the structures and methods whereby it is legislated upon, adjudicated upon and administered, within a given jurisdiction (Tetley 2000). Such systems can also be described as legal families.

According to David and Brierley's classification of world legal systems or families, there are the Romano-Germanic Law (Continental Civil Law), the Common Law, Socialist Law, Hindu Law, Islamic Law, African Law and Far East Law (David and Brierley 1985: 20–31). According to Zweigert and Kötz (1992), there are eight major groups: Romanistic, Germanic, Nordic, Common Law, Socialist, Far Eastern law, Islamic and Hindu laws. The two most influential legal families in the world are the Common Law and the Civil Law (Romano-Germanic) families, and these are the focus of most of this book. About 80% of the countries in the world belong to these two systems. Here are some examples of the two groupings. For the Common Law jurisdictions, there are England and Wales, the United States of America, Australia, New Zealand, Canada, some of the former colonies of England in Africa and Asia such as Nigeria, Kenya, Singapore, Malaysia and Hong Kong. Civil Law countries include France, Germany, Italy, Switzerland, Austria, Latin American countries, Turkey, some Arab states, North African countries, Japan and South Korea.

There are also the mixed systems of law that derive from more than one legal family. They are hybrids and examples of such mixed jurisdictions with the influence from the Common Law and the Civil Law include Israel, South Africa, the Province of Quebec in Canada, Louisiana in the US, Scotland, the Philippines and Greece. The law of the EU is also such a mixed jurisdiction. China may be considered another hybrid with influence from traditional Chinese law, the Civil Law and Socialist Law.

As David and Brierley state, each legal system or family has its own characteristics and,

> ... has a vocabulary used to express concepts, its rules are arranged into categories, it has techniques for expressing rules and interpreting them, it is linked to a view of the social order itself which determines the way in which the law is applied and shapes the very function of law in that society. (David and Brierley 1985: 19)

Due to the differences in historical and cultural development, the elements of the source legal system cannot be simply transposed into the target legal system (Sarcevic 1997: 13). Thus, the main challenge to the legal translator is the incongruency of legal systems in the SL and TL.

Then, what are the distinguishing features of the major legal systems, specifically and for our purpose, the Common Law and the Civil Law, and what are the major differences between them?[13]

One set of criteria for the classification of legal systems or families in describing the characteristics or the 'juristic or legal style' of legal systems is that proposed by Zweigert and Kötz (1992: 68–73). They include (1) the historical development of a legal system; (2) the distinctive mode of legal thinking; (3) the distinctive legal institutions; (4) the sources of law and their treatment; and (5) the ideology.

If we use these criteria to compare the Common Law and the Civil Law, firstly, the Common Law is the legal tradition that evolved in England from the 11th century onwards. Its legal principles appear for the most part in reported judgments in relation to specific fact situations arising in disputes that courts have to adjudicate. Thus, the Common Law is predominantly founded on a system of case law or judicial precedent. The key features of the Common Law include a case-based system of law that functions through analogical reasoning and an hierarchical doctrine of precedent (de Cruz 1999: 102–103).

In contrast, the Civil Law originated in ancient Roman law as codified in the *Corpus Juris Civilis* of Justinian (AD 528–534). It was later developed through the Middle Ages by medieval legal scholars. It is the oldest legal tradition in the Western world. Originally, Civil Law was one common legal system in much of Europe, but with the development of nationalism in the 17th century Nordic countries and around the time of the French

Revolution, it became fractured into separate national systems. This change was brought about by the development of separate national codes. The French Napoleonic Code and the German and Swiss Codes were the most influential ones. The Civil Law was developed in Continental Europe and subsequently around the world, e.g. Latin America and Asia (see Merryman *et al.* 1994). Because of the rising power of Germany in the late 19th century, many Asian nations translated and introduced the Civil Law. For instance, the German Civil Code was the basis for the law of Japan and South Korea. In China, the German Civil Code was introduced in the late 1800s and early 1900s and formed the basis of the law of the Republic of China, which remains in force in Taiwan today. It has also greatly influenced the legal system of the People's Republic of China. Some authors also believe that the Civil Law later served as the foundation for Socialist Law in Communist countries.

In terms of legal thinking, the Civil Law family is marked by a tendency to use abstract legal norms, to have well-articulated system containing well-defined areas of law, and to think up and to think in juristic constructions (Zweigert and Kötz 1992: 70).

The function and style of legal doctrine are different in the Common Law and Civil Law. The Common Law jurists focus on fact patterns. They analyse cases presenting similar but not identical facts, distinguishing cases and extracting specific rules, and then, through deduction, determine the narrow scope of each rule, and sometimes propose new rules to cover facts that have not yet presented themselves (Tetley 2000: 701). In contrast, the Civil Law jurists focus on legal principles. They trace their history, identify their function, determine their domain of application, and explain their effects in terms of rights and obligations (Tetley 2000: 702, see also Vranken 1997).

In terms of case law, in the Common Law, specific rules are set out to specific sets of facts. Case law in the Common Law provides the principal source of law, whereas in the Civil Law system, case law applies general principles and is only a secondary source of law (Tetley 2000: 702). The English doctrine of *stare decisis* compels lower courts to follow decisions rendered in higher courts, hence establishing an order of priority of sources by 'reason of authority'. *Stare decisis* is unknown to the Civil Law, where judgments rendered by judges only enjoy the 'authority of reason' (Tetley 2000: 702).

In the Civil Law world, the general legal principles are embodied in codes and statutes, and legal doctrine provides guidance in their interpretation, leaving to judges the task of applying the law (Tetley 2000: 702). The Civil Law is highly systematised and structured and relies on declarations of broad and general principles, often ignoring details (Tetley 2000). The key or primary sources of law in Civil Law are codes and enacted statutes. Secondary sources include court decisions (jurisprudence), learned annotations of academic lawyers or scholars' opinions or legal scholarship (*la doctrine*), textbooks and commentaries. Civil Law courts base their judgments on the provisions of codes and statutes, from which solutions in particular cases are to derive on the basis of the general principles of codes and statutes.

In terms of legal institutions, typical legal institutions of the Common Law include trust, tort law, estoppel and agency, and these are unique to the Common Law. The Common Law also has categories of law such as contract and tort as separate branches of law and two main bodies of law: common law and equity. There is no substantive or structural public/ private law distinction as that which exists in the Civil Law system (de Cruz 1999). In contrast to the Common Law, the Civil Law has such unique legal institutions as *cause*, abuse of right, the direct action, the oblique action, the *action de in rem verso*, the extent of strict liability in tort, and *negotiorum gestio*, among others. These are foreign to the Common Law. In the Germanic family, there are also the *calusulae generales*, the theory of the abstract real contract, the concept of the legal act and liability based on *culpa in contrahendo*, the doctrine of the collapse of the foundations of a transaction, the entrenched position of the institution of unjust or unjustified enrichment, and the land register (for detailed discussions of these, see Zweigert and Kötz 1992).

In short, Zweigert and Kötz summarise the major differences between the Common Law and the Civil Law succinctly:

> To the lawyers from the Continent of Europe, English law has always been something rich and strange. At every step he comes across legal institutions, procedures, and traditions which have no counterpart in the Continental legal world with which he is familiar. Contrariwise, he scans the English legal scene in vain for much that seemed to him to be an absolute necessity in any functioning system, such as a civil code, a commercial code, a code of civil procedure, and an integrated structure of legal concepts rationally ordered. He finds that legal technique, instead of being directed primarily in interpreting statutory texts or analysing concrete problems so as to 'fit them into the system' conceptually, is principally interested in precedents and types of case; it is devoted to the careful and realistic discussion of live problems and readier to deal in concrete and historical terms than think systematically or in the abstract. (Zweigert and Kötz 1992: 188)

Despite the differences, we need to recognise that the Common Law and the Civil Law families are not incompatible. We should not exaggerate the differences or believe that the translation between the two is somehow not possible. After all, both belong to the Western legal traditions and political cultures. Particularly, there has been convergence due to the mutual influence and cross-fertilisation between the two families (see Merryman *et al.* 1994). Statute laws have played an increasing role in Common Law countries, especially the US after the Second World War. More recently, the impact the EU laws on both the Common Law and Civil Law jurisdictions in Europe has also been felt (see Vranken 1997). Nevertheless, the systemic differences between different legal families are a major source of difficulty in translation.

Linguistic differences

In language for special purpose communication, the text is formulated in a special language or sub-language that is subject to special syntactic, semantic and pragmatic rules (Sager 1990b). In our present case, LLP is subject to the special rules of legal language. Legal language is used in communicative situations between legal specialists, such as judges, lawyers and law professors, and also in communications between lawyers and the layperson or the general public.

According to White (1982: 423), one of the most problematic features of legal discourse is that it is 'invisible'. He claims that 'the most serious obstacles to comprehensibility are not the vocabulary and sentence structure employed in law, but the unstated conventions by which language operates' (White 1982: 423). There are expectations about the way in which language operates in legal contexts. Such expectations are not explicitly stated anywhere but are assumed in such contexts (Bhatia 1997: 208).

Linguistic difficulties often arise in translation from the differences found in the different legal cultures in the Common Law and the Civil Law. The root of the problems lies in their varying legal histories, cultures and systems. Law and languages are closely related. Legal language has developed its characteristics to meet the demands of the legal system in which it is expressed. As said earlier, legal translation is distinguished from other types of technical translation that convey universal information. In this sense, legal translation is *sui generis*. Each legal language is the product of a special history and culture. It follows that the characteristics of the *la langue de droit* in French do not necessarily apply to legal English. Nor do those of the English language of the law necessarily apply to French.

A basic linguistic difficulty in legal translation is the absence of equivalent terminology across different languages. This requires constant comparison between the legal systems of the SL and TL. As David and Brierley state:

> The absence of an exact correspondence between legal concepts and categories in different legal systems is one of the greatest difficulties encountered in comparative legal analysis. It is of course to be expected that one will meet rules with different content; but it may be disconcerting to discover that in some foreign law there is not even that system for classifying the rules with which we are familiar. But the reality must be faced that legal science has developed independently within each legal family, and that those categories and concepts which appear so elementary, so much a part of the natural order of things, to a jurist of one family may be wholly strange to another. (David and Brierley 1985: 16)

In terms of legal style, legal language is a highly specialised language use with its own style. The languages of the Common Law and Civil Law systems are fundamentally different in style. Legal traditions and legal culture has had a lasting impact on the way law is written. Written legal language thus reflects the essential elements of a legal culture and confronts the legal translator with its multi-faceted implications (Smith 1995: 190–191).

As said earlier, there are major differences in the order of priority in Civil Law and Common Law regarding case law and legal doctrine. The functions of case law have had an apparent influence on the writing style and language of court decisions. Common Law judicial opinions are usually long and contain elaborate reasoning, whereas the legal opinions in Civil Law countries are usually short and more formal in nature and style. For instance, in France, judges normally cite only legislation, not prior case law. Such judgments are normally separated into two parts – the *motifs* (reasons) and the *dispositif* (order). The method of writing judgments is also different. Common Law judgments extensively expose the facts, compare or distinguish them from the facts of previous cases, and decide the specific legal rule relevant to the facts. In contrast, Civil Law decisions first identify the legal principles that may be relevant, then verify if the facts support their application (Tetley 2000: 702). In Civil Law countries, there are mainly two styles in presenting judicial decisions (David and Brierley 1985: 142, see also de Cruz 1999). There is the French technique of 'whereas-es' (*attendus*). Such judgment is formulated in a single sentence and is concise and concentrated. This style is mostly found in France, Belgium, Luxembourg, the Netherlands, Spain, Portugal and most of the Nordic countries. The other style of judicial decision is found in other Civil Law countries such as

Germany, Greece, Italy, Switzerland and Sweden, where the judgment is presented in the form of a dissertation that varies in length and in its organisation (David and Brierley 1985: 142). Normally, they are lengthy and discuss prior cases and academic writing extensively.

In terms of the style of legislative drafting, Civil Law codes and statutes are concise (*le style français*), while Common Law statutes are precise (*le style anglais*) (Tetley 2000: 703). Civil Law statutes generally provide no definitions, and state principles in broad, general phrases. In contrast, Common Law statutes provide detailed definitions, and each specific rule sets out lengthy enumerations of specific applications or exceptions, preceded by a catch-all phrase and followed by qualifications (Tetley 2000: 703, see also Chapter 6).

To be more specific, if we compare the Common Law with German law, the legal traditions of the Anglo-American and German Civil Law systems underscore the different styles of the two legal cultures. Common Law in English is forensic whereas Civil Law in German is scholastic (Smith 1995). In the Civil Law system, interpretation of the legal norm entails determining unforeseen and future problems. The thinking is abstract and system-oriented while the method is deductive. In contrast, in the Anglo-American system, the method of legal thinking is inductive. US judges and lawyers are deeply sceptical of abstract norms. The approach to legal problems is empirical. Consequently, in the Anglo-American context, legal writing reflects the necessity to leave the judge as little room for interpretation as possible. This is most obvious in contracts between business partners (Smith 1995). They result in wordy, lengthy texts, listing a seemingly endless array of terms with seemingly similar meanings (see Chapter 5). Typically, in an American contract, one finds phrases such as 'any right, interest, title, property, ownership, entitlement and/or any other claim . . .'. The equivalent in German would be one word *rechtasnspruch* meaning 'legal claim' (Smith 1995). In short, there are stylistic differences between the two systems.

When we translate legal texts between different legal systems or families and languages, the degrees of difficulty may vary. There are the following scenarios depending upon the affinity of the legal systems and languages according to de Groot (1988: 409–410): (1) when the two legal systems and the languages concerned are closely related, e.g. between Spain and France, or between Denmark and Norway, the task of translation is relatively easy; (2) when the legal systems are closely related, but the languages are not, this will not raise extreme difficulties, e.g. translating between Dutch laws in the Netherlands and French laws; (3) when the legal systems are different but the languages are related, the difficulty is still considerable, and the main difficulty lies in *faux amis*, e.g. translating German legal texts into Dutch, and vice versa; and (4) when the two legal systems and languages are unrelated, the difficulty increases considerably, e.g. translating the Common Law in English into Chinese. In short, the degree of difficulty of legal translation is related to the degree of affinity of the legal systems and languages in question (de Groot 1988: 410). An a priori argument of the disparity in legal systems is that variations exist in the different legal languages of individual societies using language to communicate law (Weisflog 1987). The 'system gap' (Weisflog 1987) between one national legal system and another results in linguistic differences. Generally speaking, the wider the 'system gap', the wider the legal language gap.

In short, the differences in the Common Law and Civil Law systems and the consequent differences in the language used in law in the two systems as described above have an impact on legal translation. The diverse range of linguistic differences is one of most challenging aspects that confront the legal translator irrespective of which legal language is involved. It is a major source of difficulty in legal translation.

Cultural differences

Another source of difficulty in legal translation is cultural differences. Language and culture or social contexts are closely integrated and inter-dependent. Halliday (1975: 66) has defined 'culture' as 'a semiotic system' and 'a system of meanings' or information that is encoded in the behaviour potential of the members. Snell-Hornby (1988: 39) argues that, in translation, language should not be seen as an isolated phenomenon suspended in a vacuum but as an integral part of culture, and that the text is embedded in a given situation, which is itself conditioned by its socio-cultural back-ground (Snell-Hornby 1988: 42, quoting Hönig and Kubmaul 1982). The concept of culture as a totality of knowledge, proficiency and perception is fundamental to the integrated approach to translation as advanced by Snell-Hornby (1988: 42), an approach adopted in this study.

In this connection, a legal culture is meant those 'historically conditioned attitudes about the nature of law and about the proper structure and operation of a legal system that are at large in the society' (Merryman *et al.* 1994: 51). Law is an expression of the culture, and it is expressed through legal language. Legal language, like other language use, is a social practice and legal texts necessarily bear the imprint of such practice or organisational background (Goodrich 1987: 2). 'Each country has its own legal language representing the social reality of its specific legal order' (Sarcevic 1985: 127). Legal translators must overcome cultural barriers between the SL and TL societies when reproducing a TL version of a law originally written for the SL reader. In this connection, Weston writes (1983: 207) that the most important general characteristic of any legal translation is that an unusually large proportion of the text is culture-specific. The existence of different legal cultures and traditions is a major reason why legal languages are different from one another, and will remain so. It is also a reason why legal language within each national legal order is not and will not be the same as ordinary language.

Legal Translational Equivalence: Possibility and Impossibility

Given the complexity and difficulty of legal translation, one may wonder whether law is translatable and whether true equivalence can be achieved in legal translation.

If one believes that no two historical epochs, no two social classes and no two localities use words and syntax to signify exactly the same things and to send identical signals of valuation and inference (Steiner 1998: 47), then one may question whether translation attempting to achieve equivalence is indeed possible. It is a fact that one major and frequently encountered difficulty in legal translation is the translation of foreign legal concepts. It has often been claimed that legal concepts alien or non-existent in the target system are untranslatable (see Sarcevic 1997: 233). For instance, there are those who believe that no Chinese vocabulary can be found to express the full meaning of Common Law concepts, and hence the Common Law is not translatable into Chinese. Some have contended that, because of the conceptual gaps between English and Chinese laws, difficulties inherent in translating Common Law terms into Chinese are insurmountable.[14] But are such claims true or exaggerations?

We can look at this issue from several perspectives. Firstly, it is a fact that we translate law between different legal families and legal traditions, and we have been doing so for the last few centuries. In fact, the laws and legal systems in many countries and continents have been developed on the basis of legal transplant from other legal systems (see Watson 1974) assisted to a large extent by the process of translation. Legal concepts, practices and entire legal systems have been introduced to new political, social, cultural and legal environments this way. So, real life experience, and successful experience at that, tells us that translating law, irrespective of what systems and families are involved, is not only possible, but also highly productive. This does not mean that there are no problems or the job is easy.

Secondly, if we look at this from the angle of translational equivalence, a number of factors need to be taken into account when foreign laws, legal concepts and practices are translated that have no existing equivalents in the TL. Naturally, there needs to be a link that establishes a degree of equivalent relationship between the SL and TL for translation to take place. But what kind of equivalent relationship? As Toury observes, translation is a series of operation or procedures,

> . . . whereby one semiotic entity, which is a constituent element of a certain cultural subsystem, is transformed into another semiotic entity, which forms at least a potential element of another cultural subsystem, providing that some informational core is retained 'invariant under transformation', and on its basis a relationship known as 'equivalence' is established between the resultant and initial entities. (Toury 1986: 1112–1113)

According to Toury, equivalence is a combination of, or compromise between, the two basic types of constraints that draw from the incompatible poles of the target system and the source text and system (Toury 1986: 1123). It can be argued that, conceptually and pragmatically, translation, including the legal kind, is not solely the question of crossing languages or the question of identity or synonymy. This is because the validity of a translation is independent of whether an element in one code is synonymous with a correlated element in another code (Frawley 1984: 161). Translation always takes place in a continuum and there are many kinds of textual and extratextual constraints upon the translator (Bassnett and Lefevere 1998: 123). Recodification occurs irrespective of the exact status of identity across the codes (Frawley 1984: 161). Translational equivalence is a relative notion (see Koller 1995, Henderson 1997). As pointed out, translators decide on the specific degree of equivalence they can realistically aim for in a specific text (Bassnett and Lefevere 1998: 2). Thus, translating legal texts is a relative affair.

Take legal concepts for example. Legal concepts from different countries are seldom, if ever, identical, because, firstly, the nature of language dictates that two words are rarely identical between two languages and even within the same language (for instance, the English legal language in the US, UK and Australia; the Chinese legal language used in China, Hong Kong and Taiwan; German in Germany, Austria and Switzerland, and French in France and Canada). Secondly, human societies with their own cultural, political and social conditions and circumstances are never duplicate. Law is a human and social institution, established on the basis of the diverse moral and cultural values of individual societies. Moreover, conceptually, added to this is the individual mediating process as described by Peirce within the semiotic process that impacts on the interpretive outcome (see Cao 2004). Nevertheless, the other side of the same coin is that common sense tells us human societies share many things in common. More things combine than divide us, our differences notwithstanding. Some legal concepts may overlap in different societies but seldom identical. Therefore, it is futile to search for absolute equivalence when translating legal concepts.

Thirdly, in this connection, the issue of comprehending translated law, after the initial linguistic transfer, is also a related consideration. In people's understanding of translated texts originally written for different audiences in different languages, inevitably, sometimes there are confusions and misunderstandings. Such confusion may have something to do with the often invisible crossover in translation. Words may be written and read in the same language but people's interpretations in the SL and TL differ due to the differences in language use. Others' horizons that are encoded in the original language but now represented in the translated language may not be so readily obvious as to place one's own horizons in relief (cf. Gadamer 1975, 1976), simply because the other horizons are now expressed in a deceptively familiar language, one's own language. Nevertheless, the 'fusion of horizons' is possible and experienceable in translation and understanding translated texts.

According to Gadamer (1975: 350, 1976: 59–68), language is the universal medium in which understanding is realised, and language is a social phenomenon and, as such, it is formally directed towards intersubjectivity. It is capable of opening a person to other horizons. Horizon, says Gadamer, is the range of vision that includes everything that can be seen from a particular vantage point. Horizon is used to characterise the way in which thought is tied to its finite determination, and the nature of the law of the expansion of the range of vision. According to Gadamer (1975, 1976), understanding transcends the limits of any particular language, and mediates between the familiar and the alien. The particular language with which we live is not closed off against what is foreign to it. Instead it is porous and open to expansion and absorption of ever new mediated content (Gadamer 1976: xxxi). In short, we can transcend our interpretive horizons. The event of understanding culminates in a fusion of horizons when the horizon of the self's experienceable world is transformed through contact with another (Gadamer 1975, 1976). This description of understanding applies to both situations within one language and across two languages.

In translation, including legal translation, one may say that a 'fusion of horizons' can be achieved and mediated in the transmission of meaning, creating new interpretive horizons on the part of the reader of translation.

Despite the seemingly insurmountable conceptual and linguistic gulf, alleged and real, between different laws and languages, translating law is possible, and cross-cultural understanding in law can be realised, although such understanding is always subjective and may not be identical in all languages at all time. However, one may say that no exact equivalence or complete identity of understanding can be expected or is really necessary.

Notes

1. For further reference for the characteristics of pragmatic, general and literary texts, see Delisle (1988: 8–18).
2. The term *prototypologie* was first used by Neubert (1984) as cited in Snell-Hornby (1988: 37).
3. Cf. Gémar (1995, cited in Sarcevic 1997: 11) who identifies six subdivisions of legal language: there are the language of the legislator, judges, the administration, commerce, private law, and scholarly writings.
4. Despite the importance given to the purpose of translated texts in this study, I do not agree with many aspects of the skopos theory and have doubts as to whether it is suitable for legal translation. For instance, Hönig (1998) gave an example of court interpreting where he argued that the phrase 'closing time' used by the witnesses in court should be translated into a specific time by the interpreter, say '10 p.m.'. It is a fundamental misunderstanding by Hönig of the nature of legal interpreting and of the legal process, and by extension, legal translation. For criticisms of the skopos theory in relation to legal translation, see Madsen (1997b) where it was pointed out that the skopos theory is inadequate for the description of legal texts due to the fact that it does not take into account the conventionalisation and institutionalisation of the communicative activities of the legal universe.
5. According to O'Barr (undated) and Charrow and Crandall (1978), both as cited by Danet (1980: 470), the linguistic differentiation of legal English may be great enough to warrant calling it a separate language or dialect.
6. According to Halliday *et al.* (1964), register is use-related language variety and is to be distinguished from user-related language varieties, e.g. geographical, temporal, social or idiolectal dialects.
7. Jackson (1988: 138) lists several types of legal discourse: litigation, legislative discourse, doctrine, solicitor–client relations, discourse between practitioners, media communication of the law to the general public, and communication of legal messages in advisory agencies.
8. See, for instance, Otto Jespersen (1964) who regards ambiguity as an inherent property of any natural language, cited in Kooij (1971: 3).
9. For a philosophical analysis of ambiguity and vagueness, see Scheffler (1979), and the differences between ambiguity, vagueness and generality.
10. For a linguistic discussion and description of ambiguity in natural language, for instance, ambiguity and phonology, grammar and lexicon, and related concepts of homonymy and polysemy, see Kooij (1971).
11. Hart is said to have borrowed the phrase 'open texture' from Friedrich Waismann (1968). Waismann states that regarding certain kinds of terms,

particularly nouns denoting physical objects, there is a virtually inexhaustible source of vagueness. When they form a concept, we only have some situations in mind. As a result, the concept is armed only against certain contingencies. This is the feature of open texture or possibility of vagueness. Waismann believes that this kind of vagueness can never be eliminated completely, and there will always be a penumbra of indeterminacy attaching to physical object terms as opposed to arithmetical terms.

12. For a discussion of the legal language and style in Hebrew in Israel, see Fassberg (2003). Interestingly, modern Hebrew legal language has been influenced by both the Common Law and Civil Law, and has some of the linguistic characteristics of both systems.

13. For a detailed comparative analysis of the Common Law and the Civil Law and other legal systems, see David and Brierley (1985), Zweigert and Kötz (1992), and de Cruz (1999).

14. See Sin and Roebuck (1996) for their discussion of legal conceptual problems in creating Common Law Chinese and their argument against the proposition that English Common Law is untranslatable into Chinese. It is also noted that untranslatability and incommensurability of concepts are different and should not be confused.

Chapter 3
The Legal Translator

Many descriptions have been offered of what the legal translator should be like and what skills such a translator should possess. Often, it is said that the legal translator requires both linguistic skills and some basic understand ing of law. Smith (1995: 181) believes that there are three prerequisites for successful translation of legal texts: (1) the legal translator must acquire a basic knowledge of the legal systems, both in the SL and TL; (2) must possess familiarity with the relevant terminology; and (3) must be competent in the TL-specific legal writing style. Another slightly different description of the requirements is that the legal translator must possess the ability to retrieve information from the specialised SL, and the ability to process information (Wagner 2003). In other words, the legal translator must understand all the shades of meaning of the SL so that he or she may reproduce it as faithfully and naturally as possible in the TL, and must understand all the mechanisms of the law, the way legal texts are drafted, interpreted and applied in legal practice (Wagner 2003).

Recognising the similarities between legal translation and other types of translation, Weisflog (1987, based on Nida 1964) proposes that a translator in general must ideally have an excellent background in the SL and control over the resources of the TL, an intimate acquaintance of the subject matter, an effective empathy with the original author and the content, and a stylistic facility in the TL. Specific to the legal translator, Weisflog believes that the translator must have a thorough acquaintance of law as the subject matter, including the national law in the case of translation within a multilingual country, and legal systems and national laws of the SL and TL countries in the case of transnational translation (Weisflog 1987). But Weisflog says that such ideal translators are rare. Similarly, according to Sarcevic (1997), the legal competence of the translator presupposes not only in-depth knowledge of legal terminology, but also a thorough understanding of legal reasoning and the ability to solve legal problems, to analyse legal texts, to foresee how a text will be interpreted and applied by the court. In addition to these basic legal skills, the legal translator should also possess extensive knowledge of the target legal system and preferably the source legal system as well (Sarcevic 1997). Moreover, drafting skills and a basic knowledge of comparative law and comparative methods are also required. However, Sarcevic adds that such ideal translators simply do not exist (1997: 114).

A number of comments can be made here. Firstly, the descriptions of the legal translator seem to be over-generalised guidelines. They are not a systematic description of the competence involved, with insufficient details as to the specific skills that are required, not sufficiently specific to be of great use to the legal translator or the educator of legal translators. Secondly, they say little or nothing about the nature of legal translation competence. They more resemble general observations than the results of systematic, analysis, either empirical or theoretical. Thirdly, some of the commentators describe their own descriptions as 'idealised', that they themselves believe have no real life reflection or existence. They seem to believe that their descriptions are not realisable or unrealistic.

In this study, translation is seen in terms of translator behaviour. Furthermore, translation is regarded as a knowledge-based activity (Wilss 1996a: 37), a human act and process. According to Wilss (1996a: 37), the two basic issues in translator behaviour are knowledge and skills (knowledge and experience), and they are the pillars of information-processing procedures designed to determine the conditions for situationally adequate translation processes and to substantiate them. Translation is

> a capacity for steering translator performance in a principled manner and enabling the interaction of knowing that/knowing what, i.e., the knowledge of a certain domain, and knowing how, i.e., the knowledge of how to execute something in a situationally adequate manner. (Wilss 1996a: 39)

Legal translation is no exception. It is a fact that successful legal translators are found around the world, performing important legal translation tasks that are often vital to the functioning of law. It is also a fact that some legal translators are not as effective. Legal and other consequences may result from both successful and unsuccessful attempts. Notwithstanding, the competence of the legal translator is identifiable and describable, and indeed can be identified and specified, and importantly, can be learned and developed. Such competence is not just an ideal projection, but achievable in real life. This does not mean that legal translation is identical, mechanical or static in all situations and contexts and across different languages. Nevertheless, the competence of the legal translator can be identified, described and acquired. As Wilss (1996a: 57) points out with regard to general translation competence, there are three aspects of knowledge-based behaviour: the acquisition of knowledge, either in a direct experiential or in an indirect (mediate) manner; the storing of acquired knowledge in memory; and the reactivation of internalised knowledge, normally for multiple use either in a problem-solving setting or in automaticised form. In this chapter, I attempt to offer a description of translation competence as a knowledge-based behaviour with reference to legal translation.

Translation Competence and Translation Proficiency

As described in Chapter 2, translation can be divided into general, specialist and literary translation. Furthermore, it argues that legal translation as a specialist or technical translation shares many things in common with other types of translation but also has its own characteristics. Therefore, characterising legal translation competence and proficiency presupposes the description of general translation competence and proficiency. A competent legal translator is first of all a competent translator.

In the deliberation of language competence and language proficiency and subsequently of translation competence and translation proficiency, a distinction needs to be made between competence and proficiency. 'Competence' in linguistics was originally used by Chomsky (1965) to refer to 'the speaker-hearer's knowledge of his language'. Chomsky distinguishes competence from performance, which is 'the actual use of language in concrete situations'. Thus, competence refers to knowledge of language as separate from the ability to use this knowledge. Conversely, 'language proficiency' has been used in the context of language testing to refer to knowledge, competence or ability in the use of language, irrespective of how, where or under what conditions it has been acquired (Bachman 1990: 16). Using these definitions, translation competence refers to the knowledge that is essential to the translation act. Translation proficiency is defined as the ability to mobilise translation competence to perform translation tasks in context for intercultural and interlingual communication purposes. For our current purpose, legal translation proficiency refers to the ability to mobilise translation competence to perform legal translation tasks in the legal setting for intercultural and interlingual communication purposes.

This definition incorporates both competence and the ability to activate that competence in an act of translating. It also takes into account the communicative nature of a translation act in intercultural and interlingual contexts. Translation proficiency is seen as a global skill to integrate both the competence and ability that transpire during the translation process and result in the translation product. It is this overall ability that makes translators what they are and makes translation a viable reality.

With translation proficiency defined, it is necessary to further depict what it encompasses both theoretically and in practice and to characterise its nature, both in general terms and with reference to legal translation.

A Model of Translation Competence

The model for translation competence and proficiency is based on the following premises. First of all, the model recognises that translation proficiency is multi-componential, that is, consisting of different sets of variables. The model recognises and characterises the processes by which the different variables interact with one another and with the context in which translation occurs. The interactivity is manifested both between each variable and within the overall act of translating, that is, intra-interactivity within the nexus and inter-interactivity between the nexuses. Translation is the product of the total translation behaviour as a result of the interaction among the variables and within the situational context. In addition this schema views translation as a dynamic process to achieve interlingual and cross-cultural communicative goals. Translation is a purposive activity. The model also maintains that the translation proficiency is a global skill and it can be described, developed and measured. In short, translation proficiency is multi-dimensional, interactive and developmental.[1]

In this description, as stated earlier, translation is divided into general, specialist and literary translation based on Snell-Hornby's (1988) typology (see Chapter 2). This means that these types of translation are different language uses that have their own distinctive features but also share common ground. They blend with one another although with blurred edges and overlapping as found in real life situations (Snell-Hornby 1988: 29–36). The model holds that the ability to translate general, specialist and literary texts can be learned, developed and tested as the model accommodates the fact that translation proficiency is identifiable. But proficiency, as herein defined, needs to be measured as a global ability for performing translation tasks.

Proceeding from these premises, and in keeping with the relevant principles of translation and language proficiency, translation proficiency is thus further described as consisting of three sets of variables interacting with one another in the context of situation (Cao 1996a): (1) translational language competence; (2) translational knowledge structures; and (3) translational strategic competence (see Figure 3.1).[2]

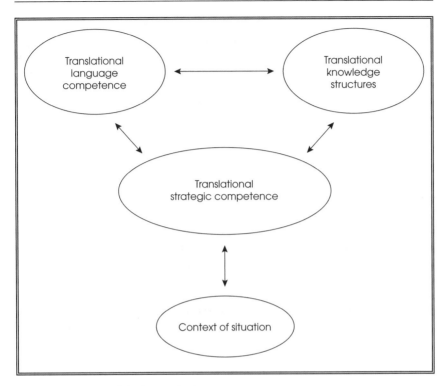

Figure 3.1 A model of translation competence

Source: Cao (1996a)

Exploring Translation Competence

Translational language competence and translational strategic competence constitute the major components of communicative language ability, and they, together with knowledge structures, are the basic components required for communicative language use in translation.

Translational language competence

Translation is a special type of communicative language use in that it requires language competence in two languages, the SL and TL. Language competence as required in translation shares many features of language competence in monolingual communicative language use, but translational language competence also has its own peculiarities. Translation as a linguistic operation in both SL and TL dictates that language competence is a prerequisite for a translator.[3] This partly corresponds to what Lörscher (1991) terms 'linguistic knowledge' and what Neubert (1994, 2000) calls 'language competence'. For translators, a high level of proficiency in the receptive and productive skills in both languages is essential. But the question remains: what constitutes this proficiency and what is the level of proficiency required for translation purpose?

In the current model, translational language competence comprises a set of specific components in both the SL and TL that are activated and utilised in the translation act of intercultural and interlingual communication. Based on Bachman's (1990) account of monolingual communicative language use, translational language competence is defined as including (1) organisational competence in the SL and TL, which consists of (a) grammatical and (b) textual competence; and (2) pragmatic competence in the SL and TL, which consists of (a) illocutionary and (b) sociolinguistic competence (see Figure 3.2).

To further describe translational language competence, organisational competence comprises two types of abilities: (a) grammatical and (b) textual. Grammatical competence in translation refers to the mastery of the language code of the SL and TL at a high level, consisting of intimate knowledge of syntax, lexis and semantic rules that determine sentence formation and the meanings of sentences in both the SL and TL. Textual

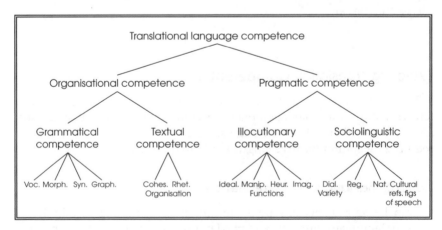

Figure 3.2 Components of translational language competence

Source: Cao (1996a)

competence in translation includes the knowledge of the conventions for joining utterances together to form a text according to rules of cohesion and rhetorical organisation. According to Bachman (1990), cohesion comprises ways of explicitly marking semantic relationships such as reference, substitution, ellipsis, conjunction and lexical cohesion. It denotes the mastery of how to combine forms and meanings to achieve a unified text in different genres by using cohesion devices to relate utterance forms and coherence rules to organise meanings. Cohesion consists of knowledge of the rules needed to produce a unified text as opposed to sentences in isolation (Bachman 1990). In translation, textual competence relies heavily on the ability to comprehend such rules and conventions in the SL and the ability to reproduce them in the TL appropriately according to the norms of the TL.

Pragmatic competence in translation includes (a) illocutionary competence and (b) sociolinguistic competence in both the SL and TL. Illocutionary competence refers to knowledge of the pragmatic conventions for performing acceptable language functions, while sociolinguistic competence refers to the knowledge of the sociolinguistic conventions for performing language functions appropriately in a given context and the mastery of appropriate language in different sociolinguistic contexts with emphasis on appropriateness of meaning and appropriateness of form with regard to two language and culture contexts. The latter comprises knowledge of the criteria governing the production and interpretation of language in different sociolinguistic contexts including the control of rules of meaning and the rules of form. These criteria, rules or norms may not correspond in the two languages concerned in translation. Sensitivity to language variety, sensitivity to differences in register, sensitivity to naturalness, ability to interpret cultural references and figures of speech in both the SL and TL are part of the repertoire. In translation, pragmatic competence particularly includes familiarity with, comprehension and interpretation of the pragmatic and sociolinguistic conventions and rules in the SL and the ability to reproduce them in an appropriate form according to the TL convention.

The prototypology of categorisation proposed by Snell-Hornby (1988) can be applied to translational language competence. Translational language competence is perceived as consisting of competence in general, specialist texts and literary uses of language. These different text types share common features and blurred edges in terms of the components of language competence. At the same time, there are different emphasis and also distinct features that characterise these text types. These features are reflected in the various facets outlined earlier (e.g. grammatical, textual, sociolinguistic).

In terms of legal translation, different languages are believed to entail distinctive features in the sub-categories of competence. It is impossible to describe them all here (see Chapter 2 for the discussion of the characterisation of legal language in terms of lexicon, syntax, pragmatics and style). So, briefly, in terms of grammatical competence, for instance, legal English has a propensity to use certain lexical and syntactical features such as archaic words and word strings, and long and complex structures (see Chapters 4 and 5). In terms of pragmatic competence, legal language relies heavily on performative verbs and they may differ in different languages (see Chapter 6). In terms of textual competence, statutes normally follow certain textual conventions peculiar to law and lawmaking (see Chapters 6 and 7). Thus, the legal translator needs to be highly sensitive to the peculiar linguistic features of the legal texts in all the aspects described above and have a sophisticated level of competency in these areas in both the SL and TL.

In short, critical to translators in terms of translational language competence is the ability to utilise, relate and mediate the SL and TL linguistic variables in the total communicative act of translating to achieve communicative goals.

Translational knowledge structures

Translation, though a linguistic activity, also requires adequate knowledge of the subject matter, i.e. translational knowledge structures. This partly corresponds to 'subject competence' described by Neubert (1994, 2000), 'factual knowledge' used by Lörscher (1991) or 'knowledge base' used by Sager (1993).

Within the present model, translational knowledge structures are defined as the knowledge that is essential to achieve interlingual and intercultural communication in translation. Translational knowledge structures include general, specialist and literary knowledge. General knowledge refers to knowledge about the world. It includes knowledge about ecology, material culture, social organisation and other areas of both the SL and TL communities. Specialist knowledge is the subject knowledge that includes technical knowledge in a specialist field such as medicine, law, economics and science and technology. In legal translation, legal knowledge is the knowledge of propositions of law in a narrow sense and the knowledge of legal culture in a broad sense, including legal systems, legal order, legal institutions, history and practices and practitioners (Salmi-Tolonen 2004: 1180–1181). Literary knowledge includes knowledge in such areas as the Bible, stage, film, lyric, poetic and literary works, cultural history and literary studies. In short, translational knowledge structures refer to the knowledge about the world and about the subject matter necessary for communication to take place in intercultural and interlingual situations.

Translational knowledge structures are characterised by the following features. Firstly, translational knowledge structures as a component of translation proficiency are dimensional and interactive. They consist of extensive sub-structures, as extensive as human activities. These sub-structures are not isolated, separated or compartmentalised, but interactive with the other variables of translation in the translation process.

The interactivity of translational knowledge structures can be perceived in at least the following three ways:

(1) Translational knowledge structures interact with translational language competence, translational strategic competence and situational variables within the translation process, i.e. inter-interactivity. It is apparent that translators activate both linguistic and non-linguistic knowledge and various strategies in order to comprehend a message contained in a text. The translator's knowledge structures and other incidental stimuli, and his or her initial and continuing encounter with the texts results in the postulation of alternatives of meaning, of which the inappropriate ones are progressively eliminated as his or her perusal of the visual configuration proceeds (cf. Ingram and Elias 1974: 64). The translator proceeds with the translational linguistic and knowledge components and postulates alternatives of meaning.

(2) Within the translation process, general translational knowledge structures interact with special or literary knowledge structures, i.e. intra-interactivity. Translational knowledge structures function in associating, optimising, eliminating processes during the translating act. General, literary and specialist knowledge structures are dimensional and spherical. They are not separated or linear. They overlap and they associate and optimise knowledge with different emphasis in different text types. In the usage of specialist subject language, the communicative and classificatory uses are maximised and the emotive and social uses are deliberately minimised or neutralised (cf. Sager 1993: 23). The interrelationship between general, specialist and literary knowledge structures is that of different emphasis. Hence, the mapping of knowledge structures in this model is a gestalt-like system of relationships between general, specialist and literary knowledge, rather than grid-like compartments of rigid classification (see Snell-Hornby 1988 and Chapter 2).

(3) Within the translation process, translational knowledge structures go through associating, networking and optimising processes, with new knowledge interacting with knowledge acquired previously. Translators relate the new information to their own knowledge structure in general and to the specific knowledge they have accumulated about a text and the purpose of the task. The established knowledge interacts with the newly acquired knowledge and permits the confirmation and expansion of a translator's knowledge structure and the specific subset of knowledge called upon for a particular task (cf. Sager 1993).

Furthermore, translational knowledge structures are both similar to and different from ordinary monolingual language user's knowledge structures. This study hypothesises that there are surface and deep translational knowledge structures. Such a distinction may be important as this may be where specialists and specialist translators differ in knowledge processing.

Mindful of the division of general, literary and specialist knowledge, this study thus assumes that there is a general corresponding division of knowledge fields in different cultures and reference to special knowledge areas presupposes that knowledge is divided into subject field or disciplines. Such a division is equivalent to defining as sets of subspaces of the overall knowledge space of a particular society and the special knowledge spaces intersect (cf. Sager 1993). General language serves for the expression of general knowledge and specialist language texts diversely combine areas of specialist knowledge and in messages knowledge subspaces overlap and interpenetrate (Sager 1993). Translational knowledge structures are a mixture of surface knowledge structures. This may be where translators, e.g. legal translators, differ from specialists, e.g. lawyers. Translators possess a considerably high degree of surface knowledge structures in different fields while specialists may possess a high degree of deep knowledge structures in a particular field. For specialist translation such as legal translation, the deep knowledge structures of the translator in a particular field can be enhanced and intensified but does not need to be the same as those of the specialist.

In this connection, Wilss's discussion of translational knowledge is particularly relevant. According to Wilss (1996a: 58), whether translators understand an LSP text depends, apart from familiarity with the respective terminology, upon their knowledge of the respective domain. Knowledge is a precondition for certainty in handling a specific discipline. A translator cannot properly comprehend and reproduce a source text belonging to a domain that is completely or partially alien. According to Wilss (1996a), translators must understand and reproduce an LSP text not in their own terms, but in its own terms. This means that in LSP translation, translators must share experiences, categories and modes of thinking with the source text author who is often a specialist (Wilss 1996a: 58). In order that the meaning of a text is determinate for the source text author, the translator and the target reader, it must be based on epistemic knowledge (Wilss 1996a). Furthermore, Wilss points out, whenever shared knowledge prevails, it exists to a large extent as tacit knowledge (pre-existing or prior knowledge), that is, knowledge the language user activates intuitively, as opposed to explicit knowledge that appears in verbalised form (Wilss 1996a: 58). Tacit knowledge is unobservable or only indirectly observable, but it is inferable from situations. The most important tool of knowledge acquisition, both explicit and tacit, is language (Wilss 1996a: 58).

Translational knowledge structures are assumed to be available in both the SL and TL regardless of in which language the knowledge is acquired. There has not been evidence to conclude in which language knowledge is stored. There is evidence to show, however, that models of the world seem not necessarily to be entirely discrete since knowledge acquired through one language often seems to be available in the other (Ingram and Elias 1974: 70). This study hypothesises that knowledge is stored in the language in which the knowledge is acquired, but it can be retrieved and transferred into the other language through the synthesising process, which is the third area of competence, translational strategic competence. It then can be stored in both languages or one or the other. Further studies are needed for such conjecture or conclusion. The study of the interrelationship between language and thought patterns and the development of bilingualism may provide some insight, but it is clearly beyond the scope of this study.

Under general translational knowledge structures in this model, knowledge of sociocultural background is also assumed, i.e. knowledge of both the SL culture and the TL culture (cf. Snell-Hornby 1988: 34). Translators translate texts, and texts are an integral part of the world around us, invariably embedded in an extralinguistic situation and dependent on their specific social and cultural background (cf. Snell-Hornby 1988). This is in contrast to Neubert's separate sub-competence of cultural competence (1994, 2000).

Translational knowledge structures can be acquired. They are accumulative through education and/or experience. Individuals acquire both general structures of the knowledge space of their society and the linguistic expression forms for accessing it (cf. Sager 1993: 42–43) through education. Translators also often acquire knowledge through translating. Translational knowledge structures are flexible, recurring, developmental and networking.

Translational knowledge structures are extensive and diverse. They vary from translator to translator. A translator's knowledge of the world is as extensive and varied as a person's experience, and is too complex for us to attempt to describe or classify in detail (cf. Bachman and Palmer 1996). The knowledge structures outlined are only a reference structure, not meant to be all-inclusive. Furthermore, many of the areas concerning translators' comprehension and the interaction between linguistic and knowledge skills are under-studied. How translators negotiate and manipulate their linguistic and knowledge structures to comprehend texts and reproduce translation effectively needs further in-depth and extensive empirical investigations.

In short, for theoretical reasons and practical purposes, translators need to possess general knowledge, specialist subject or literary knowledge, and socio-cultural knowledge to function as effective translators and carry out translation tasks in the increasingly complex world of ours.

Translational strategic competence

Translation involves a processing and synthesising ability. This is termed translational strategic competence in the present model. It includes strategic competence and psycho-physiological mechanisms, and importantly, includes the special strategic skill that is unique to translational activities.

Translational strategic competence is used to describe the integrated mental ability inherent in the translation task when a translator carries out an operation on a text and enacts language and knowledge competence for communicative purposes in translation. It characterises the mental capacity for implementing the components of translational language competence and knowledge structures in contextualised translational activities. Translational strategic competence provides the means for relating the various components of translation proficiency in the process of translation. It is seen as the linkage that relates translational language competence to translational knowledge structures and the features of the context in which translation, and hence interlingual and intercultural communication, takes place. It is a synthesising and processing ability necessary for translation to be produced. This partly corresponds to 'transfer competence' described by Neubert (1994) and 'processing knowledge' suggested by Lörscher (1991).

In translation, this mental ability is twofold. One aspect is the strategic competence that is general to all mental activity including language use by all language users (the first language included) as postulated by Bachman and Palmer (1996). The general strategic competence as applied to all language users includes 'assessment, planning, and executing' (Bachman 1990: 100).

In terms of the general strategic competence of translators, this study hypothesises that 'assessment, planning and executing' phases exist. However, this needs further investigation. These assessment, planning and executing stages include the specification, preparation, translation and evaluation/revision phases (cf. Sager 1993: 166). In short, the mental process includes initial planning, ongoing search, retrieval, monitoring and evaluation mechanisms (cf. Krings 1986, 1988, cited by Neubert 1991: 415).

A second component in translational strategic competence is unique to translation. This special strategic competence comprises the skills that are demanded during the processing and non-verbal stage of reformulation and analogy by reasoning (Delisle 1988). It is during this 'nonverbal' stage when concepts are turned over to non-linguistic cerebral mechanisms (Delisle 1988: 69). Though Delisle's study relates to translation of pragmatic texts, this study hypothesises that the mental processes for translation of literary, general and specialist texts are basically the same though further empirical studies are required to support this view. The special category of translational strategic competence performs the 'reformulation' and 'reasoning by analogy' in determining the most effective means of achieving communicative goals in translation.

Translational strategic competence also includes psychological mechanisms. This is related to the cognitive aspect of human thought processes, and in translation, it also embodies the creative aspects (cf. Delisle 1988: 69, Wilss 1990: 32–33).[4] This mental process of reformulation and analysing is still the least well understood, the most mysterious, and the most complicated to analyse (Delisle 1988: 60). Studies in bilingualism and the notion of cognitive competence to use both languages as thinking tools, that is, the ability to use one or both languages for reasoning and deliberation, might be able to provide some insight, and further studies are needed, although translation competence and bilingualism are very different in nature (see Presas 2000). There has not been any empirical evidence reported regarding how the translator's brain works. At the present phase of development in applied linguistics and translation studies, it is very difficult to establish and validate ways to establish or to measure this creative and cognitive aspect in language use or in translation. This study argues, however, that what can be measured is the final product of the translation process and the effectiveness as reflected in the communicative function of the translated texts.

Translational strategic competence is crucial to translation and can directly affect the translated works. One argument is that bilinguals are not synonymous with translators or interpreters. People may be highly proficient in two languages and sophisticated in knowledge structures but this does not automatically make them effective translators without training or practice. For instance, bilingual lawyers do not automatically become proficient legal translators without training, but they undoubtedly can acquire and develop their legal translation skills. There is a qualitative difference between knowing two languages and being a translator. Texts in one language are transferred into another language only with the intervention of a special processing ability unique to translation. Translational strategic competence is believed to constitute in large part this processing ability.

Translating as a total act

The present model of translation competence and translation proficiency reflects the view that there are three sets of variables, i.e. translational language competence, translational knowledge structures and translational strategic competence, which together constitute translation proficiency. These variables do not exist in isolation. Rather, they are closely related and interact with one another in the act of translation.

As stated earlier, the model acknowledges the full context of translation and communicative language use. Specifically, this refers to the context of discourse, of which individual utterances and sentences are intrinsic, and the sociolinguistic situation that governs the nature of that discourse in both form and function and how these features are reflected in translation. Accordingly, the model recognises the dynamic interaction between the context and the discourse and recognises translation as a dynamic process to achieve particular interlingual and intercultural communicative goals.

This study presents the view that, since external variables affect translation, they should be considered in the translation proficiency framework. There are situational variables in the internal translation process and in the cognitive translation behaviours evoked in response to those variables, and external factors and constraints that have considerable influence on the translation process and on the final product (cf. Neubert and Shreve 1992: 31, Sager 1993). Translation process, thus, is a progressive, physical production of a translated text in a context in which that production takes place, and it includes the constraints of particular institutional or personal philosophies of translation, as well as the conscious and unconscious mental operations that go on during translation. Translation proficiency is manifested only when a translation task is carried out in real life situations rather than as artificial clinical performance under idealised conditions. By direct observation of translation in action, some of these external variables (e.g. time, place, availability of resources, experience, pressure, mood, ethics, etc.) and the extent of their influence on translation can be identified and revealed.

Hence, the model holds that translation proficiency contains different sets of variables of translational language competence, translational knowledge structures and translational strategic competence within a situational context in which both the internal variables and external variables interact with one another and they together exert influence to varying degrees over the final product of translation. The internal variables are translational language competence, translational knowledge structures and translational strategic competence and external variables usually include a situation, a purpose, a target audience, time, place, and any other variables active in this operational environment. External factors are not always present simultaneously in all translation performances. Translation proficiency starts to be observable only when the three sets of variables are placed in a specific context in performing a translation task. It is in the course of performing the task that the different variables interact with one another and with external factors, both inter- and intra-interactively, exerting influences over the final product of translation. So in a sense, the translation process is a dual process including the internal and external processes, affecting the end results, but to varying degrees. The different variables can be altered and manipulated in the process of translation. The three areas of competence are different from translation techniques or methods used by translators in dealing with specific translation problems.

Of the external variables, resources available to translators are worth special mentioning. With the advent of information technology, in particular of CAT technology since the 1980s, the translator has been facing changes and new challenges in the workplace. Although the object of the translator and translation remains unchanged, that is, to transfer the message from the SL to the TL, the aids and tools available to the translator have changed a great deal (Tucker 2003: 73). This means that there is an increasing need for the translator to make use of the new resources. This also means that additional computing and CAT skills are sometimes required of the translator apart from the conventional linguistic and translational skills described previously. About twenty years ago, the tools used by the translator were pen and paper plus a dictionary, and in European languages, the typewriter. Today, a variety of new tools are on offer. These include the use of the computer, electronic document transfer such as e-mail, the Internet and search tools. For many translators, particularly those working for international organisations and multinational corporations, CAT also includes translation memories, terminological databases and machine translation (see Chapter 7 on the use of CAT at the UN and EU). For the legal translator, CAT and other computing and research skills have become indispensable, especially for those translating international instruments with a high degree of accuracy and consistency requirements.

To sum up, in this chapter, a description of translation competence is offered. This is presented as a general description applicable to most if not all translators, including specialist translators such as the legal translator. It is believed that there is an underlying competence found in all competent translators, including the legal translator. Notwithstanding, it is also believed that special characteristics exist in terms of the three sets of components, particularly translational language competence within each language pairs in translation. Furthermore, differences also exist in general, specialist and literary translation in terms of the sub-competence, accounting for the differences found in different types of translations. Moreover, within each translator and his or her translating act, different levels of competence also exist.

Notes

1. Campbell's study (1998) proposes that translation competence is divisible into components, and it follows a developmental pathway. In Campbell's model, it consists of target language textual competence, disposition and monitoring competence.
2. Cf. Neubert's (1994) description of translation competence as consisting of five parameters or sub-competences: language competence, textual competence, subject competence, cultural competence, and transfer competence.
3. Translational language competence is not the same as bilingualism. See Presas (2000).
4. Komissarov (1995: 347–354) believes that intuition is also part of the translator's competence, part of the mental process.

Chapter 4
Legal Terminological Issues in Translation

A story was told from the 1940s in China about an American official delegation visiting China. A Chinese host in conversation asked about the American 'Emperor' to the amazement of the visitors. It turned out that the Chinese host was under the impression that the US was an empire and it had an emperor as the head of state because the word 'President' in English had been mistakenly translated into Chinese as 'Emperor'. The story illustrates the kind of misunderstanding that translation, particularly, the translation of institutional terms, can cause.

In this chapter, major terminological issues in law and its translation are examined. The focus is on the lexical characteristics of legal language in general with a comparative analysis of the Common Law and Civil Law.

Major Terminological Issues

Words are the building blocks of language. It is commonly acknowledged that one distinctive feature of legal language is the complex and unique legal vocabulary. Legal terminology is the most visible and striking linguistic feature of legal language as a technical language, and it is also one of the major sources of difficulty in translating legal documents. This common feature of the language of law is found in most languages, but there are unique features in each language. The legal vocabulary in a language, including both legal concepts and legal usage, is extensive. It results from and reflects the law of the particular legal system that utilises that language. Words matter. In law, words often become points of legal contention. In translation, due to the systemic differences in law, many legal words in one language do not find ready equivalents in another, causing both linguistic and legal complications.

There are many lexical or terminological features and problems in legal translation, but here we only consider four major terminological areas that may pose problems in legal translation applicable to most languages. These are (1) legal conceptual issues and the question of equivalence and non-equivalence of legal concepts in translation; (2) legal terms that are bound to law and legal institutions; (3) legal language as a technical language in terms of ordinary vs. legal meanings, and legal synonyms; and (4) terminological difficulties arising from linguistic uncertainty such as vagueness and ambiguity.

Translating Legal Concepts

Legal concepts are abstraction of the generic legal thoughts and rules within a legal system. Concepts are important in law. Law is systematic and structured. Law is often described in categories, for instance, criminal law, property law, contract law, and torts. Legal concepts are the 'authoritative categories to which types or classes of transactions, cases, or situations are refereed, in consequences of which a series of principles, rules and standards become applicable' (Weisflog 1987: 207). Legal concepts play an important role in delineating each branch of the law. For our purpose, as legal translation involves specialised or technical language, the technical nature of legal language stems largely from the extensive use of concepts (Weisflog 1987: 207).

Consequently, a frequently encountered challenge in legal translation is the translation of legal concepts. They are often legal system-bound. Take for instance, as cited in Weisflog (1987), the concept of 'theft' in English law and its equivalent *Diebstahl* in German law. There are considerable differences in the respective laws as to what constitutes 'theft'. As Weisflog explains, in English law, 'theft' is the 'dishonest appropriation of property belonging to someone else with the intention of keeping it permanently' under the English Theft Act 1968. Under the German law, a person is guilty of *Diebstahl* (theft) if he or she takes away movable property belonging to another with the intention of appropriating it unlawfully. Furthermore, how the two legal systems define 'property' and other concepts contained in the definitions also differs (see Weisflog 1987: 210–211).

The problem of translating legal concepts is not new. Efforts have been made to find possible solutions. For instance, as Lane (1982: 224) reports, many years ago, *Internationales Institute für Rechts- und Verwaltungssprache* (the International Institute of Legal and Administrative Terminology) attempted to tackle the problem arising from the translation of legal concepts that are unknown in the target language or that do not exist in exactly the same form as in that language. The Institute developed a method for coping with this difficulty. According to the Institute (as reported by

Lane 1982, see also Sarcevic 1989), a terminological comparison between one language and the other is based on concepts and terms. In this description, a concept is a unit of thought that combines within itself the properties and relationships of things (i.e. material and immaterial objects, situations and circumstances, events actions, procedures, etc.). The properties and the relationships are called the characteristics of the concept. In the sphere of language, a concept is identified by a term that may consist of a single word or of a group of words or even of a group of words or even of letters or graphical symbols. When it is necessary to translate a term from one language into a term in another language, we may study the relevant concepts associated with the terms in question and examine whether they actually correspond (Lane 1982: 224). The Institute compiled and published volumes of the *Europaglossar der Rechts- und Verwaltungssprache* (*European Glossary of Legal and Administrative Terminology*) with detailed description and comparison of various legal and administrative terminology in different European languages (Lane 1982: 224).

In recent years, various terminological databases have been developed with CAT technology, for instance, Eurodicautom of the EU, but they remain at the terminological, not conceptual level. However, we are reminded that legal translation is not the automatic transposition of a concept from one language into another, but rather it requires thorough knowledge of the two legal systems that interface with one another as well as a comparative analysis of the text and the terms to be translated (Renis 2001).

I propose that a legal concept is three dimensional (Cao 2001) based on Peirce's semiotics, that is, it has linguistic, referential and conceptual dimensions. To ascertain whether a concept in one language can be translated as a concept in another language, we need to consider whether they are equivalent or similar in these three dimensions. However, in translation, words from different languages are rarely the exact equivalent in all three dimensions. In particular, culture-specific criteria play a role in legal concepts (Sandrini 1996). There are two major scenarios in translation here: firstly, when there are no existing equivalent concepts and words in the TL, that is, they are linguistically or conceptually absent, new words must be created or new meanings introduced; and secondly, when there are existing words in the TL that are linguistic equivalent to the SL, these words in the two languages may only carry partially equivalent meanings in law or sometimes may not be functionally equivalent in law at all. This can be seen in terms of the conceptual dimension of a term and its referential dimension, that is, how it is realised in the legal system and how it is understood by the users of the language (see Cao 2004).

For the first situation of linguistic and conceptual absence, as a result of the separate legal traditions and developmental processes, there are Common Law concepts in English unknown to the Civil Law system and vice versa. Such unique legal concepts are deployed exclusively in different legal systems. For these situations, the translators sometimes need to use borrowing or create new words. For instance, towards the end of the 19th century and beginning of the 20th century, many Chinese legal terms were borrowed from the Japanese, which had earlier been translated from Continental Europe. Legal terms that were introduced to China from the West during this period include such major concepts as *renquan* (human rights), *zhuquan* (sovereignty), *minfa* (civil law) and *xianfa* (constitution), among many others.

Similarly, many terms in modern secular legal Hebrew have been coined directly from foreign law by way of lexical or semantic loan, for instance, the English legal terms, 'precedent', 'good faith', 'restraint of trade', 'public policy, 'rule of law' and 'judicial review', the French concept 'abuse of right', and the German concept *Rechtsstaat* (see Fassberg 2003: 164).[1]

In the English legal language, there are in fact a large number of words that were originally borrowed from Latin and French. According to Tiesma (1999: 31), by far the most lasting impact of French on English is the tremendous amount of technical vocabulary that derives from French. During Norman Conquest and for a substantial period after that, Latin and French were the written legal languages of the law in England, and they remained important legal languages in England in written form as late as the 18th century (Tiesma 1999: 25, see also Mellinkoff 1963). Today, there are still many Latin words and Anglicised Latin words in English law, particularly in legal proceeding-related documents and in legal canons or maxims (sayings about law). Similarly, many French words translated, borrowed or Anglicised, and in some cases, even syntactical structures and usage, are found in legal English (Tiesma 1999).

Examples of common legal terms, both legal concepts and usage, used in English today that were borrowed from French include (as identified in Tiesma 1999:31) *agreement, arrest, arson, assault, crime, damage, felony, heir, larceny, marriage, misdemeanour, money, profit, slander* and *tort*, among many others. Words that had a French origin related to the courts include *action, appeal, attorney, bailiff, bar, claim, complaint, counsel, court, defendant, demurrer, evidence, indictment, judge, judgment, jury, justice, parole, plaintiff, plea, plead, process, sentence, sue, suit, summon, verdict* and *voir dire*. The English law of real property terminology is also overwhelmingly French: *cestui que use, chattel, conveyance, easement, estate, fee simple, feel tail, lease, licence, profit a prendre, property, remainder, rent, seisin, tenant, tenure, trespass,* among others (see Tiesma 1999: 31).

Borrowing and neologism are much more common in legal systems that are in the process of establishment or developing than in more mature or established systems.

For the second scenario in translating legal concepts, that is, similar words exist in the SL and TL, normally, such existing terms in the TL are used in translation, even if they are not completely identical. These may be near or close equivalents, partial equivalents or non-equivalents (Sarcevic 1997). Nevertheless, they need to be used as equivalents. In such cases, they may be semantic equivalents, but are partial equivalents in the conceptual or referential dimensions.

For example, the French *droit* is not identical conceptually to the English word 'law'. In terms of *droit* as a concept and how it is understood and practised in France, generally speaking, the French conception of law is broader than that of the English Common Law, encompassing political science and morality. Law is not seen as being isolated from other intellectual disciplines but encompasses the study of political, social and economic sciences and public administration, and focuses on the rights and duties recognised in society according to an ideal of justice (Dadomo and Farran 1996). Thus, in France, the essence of law lies in the general ideas it inspires, not in the technical rules by which it achieves these ends (Dadomo and Farran 1996). In contrast, the English Common Law primarily sees law as a body of rules of procedure and remedies that form the machinery of justice as administered by the courts, rather than statements of general principles and rules of ideal conduct. So, one may say that conceptually and referentially, the French word '*droit*' and the English word 'law' are not the exact equivalents. However, we have to use these two terms as linguistic equivalents in translation in many cases (see Weston 1991: 46 for examples he cited). Similarly, the French *droit constitutionnel* and *droit administratif* do not correspond exactly in content to the English 'constitutional law' and 'administrative law' (see Weston 1991: 55–57). Nevertheless, they need to be translated as equivalents, as there are no functionally equivalent alternatives, and any other translation is 'simply unthinkable' (Weston 1991: 57).

There are many examples of words that are linguistic equivalents but conceptually and/or referentially non-equivalents or partial equivalents in different languages. For instance, the English 'good faith' and its counterpart *bona fides* in French and German are not entirely the same. '*Bona fides*' in the Civil Law and 'good faith' in the Common Law both contain the notion of fair dealing, but they differ on a number of points (de Cruz 1999: 260):

(a) the English notion excludes negligence, but the continental view often regards gross negligence as the equivalent of bad faith;

(b) the continental concept covers a wider field than the English version and includes confidential relationships and minimal standards of conduct expected of parties engaging in commercial transactions.

An example cited by Renis (2001) is the term 'the Court of Appeal' in English and its equivalent in Italian, *Corte d'appello*. However, the English term is only a partial equivalent of the Italian since the two judicial authorities have different functions in the respective legal systems as Renis (2001) points out. The literal translation can be potentially misleading. *Proprietà* is another example in Italian, which is often translated as 'property'. They may look similar, but as Renis (2001) points out, the English term 'property' is deeply rooted in the Common Law and has a wider semantic scope than the Italian term, which often corresponds to 'ownership' rather than 'property'.

Other examples of semantic equivalents but functionally partial or non-equivalents and terminological incongruity include the French concept *faute*, which corresponds not to one but two German concepts – *Verschulden* and *Rechtswidrigkeit* (Sarcevic 1989: 278); *dettes* in French is much broader than the English 'debts'; the German *Vertrag* is considerably broader than its French equivalent *contrat*, which is restricted to transactions involving mutuality of agreement and obligation (Sarcevic 1989: 278); the German *höhere Gewalt* is more restricted than the English *force majeure*; and 'bankruptcy' in the law of England is not the same as the German equivalent *Konkurs* whose similarity is limited to the intension of meaning (Sarcevic 1989: 282).

A related issue here is that when translating between European languages of Latin root, as in the case of English, French and Italian among others, often words in these languages look similar linguistically but turn out to be different in legal substance. *Faux amis* are quite prevalent. Examples of common false friends include 'demand' in English and *demands* in French; 'domicile' in English, *domicile* in French and *Domizil* in German (see Weisflog 1987 for explanation). Similarly, *la doctrine* in French means 'legal writing' or 'legal scholarship', rather than 'doctrine'. *Notaire* in French is not exactly 'notary' in English. Equally, *magistrat* in French is not 'magistrate' in English. 'Common Law' in English is not *droit commun* in French (see Weston 1991 for explanation), and *Haute Cour de justice* is not the same as the 'High Court of Justice'. *Faux amis* are a common problem when translating between European languages as in the EU institutions (see Wagner *et al.* 2002), for instance, *acquis communautaire* means the body of EU laws, not 'acquis'; *opportunité* is 'advisability', not 'opportunity'; *pays tiers* is 'non-member countries', not 'third countries'; and *Statute des fonctionnaires* refers to 'staff regulations', not 'statute'.

Another example of false friends that is worth singling out is the English word 'jurisprudence'. It has different meanings as compared with its counterpart in French and Italian. In English, jurisprudence [Latin *jurispru-dentia* knowledge of or skill in law, and from Latin *juris*, genitive of *jus* right, law and *prudentia* wisdom] has two basic meanings: firstly, it means philosophy of law or legal theory; secondly, it means 'case law'. But in both French (*la jurisprudence*) and Italian (*la giurisprudenza*), the equivalent words only refer to case law or legal precedents. However, in English, 'jurispru-dence' in its 'legal philosophy' sense is more commonly used. In translation, it is necessary to ensure the right meaning is used. In international law written in English, the Continental meaning of 'jurisprudence', that is, court decision, is often adopted.

As we have seen previously, 'law' in one legal system may not be the exact 'law' in another. It seems that the approach that legal translation should be predominantly SL orientated needs reconsideration. In order to ensure that one 'law' is to approximate another 'law' in translation or to be as close as much as possible and avoid confusion, we must take into account the various TL factors. The legal usage, contextual variables, and the purposes and communicative functions of the translated texts in the TL also need to be considered.

It is also important to remember that legal concepts from different countries are seldom, if ever, identical (see Chapter 2 also). It is futile to search for absolute equivalence when translating legal concepts.

In terms of translation methods and strategies, given the vast differences and diverse situations between different language pairs and different legal systems, many different methods may be utilised. For instance, translation methods can vary from literal translation (or formal equivalence, or word for word translation), functional equivalence, to borrowing and descriptive equivalence.

We have cited examples of borrowing earlier of English from French and Latin. Another example of borrowing or loan words is Latin in the Italian legal language. Previously, we have mentioned that the English legal language has many Latin words. In fact, the Italian legal language has a large number of Latin loan words, more than there are in English (Renis 2001). Many Latin terms or phrases that remain untranslated in Italian legal texts must be rendered into English in translation. Latin terms abound in court judgments, arbitration awards, briefs and writs of summons (Renis 2001), for example, *inter vivos* (among the living), *mortis causa* (due to death), *infra* (below/hereinafter), *ex* (pursuant to), *legale rappresentante pro tempore* (acting legal representative), *vulnus* (damage), *dies a quo* (starting date), *inter partes* (between the parties), *contrariis reiectis* (after rejecting any opposite claim, action and objection), *salvis juribus* (without prejudice to any further right), *notitia criminis* (notice of crime), *inaudita altera parte* (without hearing the opposite party) (cited in Renis 2001). When such documents are reproduced in English, the Latin words must be translated (Renis 2001).

As for literal translation or formal equivalence, it is usually discouraged in other types of translation. However, sometimes, literal translation is unavoidable in legal translation. Examples from translation of law from Italian into English using literal translation method include 'mobility procedure' for the Italian *procedura di mobilità*, 'Cadaster' for *Catasto*, 'desmain' for *demanio* (Renis 2001). These are literal translations of concepts pertaining to the Italian labour and administrative law. They do not have equivalents in English. Nevertheless, the legal translator needs to be cautious in translating literally.

Legal System-Bound Words

One feature of legal language and legal translation is the use of legal terms unique to law, the so-called system-bound words. There are many such words but we will only look at three categories of such words: (1) words associated with legal personnel; (2) words associated with court structures; and (3) words associated with particular areas of law and institutions.

Words associated with the legal profession

There are stocks of words that are unique to law associated with the legal profession. A lawyer is a person licensed by the state to advise clients in legal matters and represent them in the court of law. Lawyers have many names in different countries. For instance, in English, there are 'lawyer', 'counsel', 'advocate', 'attorney', 'solicitor', 'barrister' and 'counsellor'. In the United States, lawyers are ordinarily referred to as 'lawyer' and 'attorney', or formally, 'Attorney at Law'. In contrast, in the United Kingdom, Canada, Australia and several other Common Law countries, there are generally two kinds of lawyers – solicitors and barristers. The different titles of solicitor and barrister are a reflection of division of labour in the legal profession in these countries, and the influence of the early developments of the legal profession in England over those territories. In simple terms, solicitors advise clients, and barristers argue cases in court. A solicitor is a general legal practitioner who assists clients with legal advice, drafts and prepares various legal documents such as wills, documents for business transactions and for buying and selling houses (called conveyancing), negotiates terms of commercial contracts.

When specialist legal advice is required, or when a matter goes to court, a solicitor briefs or instructs a barrister on behalf of their clients. A barrister is a legal specialist advocate who represents clients in court. Barristers often specialise in particular areas of law, such as equity, common law, criminal or family law. Sometimes barristers are referred to as counsels. They also write statements of claims, defences and cross-claims, and write advice or legal opinions on particular matters. Traditionally, both a solicitor (for advice) and a barrister (for representation) were required for legal representation before the courts.

Some Common Law jurisdictions, for example, Malaysia, Singapore, Canada (excluding the province of Quebec), and some states in Australia, have a fused legal profession, whereby a lawyer is licensed both as a barrister and solicitor and can practise as both. In Canada, in the fused jurisdictions, both names are often used. However, Quebec, which has a strong Civil Law influence, is closer to the practice of England, with *les avocats* similar to barristers practising before the courts, and *les notaires* similar to the functions of solicitors.

In England, other Commonwealth countries and former colonies, barristers are divided into senior counsel and junior counsel. Senior counsels are sometimes given the title Queen's Counsel (QC). QC is a barrister appointed to the British crown and when the sovereign is a woman. All lawyers are officers of the court, and they also belong to legal professional bodies, that is, barristers are members of Bar Associations and solicitors members of Law Societies respectively.

The United States does not draw a distinction between barristers and solicitors; all lawyers who pass the bar examination may argue in the courts of the state in which they are admitted, although some state appellate courts require attorneys to obtain a separate certificate of admission to plead and practise in the appellate court.

In Continental European countries, there are different kinds of lawyers performing different functions (see Merryman *et al.* 1994). In general, in Continental Europe, a person who possesses a degree in law is called 'lawyer'. Such lawyers can practise law as employees hired by law firms or other legal entities. However, a lawyer in the Continent may not be the same as an 'attorney' in the US or 'solicitor' in the UK. In Germany, there is one legal profession of *Rechtsanwalt* (lawyer). In France, there are *avocat, notaire* and *conseil juridique*. Spain has a division that generally corresponds to the division in Britain between barristers and solicitors. *Procuradores* represent the interests of a litigant in court, while *abogados* is the general term for other lawyers.

Thus, when translating such terms between English and other languages, it is necessary to first identify which jurisdictions the relevant words are referring to, and then determine the appropriate words. Sometimes explanatory words are used apart from indicating that these words refer to lawyers or not.

A Canadian case is relevant to our discussion here involving the meanings of words related to lawyers in English and French. In *Olavarria v Minister of Manpower and Immigration* [1973] FC 1035 (CA) (the case was discussed in Beaupré 1986), the court was asked to decide whether the word 'counsel' includes non-lawyer. The relevant Canadian act confers the right to 'counsel' in the English text, but the French version has the more strict right to an *avocat*. The relevant regulations also have the word *'ou autre conseiller'* in the French version. The court found (at 1037):

> If one referred only to the English version of section 3 of the Immigration Inquiries Regulations, one would be constrained to the view that the word 'counsel' therein had the same meaning as that word has in section 26(2) of that Act and was, therefore, used in the sense of 'lawyer'. However, when the French version is referred to, it is found that, where the English version refers to 'counsel', it unambiguously refers to both lawyer and other adviser. As the word 'counsel' in the English language has a sense that is wide enough to include an adviser whether or not he is a lawyer, it must be concluded that, in section 3 of the English version of the Immigration Inquiries Regulations, the word has been used in this wider sense.

As for other names and titles, for judicial officers, in England and Australia, there are the 'Judge', 'Justice' (abbreviated into J after the judge's name in judgments or CJ for 'Chief Justice'), and 'Magistrate' (for magistrates court), among others. There are different words of honorific to address the 'bench'. In most English speaking countries, a judge is addressed as 'Your Honour', and a magistrate in some jurisdictions is addressed as 'Your Worship'. Judges of courts of limited jurisdiction are sometimes known as 'referees'. Judges sitting in the English courts of equity are called 'Chancellors.'

In France, a judge can be a *juge*, a *conseiller* or a *magistrat*, depending upon the courts. In Germany, there is the distinction between professional judges who are trained as lawyers and honorary judges who are lay judges with their main function to assist professional judges. The position of judges in German society is quite different to their position in Common Law countries.

In translating judgments, the correct use of judicial titles is relevant. For instance, in translating judgments between French and English in Canada, *juge* is 'judge', and *juge en chef* is 'chief judge', but if he or she is from the Superior Court, 'chief justice' should be used, not 'judge in chief' (see Meredith 1979).

Finally, it is worth mentioning that there are also differences in the position and standing of legal scholars or academic lawyers in Common Law and Civil Law countries. In the Civil Law system, leading law professors and scholars enjoy a much more prestigious position in the hierarchy of the legal profession than their counterparts in Common Law countries or even lower court judges (Weston 1991: 117). For instance, in France, legal scholars are partly responsible for drawing up reasoned proposals for court decisions, and their writings have great influences over the development of case law; and legal scholars expound the law and do the basic thinking for the whole for the legal fraternity (Weston 1991: 116–117). The writings of such scholars, textbooks, annotated law reports and articles in learned journals, have been referred to as *la doctrine* (legal scholarship), as a body of opinions on legal matters (Weston 1991: 117–118). Thus, legal academic writing is much more significant as a source of law in the Civil Law system than in the Common Law, as is the standing of legal scholars.

Due to this reason, 'lawyer' in English primarily refers to a legal practitioner. In contrast, the French word *juriste* refers to a person academically qualified in the law who is as likely to be a legal scholar as to be a practitioner (Weston 1991: 117). Thus, *juriste* corresponds more closely to the English word 'jurist' (Weston 1991: 117). However, in English, 'jurist' which refers to a person who has thorough knowledge of law, is not often used, and when it is used, it often refers to judges. According to Weston (1991: 117), the French term *homme de loi*, which implies a practitioner, is a closer referential equivalent to the English word 'lawyer', but it is much less commonly used than either *juriste* in French or 'lawyer' in English.

Words associated with courts

Court hierarchies are often structured differently in different countries. In England, for instance, the court hierarchy consists of the House of Lords as the ultimate appellate court, the Supreme Court of Judicature, Court of Appeal, the High Court of Justice, the Crown Court, the County Courts and the Magistrates Court. There are also other courts such as Coroner's Court and Small Claims Court, and specialised courts such as Admiralty Court and Children's Court.

In Australia which is part of the Commonwealth and of the Common Law family, the court hierarchy is such: the High Court of Australia is the highest court of the land, the ultimate appellate court but also with original jurisdiction. Below at the federal level, there is the Federal Court and Family Court. At the state level, there are the state courts (the Supreme Court and Court of Appeal). Below are the District Courts and Magistrates Courts. There are also various tribunals.

So, in English Common Law jurisdictions, there are two words for 'court': the general term 'court' and a narrower term 'tribunal', which refers to panels and bodies that exercise administrative or quasi-judicial functions with limited or special jurisdiction.

In France, the courts are organised on the basis of general and limited jurisdiction. There are three basic words for 'court': *cour*, *tribunal* and *juridiction*. *Cours* deliver *arrêts*, while the lower courts are mostly called *tribunaux* and they deliver *jugements* (Weston 1991: 66). *Juridiction* is superordinate to *cour* and *tribunal*. Any *cour* or *tribunal* may be described as a *juridiction* whereas some *juridictions* are *cours* and others *tribunaux* (see Weston 1991). In translation, *juridiction* needs to be translated as 'court'. If it is in plural, as in *les juridictions françaises*, it needs to be translated as 'courts and tribunals'. However, *juridiction d'instruction* needs to be translated as 'judicial authority'. As Weston (1991: 67) points out, the three French terms are generally translated by a single English word because the distinctions between *cour*, *tribunal* and *juridiction*, in so far as they correspond to distinctions in the English language at all, are not reflected in the English language system. There can be confusions when the French terms are translated literally into English.

This is the situation found in *Commission des droits de la personne v AG Canada* [1978] CA 67, affirmed [1982] 1 SCR 215 (the case was discussed in Beaupré 1986). In this case, the Court of Appeal in Quebec was asked to decide whether the provincial Human Rights Commission qualified as a 'court' within the terms of Section 431 of the Canadian Federal Court Act. Based on the French *tribunal*, the jurisprudence attaching to the meaning of the same word *tribunal* in the Code of Civil Procedures and based on the English meaning of the word 'court', the Court of Appeal decided that the word 'court' in this context was not limited to a court of superior jurisdiction, but included any body exercising judicial power such as the Human Rights Commission. The court stated (at 72):

Si l'on donnait au mot 'Court' dans la version anglaise de l'article 41 de la Loi sur la Cour fédérale le sens restreint de 'Cour supérieure', de façon à en exclure la Commission appelante, l'on viendrait en contradiction avec le mot 'tribunal' dans la version française puisque ce mot, aussi bien dans son sens général que dans son sens restreint, comprend la Commission. Lorsqu'une première interprétation met en contradiction les versions anglaise et française d'une loi, alors qu'une deuxième interprétation les concilie, c'est cette dernière qu'il faut préférer (art. 8(2)(b) Loi sur les langues officielles) . . . .

In terms of court jurisdiction, there are original and appellate jurisdictions, and criminal and civil jurisdictions, federal and state jurisdictions, among others. Different courts in different countries have different rules. Some scholars have proposed that when we translate the names of the courts, we need to take into account of the differences in court jurisdiction. For instance, Geeroms (2002) argues that the terms *cassation (cour de cassation)* in the French system, *revision* in the German system (*Bundesgerichtshof*), and 'appeal' (or appellant court) in the Common Law system should not be translated as equivalent as if they were the same, because the appellant courts in these systems have different powers and jurisdictions.

As reported in Robinson (2005), during the drafting of the EU Constitution, one thorny problem was the names for the various components of the Court of Justice. Some languages have different words for 'court', signifying a hierarchy that may not be reflected in other languages. The solution finally adopted was to call the lower body 'general court' or the equivalent except in languages where single words were enough to convey the hierarchical relationship. The Directorate-General for Translation (DGT) of the European Commission (EC) has published an *English Style Guide* (DGT 2005c) in which the English translations of the judicial bodies of the Member States are suggested for use by translators, together with the English translations of the names of the various European national legal instruments.

Words Associated with Areas of Law and Institutions

In the third area of legal terms, there are different divisions and branches of law that have special sets of vocabulary. Within the Civil Law family, in both public and private law, the same fundamental branches are found in all the countries of this family: constitutional law, administrative law, public international law, criminal law, the law of procedure, civil law, commercial law, labour law etc. This same correspondence of established categories is also found at a lower level in their institutions and concepts. Thus, some believe that there are no major difficulties in the translation of the key legal vocabulary within the French, German, Spanish, Italian, Dutch, Greek or Portuguese languages across these branches of law (David and Brierley 1985: 84). The conceptual similarity facilitates the understanding of the foreign laws even though the substantive laws in each of these countries may differ (David and Brierley 1985: 84). However, this does not mean that the structural similarity of the laws of the Civil Law family is complete. Different categories or ideas found in one law may not be known to others, but it is relatively easy to understand the differences within the system (for examples of different notions in these jurisdictions, see David and Brierley 1985: 89).

However, if we compare the legal institutions and domains of law of the Common Law and the Civil Law, there are many conceptual and structural differences. For instance, the Civil Law has such institutions as *cause*, abuse of right, the direct action, the oblique action, the *action de in rem verso*, the extent of strict liability in tort, and *negotiorum gestio*, and these are foreign to the Common Law.[2] Similarly, there is the absence of such Common Law concepts as consideration or estoppel in the Civil Law of contract. Another example is the concept of 'law of obligations' in the Civil Law, a fundamental category in the laws of the Romano-Germanic family. However, it does not exist in the Common Law. It is pointed out that the phrase actually is susceptible of accurate translation in English legal vocabulary (David and Brierley 1985: 86). An 'obligation' in the Civil Law system refers to the duty of one person, the debtor, to transfer the ownership of property or create a right over it, to do or not to do something to the benefit of another person, the creditor. The obligation may derive from the law alone or it may arise by contract or even by reason of a unilateral undertaking of one person (David and Brierley 1985: 86–87). According to David and Brierley (1985), the obligation may also arise because of a *delict* or *quasi delict*, which refers to the fact that a person committed a fault or must compensate for the damage caused by a thing under his or her care or by a person for whom he or she must answer. An obligation may arise as well from the fact that a person is, by reason of a number of various circumstances, unjustly enriched at the expense of another person who has suffered an impoverishment. The law of obligations has been developed over the centuries on the basis of Roman law elements, into the central, fundamental and unique part of the Civil Law (David and Brierley 1985: 86–87).

Conversely, a branch of the English legal structure, equity, is an example that does not have an exact counterpart in the Civil Law. In the English system, there is a division of law called 'equity'. This is unique and the legal concepts and most of the legal rules found in this branch of law do not exist in other legal systems. The ordinary and lay meaning of the word 'equity' means fairness and equality. However, equity under discussion here refers to a body of legal rules formulated and administered by the Court of Chancery in England to supplement the rules and procedures of the common law. It was developed in the last few hundred years. By the Judicature Act 1837, the Court of Chancery was amalgamated with the Common Law Courts to form the Supreme Court in England, and the rules of equity are administered alongside the common law rules in all English courts. The basic principle is where there is any conflict between the rules of law and equity, equity is to prevail. Today, many legal texts and legal documents carry words such as 'equitable interest' and 'equitable remedy'. The 'equitable' in this sense carries substantive legal meanings far beyond the literal meaning of being fair, just or equitable. It refers to the body of legal principles unique in the English legal tradition. There may be specific legal principles in other legal traditions that are similar to some of equitable principles in England, nevertheless, there are systemic and fundamental legal differences. There are no exact equivalent words in the Civil Law.

To sum up, given the diversity in legal systems and practices, translating across jurisdictional boundaries is not a simple mechanical process. A basic knowledge and understanding of the relevant legal systems and their structures and a high degree of proficiency in the two legal languages are paramount for the legal translator.

Ordinary Meaning vs. Legal Meaning

Apart from the uniquely legal words as discussed in the previous section, there are also many words used in legal texts that have an ordinary meaning and a technical legal meaning. This is true in English as well in other languages. Therefore, one of the tasks for the legal translator is to identify the legal meaning and distinguish it from its ordinary meaning before rendering it appropriately into the TL.

For instance, in translating English contracts or documents related to contract law, legal terms frequently encountered include 'offer', 'consideration', 'performance', 'remedy', and 'assignment'. These words in English have an ordinary meaning used in non-legal settings. They are also legal technical terms that carry special legal significance in contract law. In English contract law, 'offer' refers to a promise which when accepted constitutes an agreement. 'Consideration' refers to the price paid, not 'thought' or 'thinking' in ordinary usage. 'Performance' specifically refers to the doing of that which is required by a contract or condition. A contract is discharged by 'performance'. The expression 'specific performance' in contract law is not literally what it says. It actually means where damages would be inadequate compensation for the breach of an agreement, the contracting parties may be compelled to perform what was agreed to be done by a decree of specific performance, e.g. the sale, purchase or lease of land, or recovery of unique chattels. The word 'remedy' is not just a way of solving a problem but a legal means whereby breach of a right is prevented or redress is given, e.g. damages and/or injunction. 'Assignment' in contract law means transfer of property or right.

Contract law in English Common Law is predominately governed by case law. It is based on precedent that has been developed over the centuries, first in England, and then spread to other Commonwealth countries. Some of the legal terms have long histories unique to the Common Law. They often present difficulties when translated into a language that is from the Civil Law and others, and meanings often get lost in translation.

Take for instance the word 'warranty' in English law. 'Warranty' has an ordinary meaning as well as a legal meaning. In a contract dispute case from England, *Oscar Chess Ltd v Williams* [1957] 1 WLR 370 at 374 (English Court of Appeal), Lord Denning LJ has this to say about the meanings of 'warranty':

> I use the word 'warranty' in its ordinary English meaning to denote a binding promise. Everyone knows what a man means when he says 'I guarantee it' or 'I warrant it' or 'I give you my word on it'. He means that he binds himself to it. That is the meaning it has borne in English law for 300 years. ... During the last 50 years, however, some lawyers have come to use the word 'warranty' in another sense. They use it to denote a subsidiary term in a contract as distinct from a vital term which they call a 'condition'. In so doing they depart from the ordinary meaning, not only of the word 'warranty' but also of the word 'condition'. There is no harm in their doing this, so long as they confine this technical use to its proper sphere, namely to distinguish between a vital term, the breach of which gives the right to treat the contract as at an end, and a subsidiary term which does not. But the trouble comes when one person uses the word 'warranty' in its ordinary meaning and another uses it in its technical meaning. When Holt CJ, in *Crosse v Gardner* [1689] Carth 90; 90 ER 656 . : . made his famous ruling that an affirmation at the time of a sale is a warranty, provided it appears on evidence to be so intended, he used the word 'warranty' in its ordinary English

meaning of a binding promise, and when Lord Haldane LC and Lord Moulton in 1913 . . . adopted his ruling, they used it likewise in its ordinary meaning. These different uses of the word seem to have been the source of confusion in the present case.

The confusion in the above example arose even just within one language.

The word 'equity' is another example of a word possessing both an ordinary meaning and a legal meaning. In English, 'equity' has the following meanings according to general dictionary definition:

(1) The state, quality, or ideal of being just, impartial, and fair.
(2) In legal usage:
   (a) Justice applied in circumstances covered by law yet influenced by principles of ethics and fairness.
   (b) A system of jurisprudence supplementing and serving to modify the rigour of common law.
   (c) An equitable right or claim.
   (d) Equity of redemption.
(3) The residual value of a business or property beyond any mortgage thereon and liability therein.
(4) (a) The market value of securities less any debt incurred.
   (b) Common stock and preferred stock.
(5) Funds provided to a business by the sale of stock.

The word 'equity', in the legal sense, refers to the principles of justice originally developed by the English chancellor as described earlier, but now it has several different meanings, both ordinary and legal. In translation, we need to distinguish its different legal meanings in different areas or branches of law as well as its legal meanings from its ordinary meanings. By the same token, 'equitable' often used in legal documents can also have several meanings, legal and ordinary.

In the next example, the words involved have both legal and ordinary meaning and the court was asked to consider which one was intended. In the Canadian case *Azdo v Minister of Employment and Immigration* [1980] 2 FC 645 CA, the Canadian Federal Court of Appeal had to decide whether to set aside a deportation order on the basis that the minor subject to the order had not been represented by his guardian at the inquiry as required by the relevant act (the case was discussed in Beaupré 1986: 59). The minor had someone with him but he was not the minor's legal guardian. The issue arose from the word 'guardian' as used in the English version of section 29 of the act but the French version of the act used the word *tuteur*. Counsel for the minor argued that the word 'guardian' was used in its technical legal sense of 'one who legally has the care and management of the person, or the estate, or both, of a child during its minority' citing the *Black's Law Dictionary*. The counsel for the minister argued that the word 'guardian' was used in its broad sense which is 'one who guards, protects or preserves' citing the *Shorter Oxford English Dictionary*. The court held that the French version was preferred, requiring the minor to be represented by his legal guardian. This is because the French version where the word 'guardian' was translated by the word *tuteur* indicates that the word 'guardian' is used in its narrow legal sense since the French word *tuteur* is a legal expression that does not have the broad general meaning of its English counterpart.

Apart from that fact that a legal term may have a legal meaning and an ordinary meaning, it may also have several legal meanings from different branches of law, as the word 'equity' shows above. It is important to be able to distinguish them. For instance, '*in rem*' and '*in personam*' in English law can have four different meanings; 'ownership' has two distinct senses of 'corporeal' and 'incorporeal', that is, ownership of things and ownership of rights; the word 'estate' can have several meaning as an estate in land and an estate in a right; 'property' can have at least seven different meanings and so forth (see Williams 1946: 179).

For the legal translator, the lesson here is that when trying to identify and ascertain the meaning of a particular word with both ordinary and legal meanings or a word with several legal meanings, one can make use of the context in which the word occurs. This includes both the wider legal context, such as a particular area of law, and the immediate linguistic context such as the sentence, the paragraph and the entire text in which the word is used. A legal dictionary will also be of great help. However, if one is not aware of the additional legal meaning that a simple everyday word may have, and assumes, wrongly, that it is the ordinary usage, one may not enlist the help of the dictionary or reference materials in the first place. So, in translating legal texts in general, the translator, especially those who do not have legal training, should not readily assume that ordinary and common words are always used in the ordinary way. General reading of and cross-reference to the relevant existing laws and other legal texts and their translations are always helpful.

Legal Synonyms

Another terminological problem is that a legal term may have several synonyms, and some of the synonyms may resemble one another, but differ in law. Such a feature can cause difficulty in translation. For instance, in English, there are many words related to 'law' – law, statute, legislation, act, enactment, regulation, ordinance, rule, decree etc. Similarly, there are several words in French for the word 'law' – *le droit* (a total set of standards that can include the notions of justice), *la justice* (the legal system) and *la loi* (legislation enacted by Parliament). As for *la loi*, there are also a number of synonyms (see Western 1991). *Loi* (law) is passed by Parliament, and promulgated by the President of the Republic; *décrets* (decree) is made by the President of the Republic or the Prime Minister; *arrêté*, means decision, rules, order or bye-law made the executive branch (see Weston 1991: 60, Dadomo and Farran 1996). Furthermore, *loi* has both a broad meaning that encompasses the constitution, international treaties and administrative regulations and a narrower meaning equivalent to the English term 'statute', and within the narrow meaning, *loi* can be further classified and distinguished (see Weston 1991: 60, Dadomo and Farran 1996).

Other examples of synonyms include *cour, tribunal* and *juridiction* in French, and 'court' and 'tribunal' in English (see earlier discussion in this chapter). In international law, there are the synonyms of 'treaty', 'convention', 'agreement', 'protocol', 'pact', 'covenant' etc. (see Chapter 7). In criminal law, there are 'manslaughter', 'murder', 'homicide' and 'killing'. This is common in most areas of law and in most jurisdictions due to the strict definitions in law.

If we take English contract law for examples, there are the synonyms of 'warranty', 'term', 'condition' and 'covenant'. A 'warranty' or a 'term' of a contract embodies a contractual undertaking. In the case of written contracts, 'terms of contract' refer to every clause in the document or, in the case of an oral transaction, every matter that the parties have agreed to govern their bargain. In this sense, the word 'term' is a synonym for 'stipulation', 'clause' or 'provision'. It is not uncommon for the words 'condition' and 'covenant' to be used in this general way although they are more frequently used in the narrower senses. Furthermore, 'condition' may refer either to terms generally or to the important terms of the contract. 'Warranty' is generally used to described any contractually binding undertaking or promise rather than in its more specific sense of unimportant undertaking or promise (see Carter and Harland 1993: 219). It is not to be confused with the 'warranty' found in the sale of goods contracts or 'warranty' used to describe a manufacturer's undertaking to repair defects in the goods within a warranty period.

As Carter and Harland (1993) point out, the word 'condition' is one of most ambiguous and difficult words in contract law. The word may refer to an event the occurrence or non-occurrence of which has been agreed by the parties to have a particular result. The occurrence or non-occurrence of the event must be uncertain. The second meaning describes any term of the contract, and a third meaning an important term (promise), the breach of which gives rise to a right to terminate the performance of the contract (Carter and Harland 1993: 310). Similarly, the word 'warranty' as can be seen from Lord Denning's judgment, is also ambiguous. According to Carter and Harland (1993), a 'warranty' is a term (promise), the breach of which does not give rise to a right to terminate. Damages are the remedy for such a breach. However, the word is also employed to describe any binding promise, as in the distinction between terms (warranties) and representations. A third meaning still applicable to insurance contracts, is to describe a term, the breach of which gives the insurer the right to avoid the contract (Carter and Harland 1993: 310).

There are many legal synonyms in different areas of law. The terms 'custody' and 'guardianship' in the Australian family law are another example. For instance, a divorce settlement may stipulate:

(1) That the husband and wife have the joint guardianship of the children of the marriage.
(2) That the wife has the sole custody of the said children.

Under the Australian family law, a 'custodian' is the person who has the responsibility for the day to day care of a child while a 'guardian' is responsible for long-term decisions and matters affecting the welfare of a child. The parents of a child can be custodians and guardians of the child. Therefore, 'custody' in relation to divorce refers to the right to have and the responsibility to make decisions concerning the daily care and control of a child (*CCH Macquarie Dictionary of Law* 1993: 47) while 'guardianship' refers to a person responsible for the long-term welfare as opposed to the daily care and control of a child (*CCH Macquarie Dictionary of Law* 1993: 79).

In English property law, there are also legal terms that look similar but are different in substance. The terms 'joint tenant' or 'joint tenancy and 'tenant in common' or 'tenancy in common' are often used in the English legal documents concerning land transaction or property in Common Law countries such as Australia. They can be confusing for the English native lay speakers as well. Under the English property law, when more than one person is to take an interest, there is the distinction between 'joint tenant' and 'tenant in common'. In one sense, 'joint tenancy' is a type of concurrent ownership of property, under which each tenant, rather than having a distinct share in the property, is to be treated as far as outsiders are concerned as the single owner of the entire property (*CCH Macquarie Dictionary of Law* 1993: 93). In other words, under a joint tenancy, all own the property together, and by the principle of survivorship, each person's interest in extinguished on death, leaving the last survivor as the sole own of the property. In contrast, 'tenancy in common' means that all the owners have distinct but undivided shares in the same property (*CCH Macquarie Dictionary of Law* 1993: 169). In strictly legal terms, a tenant is a holder of land, whether freehold or leasehold (*Osborn's Concise Law Dictionary* 1993: 320). In other words, under tenancy in common, each holder owns a separate though undivided share in the property, and there is no principle of survivorship.

In a separate area of law, tenancy and tenant are commonly used and understood to refer to a person holding under a lease. This is not to be confused with the land law meaning of 'tenant'.

Other examples of legal synonyms include 'encumbrance' in English property law, which means any 'mortgage', 'charge', 'pledge', 'lien', 'assignment', 'hypothecation', 'security interest', 'title retention', 'preferential right' or 'trust arrangement' and any other 'security agreement or arrangement'. Most of these words are synonyms, but they are not identical, each has its own connotations. When translated into other languages, the distinctions may be lost. Similarly, phrases such as 'transferring property', 'assigning property', 'disposing property', 'dealing with property' and 'selling property' all have the basic similar meaning of 'selling' but each word also carries its own meaning due to the development and evolution of English property law and legal culture and practice.

In terms of translation, one needs to remember that the translator's job is to translate, not to advise clients on the legal implications of words found in legal documents. However, the translator must be aware of such different concepts so as not to mistranslate and confuse the terms. Many languages and legal systems do not make the same distinctions as English does, and there may not be separate words for these different English terms. Sometimes, it may be difficult to find sufficient synonyms in the TL. This may present a challenge for the translator who needs to be resourceful and sometimes even creative so that appropriate choices are made to distinguish the synonyms in translation.

Linguistic and Legal Uncertainty

Another possible terminological difficulty may arise from linguistic uncertainty. 'Linguistic uncertainty' is used here as a general term to cover the uncertain and indeterminate property of language including linguistic vagueness, generality and ambiguity. It includes both lexical and syntactical uncertainty, but we are only concerned here with lexical uncertainty. There are other linguistic features that may contribute to uncertainty such as unclarity, relativity, inexplicitness and indexicality, but are not the focus

here. Vagueness, generality and ambiguity are distinguishable, but they are
also relative, and sometimes may overlap. Legal disputes often arise from
linguistic uncertainty found or allegedly found in contracts and statutes.

Firstly, a word, phrase or sentence is ambiguous if it has more than one
meaning. There are lexical and structural or syntactic ambiguities. Words
such as 'light', 'right', both as a noun and as an adjective, for example, can
have more than one meaning, depending upon how they are used. H.L.A.
Hart once cited a case where a testator leaves his 'vessels' to a legatee. Did
the testator mean to refer to his crockery or to his yachts or to both (Hart
1958, cited in Christie 1963–1964)? Furthermore, a sentence may have
structural or syntactical ambiguity, not the focus here, as in the often cited
example of 'The police shot the rioters with guns.' The courts in the US
generally regard a statute or contract as being 'ambiguous if it is susceptible
of more than one reasonable interpretation' (Solan 2004: 862). It seems that
more legal disputes arise from lexical than syntactical ambiguity.

An expression is vague or imprecise if it admits of borderline cases in
actual use.[3] To say that a concept is vague is to say that there can be no clear
fact of the matter whether the concept applies or not. For instance, words
such as 'brown', 'bald', and 'old', and concept words or cluster concepts
such as 'just', and 'intelligent' are vague, as they refer to fuzzy regions of
a scale.[4] Another example is 'serious', as in 'Serious consequence will
result' if UN resolutions are not complied with. What does 'serious' entail:
economic sanctions, use of force, or any other consequences? One type of
vagueness is intensional vagueness, with words such as 'religion', 'vehicle'
and 'fruits' (see Alston 1964, Moore 1981, 1985). This kind of vagueness is
quite common in law. Courts are often asked to define, say 'vehicle'. As in
Hart's (1961/1994) example of 'No vehicle is allowed in the park', 'vehicle'
is vague, open to different interpretation as to what may constitute a vehicle:
a car, an ambulance or a roller skater. Other examples include: What is meant
by 'disability'? How much loss of vision is required before one is legally
blind for being disabled? Who is an 'adult' as in the legal age for driving,
drinking, smoking and voting? Who should count as a 'public official' for
purposes of the bribery statute, or is a tomato a fruit or vegetable (see Solan
2004)? For these and many other situations, often there is no easy answer or
solution. But the court is never entitled, on the principle *non liquet* (it is not
clear), to decline the duty of determining the legal meaning of a relevant
enactment (Bennion 2002: 14). Courts have developed rules of construction
for such purposes, and sometimes judges come up with novel explanations
in dealing with linguistic uncertainty. One example is the judicial attempt
to distinguish the vague and similar expressions of 'slight negligence',

'negligence' and 'gross negligence' in US law where Judge Magruder once said that it was simply the difference among 'a fool, a damned fool, and a God-damned fool' (Christie 1963–1964: 899). Another example is the US Supreme Court's attempt in defining obscenity, the famous 'I know it when I see it' pronounced by Justice Potter Stewart.[5]

An expression is general when it is applicable to any one of a number of things whose differences are not denied or necessarily overlooked, for instance, 'coloured' as opposed to a specific colour of red or blue.

Law depends upon and utilises the linguistic properties of generality and vagueness (see Bix 1993, Endicott 2000). It is necessary to distinguish linguistic uncertainty and legal indeterminacy. Linguistic uncertainty refers to the various features of language including vagueness, ambiguity and other unclarity in the application of linguistic expressions that may lead to legal indeterminacy. Legal uncertainty or legal indeterminacy means that the law is indeterminate when a question of law or of how the law applies to facts has no single right answer.

The following case illustrates that ordinary words, not just legal technical terms, can be vague or ambiguous and often need clarification from the court. In *Frigaliment Importing Co. v BNS International Sales Corp.* (190 F Supp 116. SDNY 1960), the dispute arose from the different interpretation of 'chicken' with confusion over the English word chicken in relation to the German words *Huhn* (chicken) and *Suppenhuhn* (stewing chicken). The court was asked to make a determination as to what the meaning of the word 'chicken' should be. In this 'chicken case', the plaintiff, an American firm, ordered a large quantity of 'chickens' from the defendant, a Swiss firm, intending to buy young chickens suitable for broiling or frying, but the defendant believed that the order could be filled with older chickens suitable for stewing. The plaintiff argued that they used the English word 'chicken' and claimed this was done because they understood 'chicken' being 'young chicken' whereas the German word, *Huhn*, includes both *Brathuhn* (broiler) and *Suppenhuhn* (stewing chicken), and the defendant, whose officers were conversant with German, should have realised this.

The court held that both parties acted in good faith, and neither had reason to know of the difference in the meanings of the word 'chicken'. The misunderstanding went to a vitally important term of the contract. Therefore, the plaintiff's claim for breach of contract fails. The court also held that the party who seeks to interpret the terms of a contract in a sense narrower than their everyday use bears the burden of persuasion to show that is the case. In determining the intent of parties the court will turn first to the language of the contract to see whether the meaning of an ambiguous term can be raised. If unsuccessful, court must look to other evidence. The apparent purpose of parties should be given greater weight to determine the meaning.

Another example of a common everyday word that is vague and general is the word 'vehicle'. A case once came before the Supreme Court of Israel involving the Hebrew word for 'vehicle' (see Azar 2006 and also Chapter 7 for the 'vehicle' case from the ECJ, p. 134). The court here was asked to determine whether the word a *rexev* (vehicle) or a *rexev meno'i* (motor vehicle) as found in the Act of Compensation for Road-Accident Victims of Israel includes a train and a locomotive. The relevant Act reads:

> A *rexev meno'i* or a *rexev* [is] a *rexev* propelled by mechanical force, including motor-cycle with a side-car, three-wheel motorcycle, bicycle, and three-wheel bicycle with an auxiliary motor, and including vehicle towed or supported by a motor vehicle. (Translated and cited in Azar 2006: 129)

The court held that trains and locomotives are included in the definition. The judges explained that the inclusion of trains as part of the notion of motor vehicle has linguistic grounds due to the vagueness of the notion that permits the distinction between the core and the penumbra zone. As pointed out (Azar 2006: 130–131), the Hebrew term *rexev* is ambiguous and vague, designating a broad range of means of transport and a much more restricted one (Azar 2006: 130). The first meaning conforms to definitions of the kind one may find for the English equivalent term 'vehicle', and in this case, trains and locomotives are included. The second, restrictive meaning excludes trains and locomotives. It is a usual and everyday word for designating overland means of transport that run on wheels, especially motorcars and motorcycles (Azar 2006: 132). Although no modern Hebrew speaker in everyday speaking or writing will use this word to refer to trains or locomotives (Azar 2006: 132), the court nevertheless decided otherwise.

There are many cases where the court was asked to determine the meaning of words due to linguistic uncertainty. In the famous US Supreme Court case, *Smith v United States* (508 US 223 (1993)), the court was asked to determine the meaning of 'use' as in 'use a firearm'. In the decision, Justices O'Connor and Scalia (dissenting) engaged in substantial linguistic argumentation concerning the definition and clarification of the vague and general word 'use'. The basic fact of the case is that the petitioner, a certain Mr Smith, made an offer to an undercover police officer, who represented himself as a pawn shop dealer, to exchange his automatic weapon for cocaine. This was alleged to have violated the relevant US law of 18 USC & 924 (c)(1) 1988:

Whoever, during and in relation to any crime of violence or drug trafficking crime . . . *uses or carries a firearm*, shall, in addition to the punishment provided for such crime of violence or drug trafficking crime, be sentenced to imprisonment for five years . . . . (Italics added)

The relevant issue before the Supreme Court was whether bartering a firearm for drugs constitutes 'use' of a firearm within the meaning of the statute.

Justice O'Connor held that the meaning of 'use' is the ordinary or natural every day meaning. 'Use' in its dictionary meanings, cited by Justice O'Connor, includes 'to convert to one's service', 'to employ', 'to make use of', 'to avail oneself of', 'to utilise' and 'to carry out a purpose or action by means of'. If interpreted this way, Mr Smith 'used' or 'employed' a weapon in attempt to obtain drugs by offering to trade it for cocaine, and he 'derived service' from it because it was going to bring him the very drugs he sought (for linguistic analysis of the case, see Cunningham and Fillmore 1995, Geis 1995).

The legal or linguistic issue before the court was not a question of translation. However, for our purpose, it teaches us an important lesson. It demonstrates that even the most ordinary and common words such as 'chicken' and 'use' can become a point of legal contention. Extreme caution is needed in translating law texts, not just technical legal words, but every word including ordinary everyday words.

Linguistic uncertainty can be intralingual uncertainty, that is, within one language, and interlingual uncertainty, that is, uncertainty arises when two languages are considered or when one language is translated into another language. In such cases, a word, phrase or sentence in one language may or may not be uncertain, but additional uncertainty may become present when they are considered across two or more languages. For instance, in the 1972 Sino-US Shanghai Communiqué, the English version reads: 'The United States acknowledges that Chinese on both sides of the Taiwan Straits maintain that there is only one China, and that Taiwan is a part of China.' The Chinese text of the Communiqué, back translated into English, reads 'The United States recognises (*chengren*). . .', instead of 'acknowledges'. It was reported that Henry Kissinger and the then Chinese Premier Zhou Enlai had agreed on the deliberate use of the Chinese word *chengren*, not a translation error. In this case, the Chinese word *chengren* by itself is not ambiguous in Chinese, but when it is translated into English, its meaning becomes ambiguous. *Chengren* is the linguistic equivalent to 'to acknowledge' as well as 'to recognise' and 'to admit' in English.

Interlingual uncertainty includes ambiguity, vagueness, generality or other indeterminacy where words, phrases or sentences in two or more languages that are deemed to be equivalent do not correspond exactly when compared, thus giving rise to uncertainty (for discussions of different types of interlingual uncertainty in bilingual and multilingual legal texts, see Cao 2007). Such uncertainty is most often found in situations where translation is involved. We know that in translation, it is impossible to achieve absolute exactness or complete identity between any languages. As pointed out, translation always falls short of its goals of conveying the meaning and style of a text in a new text that reads like an original composition in the second language (Joseph 1995: 14). The law is always subject to interpretation. The meaning of words is never fixed: the kind of precision that law demands of language, and formal semantics attempts to represent, is based on an illusion of human linguistic behaviour (Joseph 1995: 14). As Joseph (1995: 14) notes, if indeterminacy is already the condition within languages, it holds a *fortiori* between languages.

There have been cases in bilingual and multilingual jurisdictions of Canada, Hong Kong and the ECJ where the courts were asked to solve interlingual uncertainties. To illustrate, we use two examples.

A case once came to the ECJ concerning the ambiguous meanings of words in different languages of an EU law. In Case 100/84 *Commission v United Kingdom of Great Britain and Northern Ireland* [1985] ECR 1169, the relevant law, Regulation No. 802/68 concerning the origin of goods for the purpose of customs duties refers to products of sea-fishing and other products taken from the sea. One of the issues before the court was the meaning of the phrase 'taken from the sea'. The majority of the EU language versions use expressions that stress the act of catching the fish, not the act of taking the fish out of the water. The phrase *extraits de la mer* in French and its equivalent in the Greek, Italian and Dutch versions are capable of meaning both 'taken out of the sea' and 'separated from the sea'. The English version uses 'taken from the sea' and the UK government argued that it means 'complete removal from the water'. The German version uses the term *gefangen*, meaning 'caught'. Thus, the court found that three different possibilities exist:

- Two senses are possible – 'taken out of the sea' vs. 'separated from the sea' as in the Greek, French, Italian and Dutch versions.
- Only the first sense is possible as in the English version.
- Only the second sense is possible as in the German version.

The phrase in one language as in English or German as described above may not be ambiguous, but when they are translated into different languages, uncertainty arises and different connotations are entailed. The court in this case found that a comparative examination of the various language versions of the regulation does not enable a conclusion to be reached in favour of any of the arguments put forward, so no legal consequences can be based on the terminology used. The court decided the case on the legal and other considerations with reference to the purpose and general scheme of the relevant law.

Another example of interlingual uncertainty is Case C-149/97 *Institute of the Motor Industry v Commissioners of Customs and Excise* [1998] ECR I-7053, where the interpretation of the phrase 'trade union' contained in EU Directive 77/388/EEC in relation to value added tax and its exemption was a point of contention. The court observed that the term *syndicale* in the French version and its equivalents in some languages appear to be used in a wider sense than that of the expression 'trade union' in English and its equivalents in the other language versions. And the expression 'aims of a trade union nature' in English and some language versions is capable of having a different meaning when compared with the equivalent phrase in the other language versions. For instance, in French, the equivalent phrase used was *objectifs de nature syndicale*. As the court pointed out, this phrase in French also refers to the aims of professional associations, which do not constitute trade unions.

Here we may say that the term 'trade union' in either English or French is not uncertain. It is a well-established and well-defined term and practice in the respective individual societies. However, when the two equivalent terms are compared between English and French and other languages, interlingual uncertainty arises. A comparison reveals that the two terms overlap in English and French, but they do not correspond exactly in what they encompass. The court could not really resolve the interlingual ambiguity by comparing the languages or by linguistic means alone. It stated that the wording used in one language version of a Community provision cannot serve as the sole basis for the interpretation of that provision, or be made to override the other language versions in that regard as such an approach would be incompatible with the requirement of the uniform application of Community law. To apply the law in a uniform and consistent manner, and despite the different usage and shades of meanings in different languages, the court must provide a unitary meaning. The method to achieve this for the ECJ is by examining the underlying purpose and spirit of the provision in question, and by reference to the purpose and general scheme of the rules of which it forms part. So, in this case, the court held that for the purposes of the relevant directive, an organisation with aims of a trade union nature means an organisation whose main aim is to defend the collective interest of its members and to represent them vis-à-vis the appropriate third parties.

All languages are inherently indeterminate. Furthermore, some languages may be more uncertain and indeterminate than others.[6] I have argued elsewhere (Cao 2004) that the Chinese legal language is more uncertain than English. A German jurist, Grossfeld (cited in Weisflog 1987: 206) believes that the English legal language, compared with the German legal language, is less concentrated, or more 'open-textured', and English legal concepts are vaguer. This can cause additional problems in translation.

In terms of legal translation, there are two major considerations: the demand for precision and stability from law and the inherent indeterminate nature of language. For bilingual and multilingual jurisdictions, there is also the legal principle of equal authenticity of bilingual and multilingual legal instruments, which creates a legal fiction that the words in different authentic language versions are deemed to be equivalent and have the same meaning. The legal fiction is necessary for legal certainty and consistency so that citizens are governed by the same law, being treated equally irrespective of their linguistic diversity. Consequently, despite the linguistic, legal and other differences involved in translation, words and phrases in law and other legal texts are deemed equal, linguistically and legally. This places stringent demand and enormous responsibility on the translator.

An important point for the legal translator with regard to linguistic uncertainty is that one should always bear in mind the task of the translator. The legal translator is not the lawyer. The central task of the translator is to translate, not to solve legal problems. Lawyers and courts may interpret any vague or ambiguous words very differently, and courts are often asked to adjudicate and make a determination. Only the judicial interpretations of disputed words are the correct or enforceable ones. Thus, one of the tasks for the translator in such situations is to recognise and appreciate the linguistic uncertainty that may have occurred, intentionally or unintentionally, in the first place in the original text, and then to convey and retain the vagueness or ambiguity in translation. The translator must always resist the temptation to clarify or make a word more precise or less ambiguous, thus potentially limiting the possible interpretations by the court in the future. As rightly pointed out, translators have no authority to resolve ambiguities in the original texts, although this can be brought about inadvertently if the translators do not have sufficient legal and linguistic expertise to appreciate the delicate situation in the first place (Northcott *et al.* 2001, for this point, see also Chapter 7 for the translation of international law). Conversely, in translation, new linguistic uncertainty, that is, interlingual uncertainty, may be created due to the differences in linguistic and legal systems. This sometimes is inevitable, not due to translators' mistakes, but because of the inherent nature of language. Often, the translator has to make hard decisions within the constraints of language.

One may be tempted to think that monolingualism would reduce or eliminate linguistic uncertainties or that bilingualism and multilingualism would create more uncertainties and encourage more litigation. As we know, language, any language, is indeterminate by nature. It is true that when translation is involved, errors may and do occur from time to time that can cause additional problems that may have been avoided. That is one of the reasons why legal translators need to be extremely cautious. However, I do not believe that bilingual and multilingual laws would result in more disputes, although the issues in a dispute may become more complex when more than one language is involved. In the Common Law system, for instance, courts in monolingual jurisdictions in the US, the UK and Australia have been dealing with uncertainties of the English language over the centuries. The most litigious society of all is the monolingual US. The main issue is that people litigate when they believe their rights have been infringed upon in some ways. They litigate to enforce their rights that they believe would not be enforced in any other way. Language is an additional vehicle for lawyers to argue their case. Language is not often the cause of action. Lawyers would always try to find different ways to advance their clients' case.

Notes

1. For a discussion of the legal language and style in Hebrew in Israel, see Fassberg (2003).
2. For detailed discussions of the Civil Law institutions, see Zweigert and Kötz (1992) and Vranken (1997).
3. As Solan (2004: 860) points out, legal writers and judges often use the word 'ambiguity' in a loose sense to refer to all different kinds of linguistic indeterminacy, including vagueness.
4. See Black (1949/1970: 30) for his philosophical discussions of vagueness and his mathematical definition of vagueness. Black also discussed Bertrand Russell, Wittgenstein, Charles Morris, and Ogden and Richards's theory of interpretation, emotive meaning, and semantic definition of truth.
5. See the US Supreme Court case *Jacobellis v Ohio*, 378 US 184 (1964) where Justice Stewart said regarding what was considered pornographic: 'I shall not today attempt further to define the kinds of material I understand to be embraced

within that shorthand description; and perhaps I could never succeed in intelligibly doing so. But I know it when I see it, and the motion picture involved in this case is not that.'

6. There are different views as to whether one language may be more ambiguous than others. For instance, Bally (1944) was sceptical of the idea, but Jespersen (1964) did not rule out a priori the possibility that some languages could be less inadequate than other languages, or that ambiguities may increase with the development of a language, both cited in Kooij (1971: 3–4).

Chapter 5
Translating Private Legal Documents

It is often said that lawyers write poorly, and lawyers themselves agree. To quote a description by Goldstein and Lieberman (2002: 3), two lawyers and professors, modern English legal writing is

> ... flabby, prolix, obscure, opaque, ungrammatical, dull, boring, redundant, disorgani[s]ed, gr[e]y, dense, unimaginative, impersonal, foggy, infirm, indistinct, stilled, arcane, confused, heavy-handed, jargon- and cliché-ridden, ponderous, weaselling, overblown, pseudo-intellectual, hyperbolic, misleading, incivil, labo[u]red, bloodless, vacuous, evasive, pretentious, convoluted, rambling, incoherent, choked, archaic, orotund, and fuzzy.

This may be true to some extent, but it is yet another example of lawyers' excessiveness in writing. However, what is also true and commonly acknowledged is that legal documents are difficult to read and hard to comprehend for the layperson (see Benson 1984–1985). Legal writing is idiosyncratic and legal drafting follows certain rules. So why is legal writing difficult to comprehend, and what are its basic rules and characteristics relevant to translation?

Legal writing generally includes statutory texts, judicial texts, legal scholarly works, and private legal documents, which are the focus of this chapter. Private legal documents are those documents that are drafted and used by lawyers in their daily practice on behalf of their clients. They may include deeds, contracts and other agreements, leases, wills, among others, and other legal texts such as statutory declaration, power of attorney, statements of claims or pleadings and other court documents, and advice from lawyers to clients. The translation of these documents constitutes the bulk of actual translation work for many legal translation practitioners. In this chapter, the linguistic features of major private legal documents in English are examined with regard to translation. Many of these features also apply to English statutes (see Chapter 6).

Purpose and Status of Translated Private Legal Documents

Private legal documents, either original or translated, serve many purposes. Some of the major functions include creating, conferring, varying or negating legal rights and obligations and recording such rights and obligations (Aitkin and Butter 2004). They are also used before a court or legal authorities to protect rights or enforce obligations. Private legal documents are important. It is said that drafting legal documents is like drafting statutes between private parties, setting out the relationships and ground rules in a formal or written form (Dick 1985: 1).

There are different purposes and uses for translated private legal documents. They may be requested by organisations or individuals. For instance, legal documents may be translated for business purpose, such as contracts that are used as part of business transaction. There are documents that are translated for use by individuals for various purposes, for instance, a will, a statutory declaration, or a marriage certificate. There are documents that are translated for litigation purpose, for instance, statements of claims or pleadings and witness statements. Legal advice of lawyers to their clients may also require translation if they speak different languages, as do instructions from clients to their legal representatives.

The legal status of these translated documents may vary. They may be for informative purpose or for normative purpose. For instance, contracts sometimes stipulate that two language versions are equally authentic, that is, both texts have equal legal force in the court of law. In other times, contracts may stipulate that only one language version, not both, is legally binding. They may nevertheless require translation, and such translations are mainly for informative purpose. Court documents and other litigation documents sometimes may require translations so that all the parties and the court can have linguistic access to documents written in different languages. Today, due to the increased movement of people across national borders for educational, employment, immigration and other purposes, legal certificates such as marriage, divorce, birth and death certificates are often in need of translation.

A relevant point is that the translation of private legal documents is often used by a specific entity or individual for a specific purpose. It is different from the translation of statutory and international instruments that are used for the public at large (see Chapter 7).

Linguistic Features of Private Legal Documents

Private legal documents often follow certain established patterns and rules in a particular jurisdiction. The Common Law drafting style has been inherited from the United Kingdom over the last two to three hundred years and is similar in many ways across the Common Law countries. Moreover, the use of standard documents by law firms, called 'precedents', is common, maintaining similar drafting styles. For instance, wills, contracts of sale of land, mortgages and leases of premises are normally in standard forms. Such precedents are often available in law books and now also on-line. Legal firms usually have their own precedents. For the commonly used legal forms such as marriage, divorce, death, birth certificates and statutory declaration, they are often also in standard form in a particular jurisdiction issued by the relevant authorities. In these texts, the linguistic form is often as important as the content.

Textual features

Due to the commonalities in private legal drafting in English, certain textual features can be identified. Agreements and contracts, which are among the most commonly translated private legal documents from and into English, are often written in similar styles. Such documents vary in their actual content, which can be wide ranging from intellectual property rights transfer to the sale of equipment, depending upon the needs of the clients. They also vary in terms of length and complexity. Some are short and general but most are lengthy and detailed.

In terms of textual components, with respect to general agreements drafted in English, for instance, agreements on business or research collaboration, joint business ventures, or collaborative projects, some common parts and clauses can be identified. They often include the following:

- date of the agreement;
- names and addresses of the parties;
- recital;
- definition clause;
- rights, obligations and liabilities of the parties;
- *force majeure*;
- termination;
- breach and remedies;
- dispute resolution;
- notice;

- assignment;
- waiver;
- warranty and exclusion;
- entire agreement clause;
- governing law;
- language clause if two or more languages are involved;
- signature, date and execution.

Not all agreements have these elements, but many have, covering these and similar grounds. When an agreement has a recital or 'whereas' section, it often starts with the word 'whereas'. It has long been pointed out that the use of 'whereas' is anachronistic and should be avoided (Dick 1985). Nevertheless, it is still found in legal documents. 'Whereas' in this context has the meaning of 'given the fact that', or 'as', not the sense of indicating contrast. Recitals cover the matters leading up to the signing of the document. They are usually formal statements that come before the operative part of the agreement, setting out background and introductory materials. Nowadays, some agreements use the word 'recital' stating the background facts without using the word 'whereas'.

In many agreements in English, the operative section starts with the definition clause. It is not dissimilar to definitions found in statutes (see Chapter 6). It defines and restricts the meanings of words used in an agreement. Sometimes, after the definition, there may also be an interpretation clause, for instance,

(1) The expression 'person' includes an individual, a body corporate, a joint venture, a trust, an agency or other body.

(2) Words importing the singular shall include the plural (and vice versa) and words denoting a given gender will include all other genders.

(3) A reference to any document or agreement shall be deemed to include a reference to such document or agreement as amended, annotated, supplemented, varied or replaced from time to time.

(4) References to any legislation or to any provision of any legislation will include any modification or re-enactment of such legislation or any legislative provisions substituted for, and all legislation and statutory instruments issued under such legislation.

(5) Where a word or phase is given a particular meaning in this Agreement, other parts of speech and grammatical forms of that word or phase have a corresponding meaning.

Another common clause in English agreements is the *force majeure* clause. It often reads like this:

. . . *Force Majeure* under this Agreement shall include:

(1) governmental, semi-governmental or judicial law, regulation, order, decree, directive, restriction, restraint, prohibition, intervention or expropriation, or the failure of any government or semi-government or judicial entity to act;

(2) strike, lockout or other labour dispute;

(3) act of God, fire, flood, cyclone, tornado, hurricane or any other form of weather or conditions resulting from such weather;

(4) explosion, concussion, collision, radiation, act of the public enemy, act of war (declared or undeclared), blockade, riot, civil commotion or disturbance, martial law, sabotage, insurrection or national emergency (whether in fact or law); or

(5) any other cause, whether similar or dissimilar to the cause herein specifically enumerated and which is beyond the reasonable control of such party and which such party is unable to overcome by the exercise of reasonable diligence and at a reasonable cost.

Sometimes, *force majeure* is also called 'unexpected event'. For instance,

. . . Unexpected Event affecting a party means anything outside that party's reasonable control, including but not limited to, acts or omissions of the other party, fire, storm, flood, earthquake, war, transportation embargo or failure or delay in transportation, act or omission (including laws, regulations, disapprovals or failures to approve) of any third person (including but not limited to, subcontractors, customers, governments or government agencies) . . . .

'Complete agreement' or 'entire agreement' is another common feature in English agreements. For instance:

This Agreement constitutes the entire agreement between the parties. Any prior arrangements, agreements, representations or undertakings are superseded. No modification or alteration of any clause in this Agreement will be valid except in writing signed by both parties.

Nowadays, most agreements involving parties that speak different languages have a 'language clause'. Such provisions are quite common, for instance:

The contract shall be written in both . . . and English and both language versions shall have equal force. In case of inconsistency of the two language versions, the . . . version shall prevail.

Another example:

> This Agreement and any attachments hereto are rendered in both . . . and English. In the event of any conflict between the provisions of the English version and the . . .version which the parties cannot resolve by mutual agreement, then . . . provisions shall apply.

Lexical feature: All inclusive description

Lawyers are often criticised for their old or archaic drafting style. In English legal documents, one often finds words such as 'aforementioned', 'hereinafter', 'hereinabove', 'hereunder', 'said', 'such', etc. These words do not often present enormous problems in translation once the translator gets accustomed to such usage. However, a major linguistic feature of private legal documents written in English that does present a translation challenge is the use of word strings. We have seen some examples of this in the previous section of cited contract clauses, e.g. 'judicial law, regulation, order, decree, directive, restriction, restraint, prohibition, intervention or expropriation', 'modification or alteration', and 'document or agreement as amended, annotated, supplemented, varied or replaced', 'arrangements, agreements, representations or undertakings'. Some describe this as wordiness or verbosity.

Word strings that are often synonyms. The following examples are from typical English contracts:

> Each party acknowledges that except to the extent caused directly by the other party's negligence or breach of this Agreement Party A assumes all risks for any *liabilities, expenses, losses, damages and costs* (including legal costs on a full indemnity basis and whether incurred by or awarded against a party) incurred by Party A and resulting directly or indirectly from Party A's use or disclosure of Party B's information and/or the results under this Agreement . . . .

Word strings can consist of a series of nouns, verbs, adjectives, adverbs and other phrases. For instance:

> Each party to this Agreement hereby acknowledges that it is aware that it or its *advisers, agents or solicitors* may discover facts different from and in addition to facts that they now *know or believe to be true* with respect to the subject matter of this Agreement, but it is their intention to hereby *fully, finally, absolutely and forever* settle according to the provisions of this Agreement any and all *liabilities, claims, disputes and differences* which *exist, may exist or have ever existed* between them relating in any way to the matters the subject of this Agreement.

It is believed that this tradition goes back to early history. An early Anglo-Saxon linguistic tradition was the conjoining of two similar words with closely related meanings, and they were often alliterative as well (Tiesma 1999: 13–15). Like other Germanic tribes, Anglo-Saxons made extensive use of alliteration in the legal language, and this style is found in today's ordinary English: 'aid and abet', 'fame and fortune', 'might and main', 'new and novel', 'part and parcel' and 'safe and sound' (Tiesma 1999: 13–15). Mellingkoff (1963) points out that this doubling continued in Law French in the medieval English law with some variation. It often involved the paring of a native English word first with the equivalent French word second, for instance, 'devise and bequeath', 'break and enter', 'acknowledge and confess', 'goods and chattels', 'had and received', 'will and testament' and 'fit and proper' (Tiesma 1999: 32). This tradition of doublets and triplets were later expanded into word strings or more than two or three words of synonyms (for further discussion, see Mellingkoff 1963, Tiesma 1999, Goldstein and Lieberman 2002). An example is the word string used when transferring title to land from one person to another: grant, bargain, sell, alien, release, assign, transfer, set over and confirm 'as if proliferation of words would give safety in numbers' (Aitkin and Butter 2004: 4).

The main reason for the continuation of this linguistic tradition in English legal documents is that such word strings are used to convey the meaning of all-inclusiveness, that is, to cover all possible situations and eventualities. Lawyers tend to be overly cautious and they want to guard against all possible situations that may or may not arise in the future. Because of this reason, lawyers tend towards redundancy. This has been helped by the fact that the English legal language is richly endowed with repetitive phrases that once had different legal consequences (Goldstein and Lieberman 2002: 124).

Commonly used legal word strings that essentially have one meaning include (cited in Dick 1985: 126–127):

authorise and direct;
bind and obligate;
deemed and considered;
final and conclusive;
full and complete;
furnish and supply;
over and above;
release and discharge;
finish and complete;
full force and effect;

have and hold;
null and void;
power and authority;
save and except;
assign, transfer and set over;
build, erect or construct;
cease, desist and be at an end;
costs, charges and expenses;
obey, observe and comply with;
place, install or affix;
rest, residue and remainder;
give, devise and bequeath;
documents, instruments and writings;
changes, variations and modifications;
business, enterprise or undertaking;
bear, sustain or suffer;
advice, opinion and direction.

Word strings in English legal documents can present problems in translation as other languages may not have a string of corresponding words with similar meanings. For example, 'null and void' is translated as *wuxiao* (no effect) into Chinese as one word. This is because there are no two synonyms in Chinese to correspond the English doublet. In this case, 'null and void' in English has the essential meaning of 'void' in any event. However, we also note that 'null and void' is more emphatic in English than simply 'void'. Another example is the English word string 'costs, expenses, outlays, expenditures, fees, charges and levies'. There may be a lack of the exact corresponding synonyms in the TL.

A legal consideration is that in law, sometimes each and every word may carry different legal meanings and legal consequences. When disputes arise, courts may be asked to interpret each such individual word, and give them different meanings. Thus, for the translator, it is not always possible or advisable to combine the synonyms into one word.

One example of synonym with different legal meaning is the words 'mean' and 'include'. They are often found in the definition clause of agreements. They have different meanings and should not be translated as the same. Generally, 'mean' restricts the definition to the notion set out in the clause, that is, exhaustive, whereas 'include' enlarges the definition so that its ordinary meaning incorporates an additional notion (see Dick 1985: 151–152. See also Chapter 5 with regard to the meanings of 'mean' and 'include' in statutory interpretation).

Another example of synonym is found in the following clause:

No termination of this Contract shall *release or discharge* Party A or Party B from any *debt, liability or obligation* which shall have accrued and remains to be performed by either Party A or Party B as at the date of such termination or which is intended by this Contract to survive the termination of this Contract.

Again, here 'release' and 'discharge', and 'debt', 'liability' and 'obligation' may be construed to carry substantial different meanings even though they are similar, and even if it may be difficult to distinguish them in translation. Still another example from a lease in English:

The Lessee covenants with the Lessor to *observe and perform* the *terms, covenants and conditions* contained in the Land Use Right and on the Lessor's part to be *observed and performed* in the same manner in all respects as if those *terms, covenants and conditions*, with such modifications only as may be necessary to make them applicable to this Lease, had been repeated in full in the Lease as *terms, covenants and conditions* binding on the Lessee in favour of the Lessor.

Words used in leases in English go back in history. For instance, the words 'terms, covenants and conditions' may have different meanings in English property law. Thus, it would be advisable to translate these synonyms into separate words in the TL, although in some cases, it may prove to be difficult.

Another example is the phrase 'devise and bequeath' used in wills. Often in a will, a testator will state: 'I devise and bequeath all my real and personal property to B'. If used strictly, the term 'devise' is appropriate only to real property while the term 'bequeath' is appropriate only to personal property. Accordingly, the testamentary disposition is read as if it were worded: 'I devise all my real property, and bequeath all my personal property, to B' (Bennion 2002: 1070).

In short, the linguistic feature of word strings in the English legal language was developed in the long history of the Common Law. It is related to the notion of the so-called 'preventative law', that is, to prevent the parties from having to litigate later on (Dick 1985: 1). The main reasons for having a contract or agreement are, firstly, to specify in all-inclusive terms the exact rights and obligations of each party, and importantly, to prevent possible future disputes, and secondly, if any dispute does arise, the contract also provides for possible remedies and dispute resolution methods. Lawyers in Common Law countries are trained to go to great and sometimes extreme length to draw up contracts that attempt to cover every possible situation, every conceivable event, every foreseeable matter and contingency that may or may not arise. The English legal language has developed to meet such exact and all-encompassing demands of the lawyers and the law, to be all-inclusive and self-contained. This, apart from wordiness and sometimes redundancy, also results in long-winded sentences and complex syntactical structures to be discussed next.

Syntactical feature: Long and complex sentence structures

In legal documents, a common linguistic feature is that sentences are typically long and complex. This is true in many languages, not just in English.

Syntax refers to the structure of sentences and sequences of words. While words are the basic building blocks of language that carry meanings, translation never remains at the lexical level, but goes beyond. Words in translation never exist in isolation and their true meanings cannot be fully appreciated unless they are construed with reference to the ways they are structured.

Generally speaking, sentences in legal texts are longer than in other text types (Salmi-Tolonen 2004: 1173), and they may serve various purposes (Salmi-Tolonen 2004, and see also Chapters 2 and 6). Nevertheless, complicated syntactical structure can cause comprehension difficulty for the reader including the translator. It sometimes also makes the rendering into the TL difficult.

It is common to find long and complex sentences in legal documents. For instance:

In the event of the Contractor becoming bankrupt or making a composition or arrangement with his creditors or having a proposal in respect of his company for a voluntary arrangement for a composition of debts in respect of his company to the court for the appointment of an administrator, or having a winding up order made or (except for the purposes of amalgamation or reconstruction) a resolution for voluntary winding up passed or having a provisional liquidator, receiver or manager of his business or undertaking duly appointed, or being placed under judicial management, or having possession taken, by or on behalf of the holders of any debentures secured by a floating charge, of any property comprised in or subject to the floating charge, the employment of the Contractor under this Contract shall be forthwith automatically terminated, but the said employment may be reinstated and continued if the Proprietor and the Contractor, his trustee in bankruptcy, liquidator, provisional liquidator, receiver or manager as the case may be shall so agree.

In this example, the main clause is 'In the event of . . ., the employment . . . shall be terminated.' All the other clauses and qualifications are to cover the conditions and situations in which such an event may occur. This can be better written in two or more sentences with improved clarity. Another example:

> Where the value of any materials or goods has, in accordance with clause . . . , been included in the payment, such materials and goods shall become the property of the Proprietor, and thereafter the Contractor shall not, except for use upon the Project, remove or cause or permit the same to be moved or removed from the premises where they are, but the Contractor shall nevertheless be responsible for any loss thereof or damage thereto and for the cost of storage, handling and insurance of the same until such time as they are delivered to and placed on or adjacent to the Project whereupon the provisions of clause . . . of the conditions shall apply thereto.

These examples may be unusual as compared with ordinary everyday written language, but they are not isolated or exceptional cases in English legal documents. Still another example of long and complex sentence:

> The Seller shall indemnify the Buyer against any judgment for damages and costs which may be rendered against the Buyer in any suit brought on account of the alleged infringement of any . . . patent by any product supplied by the Seller hereunder, unless made in accordance with materials, designs or specifications furnished or designated by the Buyer, in which case the Buyer shall indemnify the Seller against any judgment for damages and costs which may be rendered against the Seller in any suit brought on account of the alleged infringement of any . . . patent by such product or such materials, designs or specifications; provided that prompt written notice be given to the party from whom indemnity is sought of the bringing of the suit and that an opportunity be given to such party to settle or defend it as that party may see fit and that every reasonable assistance in settling or defending it shall be rendered.

The basic sentence is 'The Seller shall indemnify the Buyer against any judgement for damages and costs.' However, the contexts, conditions and circumstances for such damages and costs are elaborately described, resulting in the long-winded sentence: one 'which' attributive clause followed by one conditional clause starting with 'unless', to be further modified by a 'which' clause, which itself contains another 'which' clause. There is a further conditional clause 'provided that', to introduce two conditions. Within these clauses, there are more modifying phrases. The sentence can be easily written in two or more separate sentences.

When translating long and complex sentences, there are two basic steps: firstly, to conduct a careful analysis of the original sentence structure and essential meaning so as to correctly comprehend the message, and secondly, to express and convey the meaning in the TL. So, good knowledge of syntactical rules of both the SL and TL is imperative. Sometimes, it may be necessary to break long sentences up and compose two or more sentences in the TL. It is not necessary to follow and reproduce the SL structures in the TL.

Syntactical feature: Passive structures

Lawyers like to use passive structures. The passive voice is a linguistic construction that permits the writer to avoid naming or referring to the person or thing that performs the action. For instance, the sentence 'The contract was breached', simply states the fact. It does not indicate who was the wrongdoer who breached the contract. There are many instances of the use of passive structures in the examples cited above in the previous sections, e.g. 'shall be forthwith automatically terminated', 'may be reinstated and continued', 'to be observed and performed', 'may be rendered', 'prompt written notice be given' and 'indemnity is sought of'.

Lawyers like to use passive structures to avoid directly referring to or identifying the person involved or assigning responsibilities. Because of this reason, lawyers tend to prefer the passive voice to the active voice where the doer needs to be identified and spelt out. Sometimes, lawyers overuse the passive voice for this reason (Goldstein and Lieberman 2002: 131). Even when the subject or doer of an action is known and identified, passive structures are still used, for instance, in the examples cited earlier, 'to be performed by Party A or Party B,' and 'which is intended by the Contract'.

In translation, passive structures are often translated following the original pattern. However, in some languages and in some instances where passive structures are not as commonly used as they are in English, adjustments may be necessary. It is not imperative that the passive structure is carried over in the TL.

Provisos and other limiting clauses

Provisos are a traditional feature of English legal drafting in both private legal documents and statutes. They operate as conditions or qualifications. They are usually introduced by the linguistic formula:

PROVIDED THAT . . .
AND PROVIDED THAT . . .
AND PROVIDED FURTHER THAT . . .

Other variations include 'provided always that', and 'provided nevertheless that'. Such wordings are used to vary or modify a more general provision, qualifying its operation in one or more particular circumstances (Aitkin and Butter 2004: 86). A 'proviso' is to be distinguished from a provision, which is a general term used to denote a clause or section in a document or statute. The proviso evolved from the enacting words of early English statutes – *'Provisum est'* (it is provided) – used to introduce an independent section of a statute (Aitkin and Butter 2004: 86). In modern legal drafting, some have advised against using the proviso in that it is seen as an ancient archaic device that should be avoided (see Dick 1985: 92–100, see also Fung 1997). The decline in the use of the proviso has been reflected in contemporary legal drafting practice in most English speaking jurisdictions (Fung 1997). Notwithstanding, provisos are still commonly found, in particular in wills. For example:

> I GIVE DEVISE AND BEQUEATH my house property situated at . . . to my daughter for her own use and benefit absolutely PROVIDED that my said son may reside in the said house so long as he so desires . . . . (This example was quoted in *Re Potter deceased* [1970] VR 352. See Justice Menhennit's judgment in this case regarding the meaning of 'provided that')

One may think that these expressions are from old English documents of a bygone era, but not so. Here is a section from my own will drafted in 2004 in Australia:

> I DEVISE AND BEQUEATH the whole of my estate both real and personal of whatsoever nature or kind and wheresoever situated UNTO MY TRUSTEE UPON TRUST to pay transfer and assign as follows: . . . . PROVIDED ALWAYS that should in these above mentioned clauses, any share fails to take effect and there is no further direction given to that share redistribution then that such share or trust is to pass to the part of the clause or clauses which do not fail and if there are more than one part which do not fail then the failed part is to pass proportionately between those parts that did not fail.

Other limiting clauses common in private legal documents include the phrase 'subject to'. It is used to express the intent that one provision (the master provision) prevails over another (the subject provision). For instance, if clause 7 in an agreement begins with 'subject to clause 6', then any inconsistency between the two clauses is resolved in favour of the master clause, clause 6. Similarly, if subclause (1) begins with 'Subject to subclause (4)', then subclause (4) prevails. 'Subject to' is often used in ordinary agreements, and also in wills, settlements and other instruments creating interest in succession. It is also often used statutes (see Chapter 6). When used in wills, there are two principal uses of 'subject to' (Aitkin and Butter 2004: 89): (1) where a gift has been made of part of a fund and it is desired to dispose of what remains; and (2) where it is intended that any prior gift that lapses is to pass with the gift to the balance.[1]

Generally speaking, provisos, 'subject to' and other limiting clauses are common in English legal documents. Some believe that they give a document a legalistic feel, but this has the unfortunate side effect of increasing sentence length in the process. For example:

> If the performance of the contract by the seller be delayed by reason of any of the causes above mentioned, the buyer may, *subject to* previously obtaining the written consent of the seller, cancel the purchase of such portion of the material for which details and instructions have been duly furnished in accordance with the contract as may have been subjected to such delay, *provided* such portion of the material has not been manufactured nor is in process of manufacture at the time the buyer's request for such cancellation arrives at the manufacturer.

Differences between the Common Law and Civil Law

Private legal documents from different countries are not written in the same way. In particular, major differences exist in the drafting of legal documents in the Common Law and Civil Law jurisdictions. For instance, Zweigert and Kötz (1992: 275) point out that contracts and wills in Common Law in English may be drafted in a style of language that strikes the Continental jurist as positively medieval. For example, in Germany, a contract of lease will simply say: 'The lessor leases to the lessee the following dwelling . . .', but in the UK or the US, a lease might well read something like this: 'The Landlord has let and by these presents does grant, devise and let unto the Tenant and the said Tenant has agreed to hire and take, and does hereby hire and take as tenant the following space in the apartment building . . .' (quoted in Zweigert and Kötz 1992: 275).

A recent study by Hill and King (2004), 'How Do German Contracts Do as Much with Fewer Words?', comparing German and American business contracts, can provide us with some insight into the different drafting styles. Of the US complex business contracts, Hill and King (2004: 894) have found that:

- The US contracts are very long.
- There is a great deal of explanation, qualification and limitation in the language.
- There is a great deal of legalese.
- The legalese is similar from agreement to agreement, but not exactly the same.
- Contracts of a particular type of transaction are similar in general coverage, but the specific language varies considerably from contract to contract.

In contrast, the German contracts are characterised as follows (Hill and King 2004: 894–895):

- The German agreements are much lighter, about one-half or two-thirds the size of otherwise comparable US agreements.
- There is much less explanation, qualification and limitation in the language.
- There is much less legalese.
- The legalese is almost identical from contract to contract.
- Many provisions are quite similar from contract to contract.

Some of the clauses quoted in Hill and King (2004) are also interesting. For instance, contrast the standard forms of a forum selection clause (Hill and King 2004: 895):

- American clause: The exclusive forum for the resolution of any dispute under or arising out of this agreement shall be the courts of general jurisdiction of . . . and both parties submit to the jurisdiction of such courts. The parties waive all objections to such forum based on *forum non conveniens*.
- German clause: *Ausschließlicher Gerichtsstand ist . . . .*

The granting clause:

- American clause: . . . does hereby grant, bargain, sell, assign, transfer, convey, pledge and confirm, unto Indenture Trustee, its successors and assigns, for the security and benefit of the Indenture Trustee, for itself, and for the Holders from time to time a security interest in and lien on, all estate, right, title and interest of . . . in, to and under the following described property, agreements, rights, interests and privileges, whether now owned or hereafter acquired, arising or existing (which collectively . . ., are herein called the '. . . Trustee Indenture Estate').

* German clause: *Der Sicherungsgeber übereignet der Bank hiermit den gesamten jeweiligen Bestand an . . . der sich in . . . befindet und in Zukunft dorthin verbracht wird.*

Georges A. van Hecke (1962) once recounted an incident that occurred in 1962. An American company and a Belgian company wanted to engage in a share exchange transaction. The American party drafted a contract of 10,000 words. The Belgians refused to continue with the transaction because they were shocked by the length of the draft. In contrast, the Belgian draft had 1400 words, and was 'found by the American party to include all the substance that was really needed' (van Hecke 1962: 10, cited in Hill and King 2004: 897). Due to the widespread influence of the Anglo-American, especially US business legal practice the world over, the English drafting style has started to influence the business contract drafting in other jurisdictions.

The above comparison does not imply or is not used to illustrate that one legal system or one legal style is superior to another. It is intended to demonstrate that differences exist in different legal cultures and legal languages. The legal systems and legal cultures of the Common Law and Civil Law have hundreds of years of history behind them. Laws or legal texts are not formulated or construed in a vacuum. Legal documents drafted in each jurisdiction are conditioned by and cater to the demands and requirements of that particular jurisdiction, unique to the law, tradition and policy of each culture. For instance, contracts and agreements in Common Law jurisdictions, especially the US, tend to be long, and this is partly because such documents often include provisions covering possible contingency issues litigated in the courts (Ramsfield 2005: 194). Furthermore, words used in law are loaded semiotic signs with multiple layers of meanings from a particular legal culture of which they are a part. For instance, many words in the Common Law, including simple, everyday words, and words that lawyers seem to be fond of using, such as 'subject to', 'provided' and others, have histories of legal use. They have been interpreted and defined by courts in legal precedents over the centuries. They are the archaeological bricks from the past that have constructed and supported and are still supporting the four walls of the law. Whatever stories and histories these building blocks may carry does not just get erased, even though many people are not familiar with or aware of their histories.

In this connection, the English legal language and legal drafting have been undergoing reform and change in the last few decades to make them more accessible and comprehensible to the layperson. In the past twenty or thirty years, in major English speaking countries, there have been efforts by the legal profession to simplify legal drafting and writing style in the so-called Plain English Movement.[2] The movement advocates the use of plain and straightforward language to convey meaning as clearly as possible without unnecessary pretension or embellishment, that is, emphasising clarity and simplicity. For instance, in some US and Australian jurisdictions, legislation requires some consumer documents to be written in plain English and achieve a required standard of intelligibility. Such efforts are directed both at legislative language and private legal documents, and extend beyond English. The adoption of plain language appears to have worked particularly well in situations where there is a high degree of interface between consumers and documents such as standard form contracts and insurance policies etc. (Hunt 2002). However, this does not mean to abandon legal concepts, technical terms or legal usage. Simplicity does not equal being simplistic. Sometimes, complex notions and long sentences may be necessary and details may need to be spelt out due to the nature of law. Using plain language and making a legal text easier to understand does not mean that the meanings and legal effects should be changed from those if written in a more traditional drafting style (see Turnbull 1997). We need to be aware that different words very often carry different meanings. It is not the task of this chapter or the book to evaluate the merit or result of the Plain English Movement. Suffice it to say that legal English and legal drafting are and will remain different from ordinary English. Legal language carries distinctive markers. Law and legal texts are complex because human affairs and human relations are complex. Legal texts, both statutes and private legal documents, can certainly be improved in terms of comprehensibility and accessibility. However, legal language is not everyday language but a technical language. As stated earlier, it is a special register peculiar to its situational use in the legal setting. It is naive to think that law can be written in a language that everyone can fully understand and appreciate without reference to the legal institutional parameters and cultural histories. In terms of translation, unnecessarily long and convoluted sentences and unclear meanings will make translation more difficult. They will reduce the chance of the correct meanings being conveyed in translation and increase the probability of ambiguity and other linguistic uncertainty. It is a point that drafters, especially those drafting bilingual or multilingual legal texts, both private legal documents and legislation, should bear in mind.

Notes

1   See also *Macpherson v Maund* per Latham CJ (1937) 58 CLR 341 and *Re Edwards'
    Will Trusts* [1948] Ch 440, where the meaning of the words 'subject to as
    aforesaid' used in a will was discussed, cited in Aitkin and Butter (2004: 90).

2   For plain English in law, see Wydick (1998), Adler (1990) and Asprey (2003).
    There is an international body dedicated to plain legal language called Clarity:
    An international association promoting plain legal language – http://www.
    clarity-international.net. Even in the European Commission, there has been a
    campaign to promote the use of clear and plain language in EU legislation. See
    Wagner (undated) and her booklet, *Fight the FOG*. See also *The Joint Practical
    Guide of the European Parliament, the Council and the Commission for Persons Involved
    in the Drafting of Legislation within the Community Institutions* published by the
    European Commission (2003).

Chapter 6
Translating Domestic Legislation

The principles of legislative expression in English have been developed during the long history of written law in England and its descendants, and they now inform the drafting and interpretation of statutes in the UK, Commonwealth countries, and in part, the United States (Bowers 1989: 3). Such rules have also influenced the drafting of multilateral legal instruments. These principles and statutory characteristics are manifested through legislative language at the textual, lexical, syntactical and pragmatic levels in statutes written in English.

This chapter begins with an outline of two types of translation of domestic legislation. This is followed by a comparative description of the various linguistic features of statutes of the Common Law and Civil Law. It proceeds to examine the pragmatic features of statutes in English and its relevance to translation. It then outlines the judicial positions on linguistic uncertainty in bilingual legislation in Canada and Hong Kong, and sees how the courts deal with such uncertainties and the relevant rules developed for such a purpose. In this chapter, we are dealing with domestic or municipal statutes, but some of the features apply to bilateral and multilateral legal instruments as well.

Two Types of Translated Domestic Legislation

One may wonder why legislation needs translation, that is, for what purpose is legislation translated, and what kinds of such translation are there? Essentially, there are two types of situation where municipal statutes are translated. The first type is found in bilingual and multilingual jurisdictions where two or more languages are the official legal languages. Examples include Canada, Switzerland, and more recently, Hong Kong.[1] The second type of translated legislation is found in any monolingual country where its laws are translated into a foreign language or languages for information purposes.

For the first type of translated laws, in bilingual and multilingual jurisdictions, the law may be drafted first in one language and then translated into the other language(s). For instance, in Hong Kong, up until 1989, all legislation was enacted in English only, and was a monolingual English Common Law jurisdiction despite the fact that the majority of Hong Kong people have always used Chinese in their daily life. Due to the return of Hong Kong to China, both English and Chinese have been made the official legal languages in Hong Kong. Before April 1989, the Chinese translations of Hong Kong laws were for informative purpose only with no official status. In 1987, the Hong Kong Official Languages Ordinance was amended to give the official language status to Chinese in addition to English (Section 3(1)) and to require that all legislation to be enacted and published in both English and Chinese (Section 4(1)). Article 9 the Basic Law of the Hong Kong Special Administrative Region 1990 also provides that Chinese and English may be used as official languages by the executive authorities, legislature and judiciary. The new law also provided a mechanism for translating and publishing authentic texts in Chinese of statutes enacted in English, and the Chinese translated texts went through the formal legislative process of authentication. Since then, Hong Kong statute law has become fully bilingual. Now both the English and Chinese statutory texts in Hong Kong are equally authentic, that is, both have equal legal force. The Chinese legislative text is neither subordinate to nor a mere translation of its English counterpart, despite the fact that the laws were first enacted in English, and the Chinese texts were their translation (see Lu 2004). Today, in Hong Kong, there are two types of bilingual laws: the earlier laws that were enacted first in English and subsequently translated into Chinese and went through the authentication process, and the laws that have been enacted simultaneously in both English and Chinese since 1989.

In other situations in bilingual and multilingual jurisdictions, the law may be drafted in two or more languages with drafters, lawyers and linguists and translators working together producing a working document in the form of a bill that is written in all the relevant languages. Even in such a case, translation is still involved. For instance, in Canada, the practice of bilingual drafting federal legislation in both English and French as opposed to translation from one language into another was standardised in the 1980s, but still translation has been very much part of the process. According to Revell (2004), in Canada, there are three basic models of authoring or drafting bilingual laws in Canada: apart from the translation model, there are also the co-drafting and double drafting models.

Irrespective of the methods employed, whether it is translation or simultaneous bilingual drafting, in both situations, all the language versions are equally authentic, that is, they enjoy equal legal force. The different language texts do not have the status of a copy or translation, and one does not enjoy priority or paramountcy over the other. This corollary of bilingual enactment is known as the 'equal authenticity rule' (see Sullivan 2002: 75).

In this type of translation, as the law written in different languages is binding on the citizens concerned with equal legal force, the purpose of such translation is normative. It is related to lawmaking, that is, to establish new laws and to publish the law in the language or languages of the citizens so that the law can be enforced, as law must be made known and made available to people whose interests may be affected in a language they can understand.

In contrast, in the second type of translated legislation, when domestic legislation is translated in monolingual jurisdictions, such translations are used for informative rather than normative purpose. The translated text does not have any legal force, and the original law and the translated text are not equal. Take for example China. The Chinese language is the official language of China. All Chinese laws are enacted in Chinese. However, many people, including legal and other scholars, and the business and legal communities in and outside China, require translation of such laws for information purposes. There are many different translated versions of various Chinese laws, official and non-official. For instance, the Chinese government in recent years has been behind translating and publishing various English translations of all the major Chinese laws in its efforts of integration into the international community. There are private translation such as law publishers and legal academic research bodies as well. But none of such translations enjoys binding legal force in the Chinese or any other jurisdictions.

To summarise, the translation of legislation can be used for either normative or informative purposes, with similar or dissimilar legal status and consequence. Nevertheless, both types of translated domestic legislation are common and constitute part of the workload of the practising legal translator, and often bilingual lawyers, especially academic lawyers, are also engaged in this type of translation.

Textual Features of Statutes

Law in any society has a general function in prescribing, guiding and regulating human conduct. According to Hart (1961/1994), there are two basic kinds of legal norms with such primary functions as duty-imposing, that is, to establish legal obligations and commands, order and sanctions, and power-conferring, that is, to create legal power and competence. According to Watson-Brown (1997: 38), the common unit in legislation is the legislative statement that usually consists of a sentence. A section may be made up of a series of legislative statements and subsections are usually within themselves legislative statements even though they may depend upon other subsections to achieve a meaningful existence (Watson-Brown 1997: 38). There are two distinct forms of legislative statement: the substantive legislative statement and the adjective legislative statement (Watson-Brown 1997: 38). The substantive legislative statement secures some benefit to some person or persons, such as conferring a right, privilege or power and imposing liabilities or obligations on others, and these are the primary function of legislation (Watson-Brown 1997: 38). The highest level of a substantive legislative statement consists of a statutory declaration and, if the legislative statement is not of universal application, the qualifications under which the statutory declaration operates (Watson-Brown 1997: 39). In contrast, adjective legislative statements do not create substantive law in that they do not secure a benefit to some person or persons (Watson-Brown 1997: 40). Adjective legislative statements generally are flags to assist the reader with following the legislation, and they are descriptive in nature, for instance, the short title, headings and notes (Watson-Brown 1997: 40).

Generally speaking, modern statutes consist of a generic structure and standard form with the following common elements:

- title;
- date;
- the preamble;
- the enacting words;
- substantive body: the parts, articles and sections;
- schedules or forms.

The required elements are the title and substantive body. The other parts are optional. Normally, a statute starts with the title. In English statutes there are the long title and short title. The short title is the name by which an act is commonly known and cited. The long title of an act is usually a description of the aims of the act. For instance, the Animal Care and Protection Act 2001 [of Queensland, Australia] is the short title. The long title of the act is 'An Act to promote the responsible care and use of animals and to protect animals from cruelty, and for other purposes'. Some long titles are indeed long. The UK Consumer Credit Act 1974 has this long title: 'An Act to establish for the protection of consumers a new system, administered by the Director General of Fair Trading, of licensing and other control of traders concerned with the provision of credit, or the supply of goods on hire or hire-purchase, and their transactions, in place of the present enactments regulating moneylenders, pawnbrokers and hire-purchase traders and their transactions; and for related matters'.

In English statutes, the date is the date when royal assent is obtained for statutes to come into effect in England and Commonwealth countries such as Australia. In other jurisdictions, the date may include the date of the adoption of the act and the date of commencement.

Most domestic statutes nowadays do not have a preamble (cf. international legal instruments). If there is, it follows the title. A preamble in English statutes is normally brief and may comprise of more than one paragraph. The preamble begins with 'whereas' or similar phrases and continues with an explanation for the passing of the bill.

As for enacting words, in some jurisdictions, a statute contains an explicit performative verb and this part is known as the enacting formula. In the UK and the US, the enacting formula usually has the form of 'Be it enacted that . . .', and this is found at the beginning of a statute. The British enacting formula reads:

> BE IT ENACTED by the Queen's Most Excellent Majesty, by and with the advice and consent of the Lords Spiritual and Temporal, and Commons, in this present Parliament assembled, and by the authority of the same, as follows: – . . .

The US enacting formula reads:

> Be it Enacted by the Senate and House of Representatives in Congress assembled and by the authority of the people of the State of . . ., as follows: . . .

Such explicit use of performative formula in legislative texts is found only in Common Law countries. In the Civil Law system, there is no such formula, that is, 'implicit performative', since it is only the occasion – the promulgation of a law – not the linguistic form, that allows for a performative interpretation (Kurzon 1986).

As regards the substantive body of an act, it normally consists of parts and sections. In English statutes, there is also a marginal note for each section. Each section traditionally deals with one topic. Another long-established tradition in English legislation is for sections to contain one sentence, which in many cases, is very long, purportedly to indicate the unity of thought and policy that underlies it. This has since changed.

At the end of an act, in English statutes, schedules or forms are included following the last section of the act. Some schedules can be very lengthy. They are grouped into paragraphs and sub-paragraphs.

In a comparative study of a number of enactments from different countries, William Dale (1977) identified some of the features of legislative drafting in the UK as compared with France, Germany and Sweden. The English drafting is generally characterised by the following features (Dale 1977):

- The significant propositions or principles of the law not normally stated.
- The inclusion of the interpretation definition sections.
- Considerable length, with long, involved sentences and sections with lengthy details.
- Lack of brevity with repetitions; unnecessary words that add to the length and impede understanding.
- Obscurity that makes it difficult to comprehend.
- The intrusion into the sentences of phrases such as 'except where the context otherwise requires', 'subject to the provisions of this Act'; too many provisos or exception clauses; and the indication of exceptions or qualifications of a rule before the rule is stated.
- The use of blank expressions with no definite meaning, necessitating the filling of the blanks later – certain acts, relevant provisions etc.
- An indirect approach to the subject matter; subtraction – as in 'subject to . . .', 'Provided that . . .'; centrifugence – a flight from the centre to definition and interpreting clauses.
- Poor arrangement; too many long schedules; and frequent cross-references to other acts.

In contrast, the prominent features of the French, German and Swedish texts include (Dale 1977):

- The laws begin with statements of principles fundamental to their subject matter.
- There are no definition and interpretation sections.
- The style is natural and smooth without awkward or involved sentences.
- Statements are concise, flowing from one to another in a logical sequence.
- Absence, in general, of conditions, qualifications, reservations, warnings and other interceptions of the communication.

- Orderly sequence of ideas, clarity of repression and simplicity of articles; easier to comprehend and follow compared with English statutes.
- No long schedules.

Generally speaking, the above description of UK laws represents the prominent features of statutes in Common Law countries while the French and German characteristics embody the general trend in legislative drafting in Civil Law countries. The general characteristics of the law in these jurisdictions have not changed a great deal since Dale's study, although there have been efforts in Common Law countries to simplify legislative expression.

We can have a closer look at the two prominent differences of the Common Law and Civil Law legislative styles: (1) general principle provisions; and (2) definition provisions.

In Common Law jurisdictions, statutes usually include definitions and interpretation provisions but lack general principle provisions. Generally speaking, in English laws, there are two types of statutory definitions: exhaustive and non-exhaustive (see Sullivan 2002: 51). Exhaustive definitions declare the complete meaning of the defined term and completely displace whatever meanings the defined term might otherwise bear in ordinary or technical usage (Sullivan 2002: 51). An exhaustive definition is normally introduced by the verb 'means'.

Exhaustive definitions are typically used for the following purposes (Sullivan 2002: 51):

- to clarify a vague or ambiguous term;
- to narrow the scope of a word or expression;
- to ensure that the scope of a word or expression is narrowed;
- to create an abbreviation or other concise form of reference to a lengthy expression.

In contrast, non-exhaustive definitions presuppose rather than displace the meaning that a defined term would bear in ordinary usage. A non-exhaustive definition is normally introduced by the verb 'include' and is used for one of the following purposes (adapted from Sullivan 2002: 51):

- to expand the ordinary meaning of a word or expression;
- to deal with borderline applications;
- to illustrate the application of a word or expression by setting out examples.

Non-exhaustive definitions can also take a negative form 'does not include' to narrow the ordinary meaning of a word or expression. Some non-exhaustive definitions narrow the ordinary meaning of a word or expression by introducing conditions precedent (Sullivan 2002: 52). For an example of definitions, take the UK Human Rights Act 1998, we can also have a glimpse of the style and expressions used in English statutes:

21. - (1)   In this Act-

'amend' includes repeal and apply (with or without modifications);

'the appropriate Minister' means the Minister of the Crown having charge of the appropriate authorised government department (within the meaning of the Crown Proceedings Act 1947);

'the Commission' means the European Commission of Human Rights;

'the Convention' means the Convention for the Protection of Human Rights and Fundamental Freedoms, agreed by the Council of Europe at Rome on 4th November 1950 as it has effect for the time being in relation to the United Kingdom;

'declaration of incompatibility' means a declaration under section 4;

'Minister of the Crown' has the same meaning as in the Ministers of the Crown Act 1975;

'Northern Ireland Minister' includes the First Minister and the deputy First Minister in Northern Ireland;

'primary legislation' means any -

(a) public general Act;

(b) local and personal Act;

(c) private Act;

(d) Measure of the Church Assembly;

(e) Measure of the General Synod of the Church of England;

(f) Order in Council -

(i)   made in exercise of Her Majesty's Royal Prerogative;

(ii) made under section 38(1)(a) of the Northern Ireland Constitution Act 1973 or the corresponding provision of the Northern Ireland Act 1998; or

(iii) amending an Act of a kind mentioned in paragraph (a), (b) or (c); and includes an order or other instrument made under primary legislation (otherwise than by the National

Assembly for Wales, a member of the Scottish Executive, a Northern Ireland Minister or a Northern Ireland department) to the extent to which it operates to bring one or more provisions of that legislation into force or amends any primary legislation; . . .

For an example of definitions of a more recent law, the Australian Gene Technology Act 2000 provides that:

(1) In this Act, unless the contrary intention appears: . . .

Commonwealth authority means the following:
   (a) a body corporate established for a public purpose by or under an Act;
   (b) a company in which a controlling interest is held by any one of the following persons, or by 2 or more of the following persons together:
      (i) the Commonwealth;
      (ii) a body covered by paragraph (a);
      (iii) a body covered by either of the above subparagraphs.

containment level, in relation to a facility, means the degree of physical confinement of GMOs [Genetically Modified Organisms] provided by the facility, having regard to the design of the facility, the equipment located or installed in the facility and the procedures generally used within the facility.

deal with, in relation to a GMO, means the following:
   (a) conduct experiments with the GMO;
   (b) make, develop, produce or manufacture the GMO;
   (c) breed the GMO;
   (d) propagate the GMO;
   (e) use the GMO in the course of manufacture of a thing that is not the GMO;
   (f) grow, raise or culture the GMO;
   (g) import the GMO;

and includes the possession, supply, use, transport or disposal of the GMO for the purposes of, or in the course of, a dealing mentioned in any of paragraphs (a) to (g).

environment includes:
   (a) ecosystems and their constituent parts; and
   (b) natural and physical resources; and
   (c) the qualities and characteristics of locations, places and areas.

evidential material means any of the following:
  (a) a thing with respect to which an offence against this Act or the regulations has been committed or is suspected, on reasonable grounds, to have been committed;
  (b) a thing that there are reasonable grounds for suspecting will afford evidence as to the commission of any such offence;
  (c) a thing that there are reasonable grounds for suspecting is intended to be used for the purpose of committing any such offence.

facility includes, but is not limited to, the following:
  (a) a building or part of a building;
  (b) a laboratory;
  (c) an aviary;
  (d) a glasshouse;
  (e) an insectary;
  (f) an animal house;
  (g) an aquarium or tank.

gene technology means any technique for the modification of genes or other genetic material, but does not include:
  (a) sexual reproduction; or
  (b) homologous recombination; or
  (c) any other technique specified in the regulations for the purposes of this paragraph.

genetically modified organism means:
  (a) an organism that has been modified by gene technology; or
  (b) an organism that has inherited particular traits from an organism (the *initial organism*), being traits that occurred in the initial organism because of gene technology; or
  (c) anything declared by the regulations to be a GMO, or that belongs to a class of things declared by the regulations to be GMOs;
but does not include:
  (d) a human being, if the human being is covered by paragraph (a) only because the human being has undergone somatic cell gene therapy; or
  (e) an organism declared by the regulations not to be a GMO, or that belongs to a class of organisms declared by the regulations not to be GMOs.

organism means any biological entity that is:
  (a) viable; or
  (b) capable of reproduction; or
  (c) capable of transferring genetic material.

premises includes the following:
  (a) a building;
  (b) a place (including an area of land);
  (c) a vehicle;
  (d) a vessel;
  (e) an aircraft;
  (f) a facility;
  (g) any part of premises (including premises referred to in paragraphs (a) to (f)).

A number of general observations can be made with regard to the above two examples of definitions. Firstly, we can see that there are a great deal of cross-references in the definitions, either to the same act and to other laws. In translation, it is important that the same names or established translated names are used throughout for consistency.

Secondly, we can see that the definitions have detailed enumeration and specific descriptions, with precise and deliberate choice of words. Even with common words, they have strict definitions, specifying what they mean under a particular act.

Thirdly, statutory definitions are considered necessary in Common Law countries because words in a particular statute are used with specifically assigned meanings in order to give certainty to the law and its implementation. This is used for both common words and technical words. For instance, in the above example, common words such as 'facility', 'premise' and 'to deal with' are general and vague. They can mean vastly different things to different people. Therefore, they need restricted definition under a particular act so that citizens know what circumstances and what conducts are governed by the act. Definitions are also used to maintain consistency in the law, so that the same words throughout an act have the same consistent meaning.

In general, the purpose of statutory definition may include the following (Bennion 2002: 479):

- to clarify the meaning of a common word or phrase by stating that it does or does not include specified matters (a clarifying definition);
- to use a term as a label denoting a complex concept that can then be referred to merely by use of the label (a labelling definition);

- to attract a meaning already established in law, whether by statute or otherwise (a referential definition);
- to exclude a meaning that otherwise would or might be taken to be included in the term (an exclusory definition);
- to add a meaning that otherwise would or might not be taken to be included in the term (an enlarging definition);
- to provide a full statement of the meaning of the term (a comprehensive definition).

In contrast, statutes in the Civil Law countries do not normally have a definition or interpretation section, but they usually include general principle provisions. Take for instance the Swiss Federal Act on Animal Protection 1978. Its format is quite simple and straightforward. It starts with the title: Act on Animal Protection, Swiss Federal Act of March 9, 1978. It then reads:

The Federal Assembly of the Swiss Confederation,
based on the Articles 25bis, 27sexies and 64bis of the Federal Constitution, after consideration of a report submitted by the Federal Council, dated February 9, 1977,
resolves:

Section 1: General Provisions

Article 1: Purpose and Scope
1. This Act prescribes rules of conduct to be observed in dealing with Animals; it is designed to ensure their protection and welfare.
2. The Act applies to vertebrates only. The Federal Council shall decide for which invertebrates and to which extent the Act shall apply to such animals.
3. The following are reserved: Federal Act of June 10, 1925 on the Hunting and Protection of Birds, Federal Act of July 1, 1966 on Nature and Landscape Conservation, Federal Act of December 14, 1973 on Fishing, and the Federal Act of July 1, 1966 on Epizootic Diseases.

Article 2: Principles
1. Animals shall be treated in the manner which best complies with their needs.
2. Anyone who is concerned with animals shall, insofar as circumstances permit, safeguard their welfare.
3. No one shall unjustifiably expose animals to pain, suffering, physical injury or fear . . . .

It is noted that in recent years, increasingly in some Common Law juris-dictions such as Australia, statutes include an 'object' section stating the general purpose of the law.

On the whole, we can see that the linguistic manifestations of statutes in the Common Law and Civil Law jurisdictions are different. The differences in drafting styles are closely related to the way statutes are interpreted by the courts.

According to Zweigert and Kötz (1992), there are characteristic dif-ferences between the methods of statutory interpretation in the Common Law and Civil Law. They stem from the very different part played in the development of English law by statutes enacted by Parliament from the role played by legislation on the Continent. English statutes were 'originally sporadic ad hoc enactments which as legal sources had much less force than the Common Law, which had been developed by the judges through the centuries and which covered all areas of the law equally' (Zweigert and Kötz 1992: 273–274). It was believed that every statute that deviated from the Common Law must be of an exceptional nature and therefore must be narrowly construed and applied only to the precise situations that were covered by its terms; if the statute so construed did not cover the case in issue, then the case fell to be decided according to the general rules of the Common Law (Zweigert and Kötz 1992: 274). These historical developments have left their traces.

Specifically, in statutory interpretation, in Civil Law jurisdictions, a major statutory interpretation rule is the so-called purposive approach. The first step in interpreting an ambiguous law is to discover the intention of the legislator, or the legislative intent, by examining the legislation as a whole, including the *travaux préparatoires*, as well as the provisions more immediately surrounding the obscure text (Tetley 2000: 704).[2] In contrast, in Common Law jurisdictions, statutes are to be construed according to a host of rules developed by the courts such as the literal rule, the golden rule, the mischief rule, and other statutory rules of interpretation (see Bennion 2002).[3] Generally speaking, in the Civil Law statutes, general principles need not be explained because they are not read restrictively, but need to be stated concisely if the code is to be exhaustive. Common Law statutory provisions need not be concise, because they cover only the specific part of the law to be performed, but must be precise, because the Common Law courts restrict rules to the specific facts they are intended to cover (Tetley 2000: 703). According to Tetley (2000), these styles can also be found in international conventions that are influenced by the two systems. The Hamburg Rules were drafted in the Civil Law style with the rule of responsibility in one sweeping article. The Hague Rules, by comparison, were drafted in the Common Law style, with very long and detailed articles (see Tetley 2000: 704).

The adoption by English judges of the restrictive techniques of construction helps to explain the peculiarities of the drafting of English statutes. It is observed that Continental lawyers are often struck by the pedantic and prolix detail in which states deal with the simplest matters, obviously so as to make it more difficult for the judges to get round them: where a Continental legislator would be satisfied with a single comprehensive notion, the English legislature will use five specific terms without adding anything to the meaning (Zweigert and Kötz 1992: 275). The Continental lawyer finds it amazing that terms used in English statutes are collected together in a kind of lexicon and defined in what is often a rather pedagogic manner, 'the device of making a statute contain its miniature dictionary' (Amos 1933: 170, cited in Zweigert and Kötz 1992: 275). In fact, many statutes today in English contain a section called 'Dictionary'. But for the Continental lawyer, such provisions may look strange. Take for instance, the British Interpretation Act 1978, which has the following provision:

> In any Act, unless the contrary intention appears, -
> (a) words importing the masculine gender shall include the feminine;
> (b) words importing the feminine gender shall include the masculine;
> (c) words in the singular shall include the plural and words in the plural shall include the singular . . . .

Zweigert and Kötz comment that 'the technique of statutory construction in a country has to be in a parlous condition to require trivial aids of this sort' (1992: 275). Zweigert and Kötz attribute the 'pedantry and pettiness' of the English legislative language to the desire to leave judges the least possible scope for construction, and also to a certain formalism of legal thought still prevalent in the Common Law today (1992: 275).

Pragmatic Feature: Illocutionary Force

One prominent linguistic feature of legislative texts is the illocutionary force as a pragmatic consideration. This pragmatic feature is a crucial and prominent linguistic aspect of statutes, for both domestic or municipal statutory instruments and multilateral legal instruments. It is universally important. The legal rules conveyed in legislation may and do vary considerably from country to country and from jurisdiction to jurisdiction in terms of content, legal force, and linguistic expression. However, they are all linked to the basic function of law in regulating human behaviour and relations by setting out obligation, permission and prohibition in society. This primary function of law is closely connected to the illocutionary force of legislative provisions as expressed in language. As we are also aware, languages differ considerably in how to express obligation, permission and prohibition.

Domestic statutes can be considered legislative speech acts, as opposed to other types of speech acts such as judicial speech acts. Normally, legislative speech acts must follow the relevant legal institutional conventions. Statutes are written in a linguistic structure different from that of ordinary speech acts. In ordinary speech acts, the standard form is the first person pronoun followed by the simple present tense of the verb, for instance, 'I promise . . .' or 'I declare . . .'. Statutory provisions are often written in the third person. However, they may be paraphrased in the first person. For instance, 'We (the lawmaking body or authorities) hereby declare that . . .' or 'We hereby enact that . . .' is said to be omitted, thus may be added to the beginning of a statute. In some jurisdictions, a statute contains an explicit performative verb and this part is known as the enacting formula (see p. 105).

A legislative text as a rule-enacting document is a speech act with illocutionary forces. As Kurzon (1986: 9–15) argues, statutes as a speech act can be seen through the linguistic features of statutes that demonstrate their performative nature, and the various felicity conditions such as the authority of the speaker and the function of the relevant convention.

Bowers (1989: 30–31) classifies the illocutionary forces of legislative provisions into (1) facultative language, which confers a right, privilege or power through the use of 'may'; (2) imperative language, which imposes an obligation to do an act through the use of 'shall'; and (3) prohibitive language, which imposes an obligation to abstain from doing an act through the use of 'shall not'. Thus, 'shall', 'may' and 'shall not' are the main legal performative markers in English. In legislative texts, sentences containing such performative markers function as speech acts with the illocutionary forces of permission (may), ordering (shall) or prohibition (shall not) (see Bowers 1989).

Specifically, according to Sullivan (2002: 56–57), 'may' and 'shall' (including 'shall not') have the following usage:

'May' is used to

- confer an authority or a power: a person may lawfully do something that would otherwise be unlawful;
- confer a right: a person may claim a benefit or protection under the law;

- impose conditions on a grant of authority or a right: the authority is exercisable, the right can be claimed only if certain conditions are met;
- impose procedural limitations: a person may do something (only) by proceeding in a stipulated way; and
- refer to future actions or events.

'Shall' is used to
- impose a duty – 'a person shall . . .';
- prohibit conduct – 'no person shall . . .' or '. . . shall not. . .';
- create formal or substantive conditions precedent – 'to achieve x, a person shall . . .'; and
- declare legal effects – 'the contract shall be deemed valid', '. . . [a particular word] shall mean . . .'.

In recent years, as part of the efforts to simplify legislative language and make it more accessible to the general public, in some English speaking jurisdictions, 'must' instead of 'shall', 'must not' instead of 'shall not' have been increasingly used. But the meanings of compulsory obligations for 'shall'/'must' and of prohibition for 'shall not'/'must not' have not changed.

In essence, 'shall' is used to indicate obligations. Such obligations are mandatory or directory; 'may' signifies permission, indicating discretionary obligations; and 'shall not' is a prohibition. When a prohibition is imposed, legal consequence or penalty will arise for violation.[4]

Other commonly used performative verbs in law include 'declare', 'announce', 'promise', 'undertake', 'enact', 'confer' and 'amend'.

In sum, statutes as legislative speech acts carry various illocutionary forces, communicating a range of propositions – empowering rights and obligations, establishing institutional facts, and imposing prohibitions.

In terms of translation, when translating performative verbs from English into other languages or vice versa, a number of issues may arise that deserve our attention. Firstly, there may not be the exact equivalence of the legal performative markers in different languages. The performative words may not be the same. Care is needed so as not to confuse different types of obligations. For instance, in Chinese, apart from the equivalent of 'shall' for mandatory obligations, there is an additional performative marker of 'should' that also indicates compulsory duties (see Cao 1999).

Secondly, there may be uncertainty when the auxiliary verbs are not used. In some European languages, no performative auxiliary verbs are needed or used. Instead, the simple present tense is employed. In such cases, caution is needed when translating into English. Furthermore, in such cases, as the legislation concerned is a speech act, and its legal status endows the entire text with the legal authority, which Kurzon (1986: 20) referred to as the master speech acts, the speech act of enactment determines the occurrence of certain other speech acts within the text (Kurzon 1986: 20). In other words, the entire statute may be seen as a speech act with the illocutionary force of enactment, and many of the sentences in the statute may also have the status as speech acts. Therefore, even if there are some sentences in a statute that do not contain performative markers or auxiliary verbs, they may still be considered as speech acts and each provision is a speech act that has the illocutionary force of enacting and ordering.

Thirdly, where performative modal or auxiliary verbs are used in the original text, they must not be omitted or changed in translation as there may be legal consequences (see the Hong Kong *Lau San Ching* case concerning the translation of 'may' later in this chapter, pp. 129–131).

In short, the importance of legal texts as speech acts goes to the very heart of the nature of law, legal language and legal translation. For the legal translator, such understanding, recognition and appreciation are fundamentally important. This is also where legal translation and translation of other text types differ significantly. Translating law involves more than just the choice of phraseology. Words are not just words. They are acts that can and do create facts, affecting society and citizens and producing legal consequences. Legislation, as rule-enacting documents, is a speech act with various illocutionary forces. A legal translator, therefore, needs to have a basic understanding of the nature and function of law in society as such a legal knowledge is essential, not for the purpose of interpreting or applying the law, but to understand the message and re-present it in another language appropriately.

Other Common Linguistic Features of Legislative Texts

Statutes have their own lexical and syntactical idiosyncrasies. At the lexical level, different languages may differ in their lexical features. For instance, in English legislative language, nominalisation of words and extensive use of prepositional phrases are prevalent. At the syntactical level, typically, legislative texts are long and complex in sentence structure with a heavy use of qualifications. Long and complex sentences are common in legislative texts in many languages.

Here are some examples of long and complex sentences from the US. The provisions are complete with multiple qualifications, conditions, and heavy use of 'except for', 'provided', 'notwithstanding' and 'if' and other clauses. They are from the US Copyright Act, 17 USC:

§108. Limitations on exclusive rights: Reproduction by libraries and archives

. . .

(a) *Except* as otherwise provided in this title and *notwithstanding* the provisions of section 106, it is not an infringement of copyright for a library or archives, or any of its employees acting within the scope of their employment, to reproduce no more than one copy or phonorecord of a work, *except* as provided in subsections (b) and (c), or to distribute such copy or phonorecord, under the conditions specified by this section, *if* –

(1) the reproduction or distribution is made without any purpose of direct or indirect commercial advantage;
(2) the collections of the library or archives are
  (i) open to the public, or
  (ii) available not only to researchers affiliated with the library or archives or with the institution *of which* it is a part, but also to other persons doing research in a specialised field; and
(3) the reproduction or distribution of the work includes a notice of copyright that appears on the copy or phonorecord that is reproduced under the provisions of this section, or includes a legend stating that the work may be protected by copyright *if* no such notice can be found on the copy or phonorecord *that* is reproduced under the provisions of this section . . . .

§ 111. Limitations on exclusive rights: Secondary transmissions

. . .

(b) . . . *Notwithstanding* the provisions of subsections (a) and (c), the secondary transmission to the public of a performance or display of a work embodied in a primary transmission is actionable as an act of infringement under section 501, and is fully subject to the remedies provided by sections 502 through 506 and 509, *if* the primary transmission is not made for reception by the public at large but is controlled and limited to reception by particular members of the public: *Provided,* however, *That* such secondary transmission is not actionable as an act of infringement *if* –

(1) the primary transmission is made by a broadcast station licensed by the Federal Communications Commission; and
(2) the carriage of the signals comprising the secondary transmission is required under the rules, regulations, or authorisations of the Federal Communications Commission; and

(3) the signal of the primary transmitter is not altered or changed in any way by the secondary transmitter . . . .

. . . (3) *Notwithstanding* the provisions of clause (1) of this subsection and *subject to* the provisions of subsection (e) of this section, the secondary transmission to the public by a cable system of a performance or display of a work embodied in a primary transmission made by a broadcast station licensed by the Federal Communications Commission or by an appropriate governmental authority of Canada or Mexico is actionable as an act of infringement under section 501, and is fully subject to the remedies provided by sections 502 through 506 and sections 509 and 510, *if* the content of the particular program *in which* the performance or display is embodied, or any commercial advertising or station announcements transmitted by the primary transmitter during, or immediately before or after, the transmission of such program, is in any way willfully altered by the cable system through changes, deletions, or additions, *except for* the alteration, deletion, or substitution of commercial advertisements performed by those engaged in television commercial advertising market research: *Provided, That* the research company has obtained the prior consent of the advertiser who has purchased the original commercial advertisement, the television station broadcasting that commercial advertisement, and the cable system performing the secondary transmission: *And provided further, That* such commercial alteration, deletion, or substitution is not performed for the purpose of deriving income from the sale of that commercial time [italics added].

This last paragraph consists of 226 words. Not all provisions in the US or other Common Law countries are this long, but these examples give us a glimpse of how legislative provisions are often structured and expressed.

In recent years, there have been efforts to simplify legislative language in English speaking countries. For instance, in Australia, in the past ten years or so, statutes have seen simplification in language and reduction in sentence length and complexity. Take for example, the Australian Patents Act 1990. The following sentence is one of the longest and most complex sentences in the whole act, which compares favourably in terms of length with the examples from US laws:

7(2). For the purposes of this Act, an invention is to be taken to involve an inventive step when compared with the prior art base unless the invention would have been obvious to a person skilled in the relevant art in the light of the common general knowledge as it existed in the patent area before the priority date of the relevant claim, whether that knowledge is considered separately or together with either of the kinds of information mentioned in subsection (3), each of which must be considered separately.

In the Australian Gene Technology Act 2000, the sentences are generally much shorter, but there are still many 'if' clauses:

(1) This Act is not intended to exclude the operation of any State law, *to the extent* that the State law is capable of operating concurrently with this Act, other than a State law prescribed by the regulations for the purposes of this section.

(2) The Governor-General may prescribe a State law under subsection (1) *only if*:
   (a) there is no corresponding State law in effect in relation to that State; *and*
   (b) *either*:
      (i) the State law relates specifically to dealings with GMOs; *or*
      (ii) for the purposes of a decision under the State law as to whether or not a licence, authority or approval (however described) is granted under the State law, the State law distinguishes between dealings with GMOs and dealings with other things . . . .

S18 . . .

(1) *If*:
   (a) an act or omission is an offence against this Act and is also an offence against a corresponding State law; and
   (b) the offender has been punished for the offence under the corresponding State law;
   the offender is not liable to be punished for the offence under this Act.

(2) *If* a person has been ordered to pay a pecuniary penalty under a corresponding State law, the person is not liable to a pecuniary penalty under this Act in respect of the same conduct . . . .

S185

(3A) *If*:
   (a) the Regulator declares that particular information is confidential commercial information; *and*
   (b) the information relates to one or more locations *at which* field trials involving GMOs are occurring, or are proposed to occur;

the Regulator must make publicly available a statement of reasons for the making of the declaration, *including, but not limited to*:

(c) the reasons why the Regulator was satisfied as mentioned in subsection (1); *and*

(d) the reasons why the Regulator was not satisfied under subsection (2) that the public interest in disclosure of the information outweighed the prejudice that the disclosure would cause; *and*

(e) the reasons why the Regulator was satisfied under subsection (2A) that significant damage to the health and safety of people, the environment or property would be likely to occur *if* the locations were disclosed.

A number of observations can be made here. Firstly, it is necessary for the translator to be aware of the nature of statute laws and the various reasons for them to be written the way they are, in particular regarding the long and complex sentence structures and the seemingly wordiness that are often found in Common Law statutes.

According to Bentham, law is either a proposition or an assemblage of propositions (cited in Bennion 2002: 338). Legal propositions are laid down in an act or other legislative text with the effect that, when facts fall within an indicated area, specified legal consequences are called forth (Bennion 2002: 337). Therefore, the facts and acts and their precise consequences need to be spelt out. Furthermore, statute laws are prospective. They need to be broad to cover various conceivable or possible future acts and situations. They deal with a multiplicity of circumstances. Thus, the language used needs to be precise and also flexible.

From the cited statutes, we can identify some of the common features in sentence pattern and usage in statutes written in English. One such a feature is the extensive use of conditional clause. According to Crystal and Davy (1969: 203), a common linguistic formula in legal texts is 'If X, then Z shall be Y' or 'If X, then Z shall do Y.' There are many variations of this but in most cases 'If X' is essential: every action or requirement, from a legal point of view, is hedged around with and even depends upon, a set of conditions that must be satisfied before anything can happen (Crystal and Davy 1969: 203). In sentence structures, 'If X' is often accommodated by means of adverbial clauses, conditional or concessive. Because of this reason, legal sentences are invariably complex (Crystal and Davy 1969: 203).

Thus, the most important overall strategy governing the syntax of the sentence in legal English is the 'If ' structure, and the great majority of legal sentences have the logical structure of the 'If' conditional clause

(Salmi-Tolonen 1994). Studies have found the frequency of conditional clauses in statutory language is higher than in English written language in general (Salmi-Tolonen 1994). Other common conditional expressions include 'except', 'unless', 'in the event', 'in the case', 'if and so far as' and 'if, but only if' (see Salmi-Tolonen 1994).

Another common and related syntactical feature is the extensive use of qualifications and exceptions as we can see from the above examples. This includes the use of 'provided that', 'subject to' and 'notwithstanding', among others. These provisos (as expressed in 'provided that', see also Chapter 5) are used to narrow the effect of the relevant sections. As said in Chapter 5, provisos are an ancient verbal formula. It enables a general statement to be made as a proposition so that any necessary qualifications are kept out and relegated to a proviso (Bennion 2002: 616). A proviso is usually construed as operating to qualify that which precedes (see *Mullins v Treasurer of Surrey* (1880) 5 QND 170, cited in Bennion 2002: 617). The use of provisos has declined in contemporary legislative practice in most English speaking jurisdictions (Fung 1997).

On the whole, legislative language has its own characteristics. They are conditioned and influenced by the nature of legislation and its functions in society. Generally speaking, there are three constraints on the accessibility of legislative expression according to Bowers (1989): firstly, legislative language has to convey complex substance to a wide public, lay and legal; secondly, legislative language must anticipate a world that does not exist at the time of expression and must be prepared for an infinity of possibilities. Every new act itself brings a new world into existence and must prognosticate a whole variety of states, conditions and events that might fall within the terms of this new world. The third constraint is one of language history, and the development of legal language (Bowers 1989).

In recent years, there has been the trend of simplifying legislative language, making it simpler, significantly shorter and more accessible. However, this does not mean that legislative language in English is the same as ordinary English. It still tends to be more complex with heavy use of conditions and qualifications.

Bilingual Statutory Interpretation and Linguistic Uncertainty

Often words in legislation are points of legal contention. The courts are frequently asked to adjudicate. This is true for both monolingual and bilingual jurisdictions. In monolingual jurisdictions, there are a number of long-established statutory interpretation rules in the Common Law.

As said: 'An Act of Parliament is not something that can be read like a book' (Gifford 1990). Over the years, the courts in Common Law countries have developed special rules and a uniform approach that govern the reading of ambiguous acts of Parliament, to maintain consistency and certainty in law. These rules are commonly used in statutory interpretation in Common Law countries including England and Australia. Some of the general rules include the plain meaning rule, the golden rule (that manifest absurdity and injustice are to be avoided) and the purposive approach.[5] There are also many other specific rules (see Bennion 2002).

For our purposes, there are added complications in interpreting statutes in bilingual jurisdictions where two languages and translation are deemed equivalent. It is worthwhile having a look at the general principles of bilingual interpretation and the approaches the courts have developed in the bilingual jurisdictions of Canada and Hong Kong to achieve the unity of interpretation and certainty in the law and its application.

Bilingual statutory interpretation in Canada

The Canadian experience in the interpretation of bilingual laws goes back to 1866. It is said that the Canadian statute book is considered a model by many jurisdictions around the world because of its bilingual and bijural character (Sullivan 2002: 73).[6]

There exists an established legal regime for bilingual statutory interpretation in Canadian law. The two general principles, the 'equal authenticity rule' and 'shared meaning rule' are selectively and briefly discussed below in relation to translation. For comprehensive and detailed analysis of Canada's bilingual statutory interpretation, see Sullivan (2002, 2004) and Beaupré (1986).

Firstly, the 'equal authenticity rule', that is, both language versions of a bilingual statute are the official, original and authoritative expressions of the law, is a fundamental principle. In Canada, it means that neither the English nor the French version has the status of a copy or translation, and neither enjoys priority or paramountcy over the other (*CPR v Robinson* [1891] 19 SCR 292; *R. v Dubois* (1935) SCR 378). This rule was first formulated in 1891 by the Canadian Supreme Court in *CPR v Robinson* wherein the Court stated:

> . . . whether the article was first written in French or in English is immaterial . . . In the case of ambiguity, where there is any possibility to reconcile the two, one must be interpreted by the other. The English version cannot be read out of the law. It was submitted to the

legislature, enacted and sanctioned simultaneously with the French one, and is law just as much as the French one is.

This rule has also been codified in statutes including the Canadian Constitution Act 1982 and the Official Languages Act 1970. S18(1) of the Constitution Act provides that the statutes of Parliament of Canada shall be printed and published in both English and French, and both language versions are equally authoritative. S8(1) of the Official Languages Act stipulates that in construing an enactment, both its versions in the official languages are equally authentic.

Furthermore, for the construction of an enactment where there is a difference between the two versions, regard must be had to both versions (S8(2) of the Official Languages Act). This means that where there are discrepancies between the versions, the court must read both versions with care and both must be considered in resolving interpretative issues, to determine the intention of the legislature and both versions should be attributed the same importance or weight.

The basic rule governing the interpretation of bilingual legislation in Canada is the 'shared or common meaning rule', that is, where the two versions of bilingual legislation do not say the same thing, the meaning that is shared by both ought to be adopted unless that meaning is for some reasons unacceptable *(R. v O'Donnell* [1979] 1 WWR 385 (BCCA)). Furthermore, if one is ambiguous and the other is clear, then the meaning shared by both is presumed to be the meaning intended by the legislature. Thus, it is necessary to extract the 'highest common meaning' from the two versions that is consistent with the context of the provision (Sullivan 2002, 2004). Where there is a conflict between the English and French versions, courts must examine the legislative history of the two linguistic versions of the provision, looking to the purpose and object of the statute. The true spirit, intent and meaning of the enactment must be given priority to best ensure the attainment of its objects. One must therefore go further than mere verbal comparisons, looking to the highest common meaning of the two versions (Sullivan 2002, 2004). In addition, discrepancies in the two versions are to be treated as any other ambiguity and must be resolved by resorting to the usual method of interpretation (Sullivan 2002, 2004).

Regarding the shared meaning rule, such shared meaning is usually the ordinary meaning of the words as established in both languages. For instance, in *R. v Barnier* [1980] 1 SCR1124, the Supreme Court of Canada was concerned with the Criminal Code definition of insanity and what it means to be incapable of 'appreciating the nature and quality of an act' or 'of knowing that an act is wrong'. The issue was whether these two formulations established two tests or one. To determine their meaning, the court examined both the English words 'know' and 'appreciate' and the equivalents *saviour* and *juger* in the French version. The court found that in both languages, the meaning of the words differed in small but significant ways, and these differences were similar in the two languages. Thus, the plain meanings of the words in both languages are the meanings intended (see Sullivan 2002: 81).

This approach is also found in *Reference re Education Act of Ontario and Minority Language Education Rights* (1984) 10 DLR (4th) 491 (Ontario Court of Appeal). In this case, the court dealt with the interpretation of subsection 23(3) of the Canadian Charter on minority language rights. The English version of the section referred to 'minority language educational facilities' while the French version spoke of '*établissements d'enseignement de la minorité linguistique*'. While a common meaning of these terms reduced to their lowest common meaning was equivalent to a guarantee of classrooms, the Court of Appeal opted for the highest common meaning when reading the two versions together, and accorded a guarantee of schools managed by Francophone, rather than mere physical facilities within the language facilities of the majority.

The shared meaning rule has also been used to resolve ambiguities in one or both language versions or to clarify the scope of vague terms. For instance, in *R. v Mac* [2002] 1 SCR 856, the Supreme Court of Canada examined the word 'adapted' in the Criminal Code in English as compared to the corresponding '*adapté*' in the French version. The court found that 'adapted' in English was ambiguous, capable of meaning either 'suitable for' or 'physically modified or altered', but '*adapté*' in French was clear, having the meaning of 'suitable for' only. When the meaning of 'modified' was intended by the legislature, the French word '*modifié*' was used. Thus, the court concluded that the meaning of 'adapted' and '*adapté*' being 'suitable for' shared by both words is the proper meaning intended in the statute (see Sullivan 2002, 2004).

Another important consideration of bilingual statutory interpretation in Canada is that Canada is not only bilingual but also bijural. Bijuralism refers to the coexistence of two legal traditions within a single state (Bastarache 2000, cited in Wellington undated). Canada is one of the rare bijural countries where the English Common Law and the French Civil Law coexist within the federal state. There are often discrepancies in the laws due to the differences in the two legal systems and traditions.

To illustrate, in *Gulf Oil Canada Ltd v Canadien Pacifique Ltée* [1979] CS 72 (discussed in Beaupré 1986, Sullivan 2002), the Supreme Court of Quebec was asked to interpret an Order in Council made pursuant to the federal

National Transportation Act of Canada. Under this Order carriers such as the defendant railway were not liable for losses caused by 'acts of God' while the French version provided non-liability for *cas fortuit* or *force majeure*. The court took into account the Civil Law system in interpreting this provision, recognising that in the English and French provisions, the legislature tried to take into account the two legal systems in Canada. It concluded that in the Common Law the meaning of 'acts of God' would not include third party negligence, but under Quebec's Civil Code, *cas fortuit* included the negligent act of a third party. The court held that in these circumstances, the Civil Law meaning should prevail. This meant that the civilian understanding of *cas fortuit* or 'acts of God' was applicable in Quebec regardless of which language version was read and relied on by the parties to the case. In particular, the court held that if 'act of God' had been translated by the words '*Acte de Dieu*' in the Order, it would not be possible to appeal to the Civil Law concept of *cas fortuit* consisting of the act of a third party (see Beaupré 1986, Sullivan 2002: 100). The ambiguity basically arose from the different laws in the two systems.

In recent years, there have been considerable legislative and other legal efforts in Canada to harmonise the federal law with Quebec Civil Law. Directly relevant to translation, for instance, the Department of Justice of Canada has developed and maintained a website of bijural terminology records at http://www.justice.gc.ca/en/ps/bj/harm/Index.html. This is part of the Harmonisation Program undertaken as a result of the coming into force of the Civil Code of Quebec in 1994, which substantially changed the concepts, institutions and terminology of the Civil Law. It is part of the efforts to harmonise Canadian federal statutes and regulations. In the records, commonly used Common Law and Civil Law legal terms are compared and the relevant Canadian legal provisions where the words appear are cited. There are also descriptions of the differences between the terms in the Common Law and Civil Law, the problems and solutions when translating them between French and English.

A number of methods of drafting bijural legislation have been adopted in Canada including the following (Sullivan 2002: 96–97):

(1) to set out in each language the preferred solution for each legal system;

(2) to find general French and English expressions that are comparable in scope and can be applied in roughly equivalent ways in the two systems;

(3) to use Common Law terminology in the English version and analogous Civil Law terminology in the French; and

(4) to draw on the legal terminology of one of the legal systems and to translate this terminology into the language of the other system using ordinary as opposed to technical legal language.

Other specific drafting techniques include the use of common, neutral, generic or general terms, the use of legislative definition, among others (see Wellington undated).

A drafting and interpreting issue in Canada that concerns the legislative drafters and translators, also relevant to other bilingual and multilingual jurisdictions, is consistency in legislation. The general principle of linguistic consistency is that within a statute or other legislative instrument, the same words have the same meaning and different words have different meanings. As stated in *R. v Zeolkowski* [1989] 1 SCR 1378, giving the same words the same meaning throughout a statute is a basic principle of statutory interpretation. This is a basic legal presumption. Thus, stylistic variation in the choice of words or patterns of expression must be avoided.

Given the presumption of consistent expression, when different words or forms of expression are used, it is possible to infer an intended difference in meaning. In *Jabel Image Concepts Inc. v Canada* [2000] 257 NR 193 (FCA), it was held that when an act uses different words in relation to the same subject such a choice by Parliament must be considered intentional and indicative of a change in meaning or a different meaning. For instance, in *R. v Schwartz* [1977] 1 SCR 673, Justice Dickson stated that the word 'wrong' as used in the Criminal Code in relation to insanity must mean morally wrong and not illegal because elsewhere in the Code the term 'unlawful' is used to express the idea of illegality. But using the word 'wrong' the legislature must have meant to express a different idea. Similarly, in *R. v Barnier* [1980] 1 SCR 1124, the court held that the words 'appreciating' and 'knowing' in a statute do not mean the same thing. Consistency extends to patterns of expression (see Sullivan 2002).

In terms of translation, this entails two kinds of consistencies, that is, consistency of terms within a legal document, and consistency of terms in relation to existing or past laws. Whenever words are repeated, their translated corresponding terms need to be employed consistently. Any variation could potentially introduce extra uncertainty. This is in contrast to other types of translation, e.g. literary translation.

Bilingual statutory interpretation in Hong Kong

Hong Kong provides another interesting case for the study of bilingual statutory interpretation. It can teach some important lessons for the legal translator.

Hong Kong, as explained earlier, is a new bilingual jurisdiction. Hong Kong courts in recent years have dealt with the issues arising from bilingual legislation in a limited number of cases. The methods used are not exactly the same as in Canada.[7]

The departure point for bilingual statutory interpretation in Hong Kong is the statutory provisions that provide the basic legal framework. According to Section 10B of the Hong Kong Interpretation and General Clauses Ordinance:

(1) The English language text and the Chinese language text of an Ordinance shall be equally authentic, and the Ordinance shall be construed accordingly.

(2) The provisions of an Ordinance are presumed to have the same meaning in each authentic text.

(3) Where a comparison of the authentic texts of an Ordinance discloses a difference of meaning which the rules of statutory interpretation ordinarily applicable do not resolve, the meaning which best reconciles the texts, having regard to the object and purposes of the Ordinance, shall be adopted.

These rules can be summed up as the equal authenticity rule, the presumption of the same meaning rule, and the two-step approach to reconciliation in case of divergence. Section 10B(3) also recognises that ordinary rules of statutory interpretation apply to bilingual laws. Such ordinary interpretive rules include the literal rule, the golden rule and the purposive or mischief approach and many others used in Common Law jurisdictions (see note 4 in this chapter, and Bennion 2002). Other relevant provisions in the Interpretation and General Clauses Ordinance include:

- Section 9
  Chinese words and expressions in the English text should be construed according to Chinese language and custom. Reciprocally, English words and expressions in the Chinese text should be construed according to English language and custom.
- Section 10C
  If an expression of the common law is used in the English text while an analogous expression is used in the corresponding Chinese text, the statute should be construed in accordance with the common law meaning of that expression.
- Section 19
  A statute is deemed to be remedial and shall receive such a fair, large and liberal construction and interpretation as will best ensure that

attainment of the object of the ordinance according to its true intent, meaning and spirit.

Section19 is said to be an embodiment of the purposive approach. Its essence is to take and give effect to the overall purpose if that can be done without straining the words or violating the intention of the legislature (see Law Drafting Division Discussion Paper 1998).

Some of these bilingual interpretive rules have been applied by the courts in Hong Kong. In *R. v Tam Yuk Ha* HCMA933/1996, the court, citing Section 10B of the Interpretation and General Clauses Ordinance, held that under bilingual legislation, both the English and Chinese language texts of an ordinance are equally authentic. It is not the English language text that prevails over the Chinese language text nor vice versa. It is the two authentic texts together which make up the legislation enacted by the legislature. In *Hong Kong Special Administrative Region* (HKSAR) *v Tam Yuk Ha* HCMA1385/1996, the court held that the English and Chinese texts are presumed to have the same meaning, and both are equally authentic. It is on this basis that the court must interpret the relevant provision. It is only when there is clearly a difference of meaning that the court has to reconcile the two texts.

In *HKSAR v Leung Kwok Hung and Others* HCMA16/2003, the court has also ruled that in reading the authentic texts in the official languages, the court is not entitled to read down an authentic text in either of the official languages, but is obliged to reconcile the authentic texts in both official language, having regard to the object and purposes of the Ordinance.

In *HKSAR v Lau San Ching and Others* HCMA98/2002, the court went into considerable length discussing the issue of bilingual interpretation. One of the issues before the court in this case concerns the discrepancy found between the equally authentic English and Chinese laws. The English version of an Ordinance has the word 'may' but it was omitted in the Chinese version.

The relevant section in this case is Section 4(28) of the Summary Offences Ordinance. Its English text reads:

> Any person who without lawful authority or excuse . . . does any act whereby injury or obstruction whether directly or consequentially, *may* accrue to a public place or to the shore of the sea, or to navigation, mooring or anchorage, transit or traffic. . . . shall be liable to a fine of $500 or to imprisonment of 3 months [italics added].

The equally authentic Chinese text when back translated into English reads:

> Any person who without lawful authority or excuse . . . does any act whereby injury or obstruction whether directly or consequentially,

accrues to a public place or to the shore of the sea, or to navigation, mooring or anchorage, transit or traffic. . . . shall be liable to a fine of $500 or to imprisonment of 3 months [italics added].

Thus, there is a significant discrepancy between the English and Chinese texts. According to the Chinese text, actual obstruction, be it direct or consequential, must have accrued to a public place before the offence can be made out. But according to the English text, obstruction may accrue to a public place to create an offence. The Chinese text gives the offence a narrower meaning in that actual obstruction must be caused before an offence can be made out. As no actual obstruction occurred in this case, the appellant argued that there was no case to answer. So, there is a clear conflict between the two authentic texts.

We do not know how the variation in the two versions occurred and why an important word 'may' was left out of the Chinese translation. Possibly, it was an oversight or a translation error. The court relied on a number of principles and factors to resolve the discrepancy. The court noted the different times the two versions were authenticated. The court confirmed the lower court's rejection of the defence's submission that the word 'may' means 'must' as there is a difference in the use of 'may' and its omission. The court also held that the words 'may accrue' should be given their ordinary meaning. The court summarised the issue this way:

> In this case there is a clear conflict between the two authentic texts. The original official English text creates an offence when any person does any act whereby obstruction, whether directly or consequentially, *may accrue* to a public place, but the Chinese text creates an offence when any person does any act whereby obstruction, whether directly or consequentially, *actually accrues* to a public place [emphasis in the original and paragraph number omitted].

In resolving the apparent conflict between the two versions, the court cited Section 10B of the Interpretation and General Clauses Ordinance, and explained how it applied the law by using the two-step approach in Section 10B(3). In ascertaining the legal meaning and the legislative intent, the court gave more weight to the English original text given its original status compared with a later Chinese translation even though they are both authentic. The court stated:

> In this case, any attempt to reconcile the two conflicting texts would be doomed to failure or, at the very least, be wholly artificial. Section 10B(2), which presumes that they are to have the same meaning, provides no assistance in resolving the matter and therefore recourse

has to be had to s.10B(3), which deals with a difference of meaning. Section 10B(3) provides for a two step approach: firstly there must be an attempt to resolve the differences of meaning by applying the rules of statutory interpretation. If this fails, then the interpreter has to adopt the meaning which best reconciles the texts with regard to the object and purposes of the legislation.

From that it necessarily follows that if the Ordinance was initially enacted in English, the English text was the original official text from which the Chinese text was subsequently prepared and declared authentic. In ascertaining the ordinance's legal meaning, the English text should be taken as more accurately reflecting the legislature's intent at the time it was originally enacted. In this case, the meaning borne by the original official English text, which was already in existence as early as 1932, should take precedence over the Chinese authentic text.

A different possible approach in bilingual interpretation was contemplated, that is, when the two authentic texts cannot be reconciled with one another in case of discrepancy, then the court should give effect to the text that favours the defendant in criminal cases (*R. v Tam Yuk Ha* HCMA933/1996). But this approach was rejected in *Chan Fung Lan v Lai Wai Chuen* HCMP4210/1996, where the court held that when it is not possible to reconcile the two texts,

> ... the solution does not lie in giving effect to a text which favours one party as in the recent criminal case of *R. v Tam Yuk Ha* .... This is not a workable approach because ambiguities of the two texts do not arise solely in criminal cases but in civil matters as well where there are two or more litigants.

In *HKSAR v Leung Kwok Hung and Others* HCMA16/2003, the court also confirmed that the approach in *R. v Tam Yuk Ha* was incorrect.

With regard to errors and inaccuracies in legislation, for those statutes that were initially enacted only in English with their Chinese texts subsequently translated and declared authentic, the court held in *Chan Fung Lan v Lai Wai Chuen* HCMP4210/1996 that the English versions were considered the original official texts on the sole basis of which the Chinese counterparts were prepared. In ascertaining the legal meaning of such a statute, the English text should be taken as more accurately reflecting the legislature's intent when the statute was initially passed. The meaning borne by the English version thus takes precedence over the Chinese one.

In *Chan Fung Lan v Lai Wai Chuen*, the authenticated Chinese text of the proviso to Section 18 of the Estate Duty Ordinance was found to be incorrect. The inclusion of the word *yaji* (charge) does not appear in the English text. The court held that if the authenticated Chinese text of a piece of legislation is incorrect, then it should not be acted upon. Cheung J found that:

> One must bear in mind that the authenticated Chinese text started life simply as a translation of the original legislation and if there are errors in the translation, which are bound to arise in such a mammoth undertaking, such errors should not be given effect simply because under s.10B of the Interpretation Ordinance the two texts are said to be equally authentic.
>
> . . . When the court comes to the view that the authenticated Chinese text contains inaccuracies then it should not give effect to that text but should rely on the original legislation. This approach is justified because under s.4B of the Official Languages Ordinance (Cap 5) where the Governor in Council has declared a text to be an authenticated text of an ordinance and it appears to him that there is any manifest error, omission or inaccuracy in that text, he may by order in the gazette correct that error and such correction shall be deemed to be incorporated in the text at the time when it was declared to be the authentic text.

This approach was also applied in *HKSAR v Lau San Ching and Others* HCMA98/2002. Similarly, in *The Commissioner of Rating and Valuation v Chan Ho Chin* LDMR48A/2000, the Lands Tribunal of Hong Kong adopted the same approach. In this case, the Chinese and the English versions of Section 53A(5)(b) Landlord and Tenant (Consolidation) Ordinance have a conflict. The English provision provides:

> Where there is a breach of a condition imposed under paragraph (b) of subsection (2), the Tribunal may, on the application of the Commissioner, – . . .
>
> (ii) *in any case*, impose a penalty not exceeding the market value of the premises at the time of the imposition of the penalty [italics added].

In the Chinese text, instead of 'in any case', the literal translation of the Chinese expression is 'in any other case'. The court adopted the same approach in *Chan Fung Lan v Lai Wai Chuen* and held that as the two versions could not be reconciled, the court relied on the English text and treated the Chinese version as an error or inaccuracy.

As bilingual law is still new in Hong Kong, both bilingual drafting and judicial interpretive approaches are in the process of development and maturity. Hong Kong has much to learn from the Canadian experience. Nevertheless, the two jurisdictions are quite different and Hong Kong is sure to develop its own approach in the resolution of bilingual divergence unique to its situation.

Notes

1 For discussion of the bilingualism in law in Finland, see Salmi-Tolonen (2004).
2 According to Tetley (2000), two reasons can be advanced to explain the difference in statutory interpretation between the Common Law and the Civil Law. Firstly, Common Law statutes have to be read against a case law background, while Civil Law codes and statutes are the primary source of law under Montesquieu's theory. Secondly, Civil Law judges are influenced by Rousseau's theory that the state is the source of all rights under the social contract, while English judges favour Hobbes's theory that the individual agreed to forfeit to the state only certain rights.
3 For a comparative analysis of the literal and purposive techniques in legislative interpretation of the English Common Law and European Community law, see McLeod (2004).
4 Contrast the usage at the EU. According to the *English Style Guide* of the DGT of the European Commission (DGT 2005c), 'shall' is used for a positive command; 'may' is used for a positive permission; 'may not' is used to express a prohibition, 'shall not' is used where no prohibition is meant and 'need not' is used for a negative permission.
5 See the Law Drafting Division of the Department of Justice of Hong Kong (1998) for its explanation. Briefly, the plain meaning or the literal rule applies words of a statute in their natural and ordinary meaning with nothing added or taken away, even if an inexpedient, unjust or immoral outcome occurs. The purposive approach or the mischief rule refers to the legal position before the statute was passed and the mischief that the statute was intended to cure. The statute is then construed in such a way as to suppress the mischief and to advance the remedy. The golden rule means that a statute should be construed in such a way as to avoid manifest absurdity or anomalies. This means that the court may adopt a secondary meaning that is linguistically possible in order to produce a reasonable result. For discussions of statutory interpretation rules in Common Law jurisdictions, see Cross *et al.* (1995) and Bennion (2002). For a comparative study of statutory interpretation in different countries including France, Germany, Italy, the UK and US, see MacCormick and Summers (1991).
6 For information about bilingualism and bijuralism in Canadian law, see the publications and resources at http://www.canada.justice.gc.ca/en/jl/index. html and bijuralism and http://www.canada.justice.gc.ca/en/ps/franc/41/ publications.html.
7 In order to promote bilingualism in Hong Kong law, the Law Drafting Division has published *The English-Chinese Glossary of Legal Terms*, and *The Chinese-English Glossary of Legal Terms* as guides for Hong Kong's bilingual legislation. They are both in print form and on-line at http://www.justice.gov.hk. They list the legal terms in English and Chinese and where they appear in specific Hong Kong statutes.

Chapter 7
Translating International Legal Instruments

If the law says: 'No vehicle is allowed in the park', what would 'vehicle' mean? Hart (1961/1994) asks in his classical example to illustrate linguistic and legal uncertainties inherent in legal language. In this hypothetical case, the word 'vehicle', Hart says, may refer to a number of things – a car, an ambulance or even a roller skater. In 2005, a case came before the ECJ, asking the same question, not just with regard to English, but multiple languages.[1] An EU law has a provision with the wording 'the letting of premises and sites for parking vehicles'.[2] A Danish company letting a site for boats argued that this was not covered by the word 'vehicles'. The court examined the various language versions of the EU law and found they are not consistent. The French, English, Italian, Spanish, Portuguese, German and Finnish versions encompass means of transport in general including aircraft and boats. However, the Danish, Swedish, Dutch and Greek versions have used a more precise term with a more limited meaning that serves to designate principally land-based means of transport, and the Danish word refers to land-based transport on wheels only. By reference to the purpose and scheme of the relevant law, the court held that the word 'vehicles' used in the provision must be interpreted as covering all means of transport, including boats.

The translation of legal instruments in international or supranational bodies such as the UN and EU forms a special area of legal translation practice. Such translational activities can entail translating multilingual documents such as international instruments of the UN involving several languages, and translating bilateral treaties involving two languages. The translation of such legal documents of international nature as opposed to domestic laws has its own idiosyncrasies as well as sharing the characteristics of translating law in general.

In this chapter, the basic concepts and usage of international law and international legal instruments are explained. The legal and linguistic features of such instruments are also described. The chapter proceeds to describe the process of bilateral treaty negotiation involving translation as an example for insight into the treaty making process involving two languages. Then, aspects associated with drafting and translating multilingual instruments at the UN and EU are briefly discussed. This is followed by a brief outline of the interpretive rules and approaches of the ECJ concerning multilingual law and the relevant case law. Lastly, the use of language and translation technology in the assistance of translating multilingual documents is discussed.

International Instruments and their Legal Status

International law, or law of nations, is regarded as a set of objectively valid norms that regulates the mutual behaviour of states (Kelsen 1967). International law is normative and binding on states. According to Article 38(1) of the Statute of the International Court of Justice (ICJ), the sources of international law include international conventions, international custom, the general principles of law recognised by civilised nations, and judicial decisions and the teachings of authoritative publicists of various nations.[3]

For our purpose, international conventions and agreements are the most commonly translated texts of the legal sources cited above and are thus the focus of discussion here. Judicial decisions are also translated but are more limited. For instance, the decisions of the ICJ are translated but they are published in English and French only. The ECJ also undertakes translations of its decisions.[4]

International conventions or agreements are those binding at international law that are created and voluntarily agreed to by states. Such international legal instruments include treaties, agreements, conventions, charters and protocols. Other types of international instruments include declarations, memoranda of understanding, *modus vivendi* and exchange of notes that may or may not have any legal force.

Over the years, a variety of terms have been used to refer to international legal instruments by which states establish rights and obligations among themselves, including 'treaty', 'agreement', 'convention', 'charter', 'protocol', 'covenant' and 'accord', for instance, Biological Diversity Convention 1992, International Covenant on Civil and Political Rights 1973, Maastricht Treaty 1993, Pact of Paris 1928, African Charter on Human and People's Rights 1982, Kyoto Protocol to the United Nations Framework Convention on Climate Change 1997, Statute of the International Court of Justice 1945, Agreement Governing the Activities of States on the Moon and Other Celestial Bodies 1979 (also known as the Moon Treaty), the United

Nations Standard Minimum Rules for the Administration of Juvenile Justice 1985, and the Uniform Law on International Sale of Goods 1964.

Different international legal instruments may have different titles, but they all have common features, and international law applies to all such instruments. Such rules of international customary law are codified and stipulated in the 1969 Vienna Convention on the Law of Treaties (the 1969 Vienna Convention), which contains rules for treaties concluded between states, and the 1986 Vienna Convention on the Law of Treaties between States and International Organisations or between International Organisations (the 1986 Vienna Convention). Neither convention distinguishes between the different designations of international instruments.

Given the varied terminology, no precise terminology exists. In fact, the meaning of the terms may vary, changing from state to state, region to region and instrument to instrument. Some of the terms can be interchanged: an instrument that is designated 'agreement' may also be called 'treaty' (see *Treaty Reference Guide*, United Nations 1999). The title assigned to such international instruments normally has no overriding legal effects. The title may follow habitual use or may relate to the particular character or importance sought to be attributed to the instrument by its parties. The degree of formality chosen will depend upon the gravity of the problems dealt with and upon the political implications and intent of the parties (see United Nations 1999).

International legal instruments can create legal rights and obligations on the part of states. If a state by its act or omission breaches an international obligation, it incurs international responsibility. In fact, it is a principle of international law that the breach of an agreement involves an obligation to make reparation in an adequate form (*Corfu Channel Case* [1949] ICJ Rep 4). In this connection, an important principle in international law is that an international agreement is not legally binding unless the parties intend it to be. A treaty or international agreement is said to require an intention by the parties to create legal rights and obligations or to establish relations governed by international law (Henkin *et al.* 1993: 426). If such an intention does not exist, an agreement is considered to have no legal effect. States are free to enter into such non-binding agreements. However, as pointed out, questions have often arisen as to the intention of the contracting parties. The main reason is that governments tend to be reluctant to state explicitly in an agreement that it is non-binding or lacks legal force. An important language consideration in this regard, particularly important for the legal translator to bear in mind, is that, consequently, inferences as to such intent have to be drawn from the language of the instrument and the attendant circumstances of its conclusion and adoption (Henkin *et al.* 1993: 426). Emphasis is often placed on the lack of precision and generality of the terms of the agreement. Statements of general aims and broad declarations of principles are considered too indefinite to create enforceable obligations and therefore agreements which do not go beyond that should be presumed to be non-binding (Henkin *et al.* 1993: 426–427). It is also said that mere statements of intention or of common purposes are grounds for concluding that a legally binding agreement was not intended. Because of this reason, there is often calculated ambiguity about the obligatory force of such instruments. Not infrequently, imprecision and generalities are found in treaties of unquestioned legal force. If strict requirements of definiteness and specificity are used to measure all treaties, many of them would have all or most of their provisions considered as without legal effect (Henkin *et al.* 1993: 427). Examples of such treaties may be found among agreements for cultural cooperation and of friendship and trade that express common aims and intentions in broad language. Other examples of highly general statements can be found in the Charter of the United Nations and similar constitutional instruments, but these general and abstract principles have been given determinate meanings by the relevant international organs (Henkin *et al.* 1993: 427; see pp. 148–149 for arrangements less than treaty status). Thus, the translator should not attempt to clarify vague or ambiguous wording when translating such instruments.

Another relevant aspect is the interpretation and application of treaty provisions. Treaties may be interpreted by an international court, the state parties in their diplomatic relations, and by municipal courts (Janis 2003: 29). In this regard, the Vienna Convention provides in Article 3(1) that a 'treaty shall be interpreted in good faith in accordance with the ordinary meaning to be given to the terms of the treaty in their context and in the light of its object and purpose'. Furthermore, if the texts in different authentic languages of a treaty cannot be reconciled on their face, then Article 33(4) of the 1969 Vienna Convention, which provides that 'the meaning which best reconciles the texts, having regard to the object and purpose of the treaty, shall be adopted', can be revoked (see Sarcevic 1997, Janis 2003: 29–33, for discussions of treaty interpretation). For our purpose of translation, the translator is under constant pressure to translate accurately, ambiguity and vagueness included, and needs to give extra thought to every word of the treaty under translation. It is the court or other competent bodies that interpret treaty provisions and determine their meanings, not the translator.

A requirement for international instruments is registration. Under the Charter of the United Nations, a treaty must be published and capable of registration with the UN. Article 102 of the Charter provides that 'every treaty and every international agreement entered into by any Member State of the United Nations after the present Charter comes into force shall as soon as possible be registered with the Secretariat and published by it'. All treaties and international agreements registered or filed and recorded with the Secretariat since 1946 are published in the United Nations Treaty Series (UNTS) in their original language or languages, together with a translation in English and French, as necessary. International agreements have proliferated since the end of the Second World War. More than 50,000 treaties have been registered with the UN since 1945. Most of them are bilateral treaties or agreements among a small number of states. A few thousands of them are believed to be multilateral agreements.

The UN treaty database at http://untreaty.un.org is an invaluable resource for international lawyers and translators of international law. It contains the treaties and statements of treaties and international agreements registered or filed and recorded with the UN Secretariat in official languages since 1945. It also has the treaties from the League of Nations concluded between 1920–1944, among other resources.

Designation of International Instruments

As discussed in Chapter 4, one problem in translating law is synonyms of legal terminology that can have similar or substantively different meanings. In international law, this is no exception. One area of synonyms is found in the designations of instruments. The commonly used terms, 'treaty', 'agreement' and 'convention', are discussed next.

Treaties

According to Article 2(1)(a) of the 1969 Vienna Convention on the Law of Treaties, a treaty means an international agreement concluded between states in written form and governed by international law, whether embodied in a single instrument or in two or more related instruments and whatever its particular designation. It is a major and primary source of international law.

The term 'treaty' can be used as a common generic term or as a particular term (United Nations 1999). Treaty used as a generic term covers all instruments binding under international law concluded between international entities, giving rise to international rights and obligations. A treaty may be called an 'agreement', 'convention', 'protocol' or 'covenant'. Other terms used include statute, arrangement, *precès-verbal*, declaration, *modus vivendi*, exchange of notes or letters, final act and general act (for their explanation, see United Nations 1999). There are no international rules as to when an international instrument should be entitled a treaty. Both the 1969 Vienna Convention and the 1986 Vienna Convention confirm this generic use of the term 'treaty'. A 'treaty' in the generic sense has to meet the criteria of the 1969 Vienna Convention definition: that is, an instrument has to be a binding instrument, which means that the contracting parties intend to create legal rights and duties; it must be concluded by states or international organisations with treaty making power; it is governed by international law, and needs to be in writing.

Not all agreements involving foreign states are treaties. For instance, an agreement between an Australian state or territory and a foreign government will not be a treaty. However, this is in contrast to some countries of federal union such as Canada, Germany, Switzerland and the United States. In these countries, there are limited treaty making powers available to the component states of these countries (Janis 2003: 19). Furthermore, even if a document is agreed between two or more sovereign countries, it will not be a treaty unless those countries intend the document to be binding under international law. If a document is intended by the parties to have political or moral weight, but not legally binding, it is not a treaty. If an agreement is governed by the domestic law of a country, such a document is a contract, not a treaty.

Treaty is also used as a specific term. There are no consistent rules when state practice employs the terms 'treaty' as a title for an international instrument (United Nations 1999). It is believed that usually the term 'treaty' is reserved for matters of some gravity that require more solemn agreements. Their signatures are usually sealed and they normally require ratification. Typical examples of international instruments designated as 'treaties' are peace treaties, border treaties, delimitation treaties, extradition treaties and treaties of friendship, commerce and cooperation. It is noteworthy that the use of the term 'treaty' for international instruments has considerably declined in the last decades in favour of other terms (United Nations 1999).

There are three classes of treaties: (1) general multilateral treaties open to all states or all members, for instance, the Charter of the United Nations; (2) treaties that establish a collaborative mechanism for states to regulate or manage a particular area of activity, for instance, the UN Convention on the Law of the Sea (1982); and (3) bilateral agreements between two state parties. Multilateral treaties today are generally developed under the auspices of international or inter-governmental organisations such as the UN or its specialised agencies, for instance, the International Labour

Organisation (ILO) or the World Health Organisation (WHO). There are also regional multilateral treaties.

Treaties take many forms and can perform different functions. They may play the role of contracts between two or more parties, function as legislation for the members of the international community to regulate a particular aspect of their relations, and as the constitutions of international organisations (Greig 1970: 7–15).

Agreements

Generally speaking, the term 'agreement' is an instrument less formal than a treaty or convention. The word can have a generic and a specific meaning. Firstly, the term 'agreement' is used as a generic term. For instance, the 1969 Vienna Convention on the Law of Treaties employs the term 'international agreement' in its broadest sense. On the one hand, it defines treaties as 'international agreements' with certain characteristics. On the other hand, it employs the term 'international agreements' for instruments that do not meet its definition of 'treaty', for instance, 'international agreements not in written form'. Thus, the term 'international agreement' in its generic sense embraces the widest range of international instruments (United Nations 1999).

Secondly, the term 'agreement' is also used as a specific term. Agreements are usually less formal and deal with a narrower range of subject matter than treaties. According the UN *Treaty Reference Guide*, there is a general tendency to apply the term 'agreement' to bilateral or restricted multilateral treaties. It is employed especially for instruments of a technical or administrative character, which are signed by the representatives of government departments, but are not subject to ratification. Typical agreements deal with matters of economic, cultural, scientific and technical cooperation. Agreements also frequently deal with financial matters, such as avoidance of double taxation, investment guarantees or financial assistance. The UN and other international organisations regularly conclude agreements with the host country to an international conference or to a session of a representative organ of the organisation. In international economic law, the term 'agreement' is also used for broad multilateral agreements.

Thirdly, the term 'agreement' is used in regional integration schemes. Regional integration schemes are based on general framework treaties with constitutional character. International instruments that amend this framework at a later stage are also designated as 'treaties'. Instruments that are concluded within the framework of the constitutional treaty or by the organs of the regional organisation are usually referred to as 'agreements', in order to distinguish them from the constitutional treaty. For example, whereas the Treaty of Rome of 1957 serves as a quasi-constitution of the European Community, treaties concluded by the Community with other nations are usually designated as agreements. The Latin American Integration Association was established by the Treaty of Montevideo of 1980, but the subregional instruments entered into under its framework are called agreements (see United Nations 1999).

Conventions

Generally speaking, the term 'convention' is used for a formal instrument of multilateral character. Before the Second World War, it was also used for a bilateral treaty but now such usage is rare.

The term 'convention' can have both a generic and a specific meaning. Firstly, the term 'convention' is used as a generic term. Article 38(1)(a) of the Statute of the ICJ refers to 'international conventions, whether general or particular' as a source of law. This generic use of the term 'convention' embraces all international agreements, in the same way as does the generic term 'treaty' (see United Nations 1999). Black letter law is also regularly referred to as 'conventional law', in order to distinguish it from the other sources of international law, such as customary law or the general principles of international law. The generic term 'convention' thus is synonymous with the generic term 'treaty'.

Secondly, 'convention' is used as a specific term. In the 19th century the term 'convention' was regularly employed for bilateral agreements, but it now is generally used for formal multilateral treaties with a broad number of parties. Conventions are normally open for participation by the international community as a whole, or by a large number of states. Usually the instruments negotiated under the auspices of an international organisation are entitled 'conventions', for instance, Convention on Biological Diversity 1992, United Nations Convention on the Law of the Sea 1982, Vienna Convention on the Law of Treaties 1969. The same holds true for instruments adopted by an organ of an international organisation, for instance, the WHO Framework Convention on Tobacco Control 2003.

Other international instruments

In addition to treaties, agreements and conventions, there are many other universal instruments. The legal status of these instruments varies: resolutions, declarations, principles, guidelines, standard rules and recommendations are generally considered to have no binding legal effect and they do not constitute a source of international law (see Article 38(1) of the Statute of the ICJ). It is debatable whether UN resolutions and declarations have any legal effect, form part of international custom or express general principles (see *Filartiga v Pena-Irala*, US Court of Appeals, 630 F 2d 876 (1980) in which the court discussed the status of the Universal Declaration of Human Rights and the 1975 Declaration on the Protection of all Persons from Torture). However, at the minimum, such instruments may have a moral force and provide practical guidance to states in their conduct. They may be considered 'soft law'. For instance, the Declaration on the Rights of the Child adopted by the UN General Assembly is not a treaty. It may not be intended to be binding by its adoption, but it was part of a long process that led ultimately to the negotiation of the UN Convention on the Rights of the Child 1989. It may also assist in the interpretation of the relevant treaty.

Subject Matters Covered by International Legal Instruments

International instruments are negotiated and concluded by sovereign states. International organisations also possess such instrument making capacity and personality. Today, many multilateral instruments are concluded under the auspices of the UN, and other international entities.

The issues subject to international instruments are wide ranging, covering almost every aspect of life. There are international agreements on human rights, the environment, wildlife, on peaceful settlement of international disputes, the use of force, health, narcotic drugs and psychotropic substances, defence and security, nuclear non-proliferation, civil aviation, maritime delimitation, technological exchanges, international trade and development, transport and communications, navigation, economic statistics, educational and cultural matters, status of women, international penal matters, commodities, outer space, telecommunication, disarmament, the treatment of civilians in time of war, on the outlaw of the use of weapons of mass destruction, anti-terrorism, the law of the sea and the international trading system.

For the translator, this means that considerable basic subject knowledge is necessary to competently translate such texts. Some international instruments are of the general nature, such as the various human rights conventions, while other instruments are highly technical, such as Stockholm Convention on Persistent Organic Pollutants 2001. In translating such technical documents, close collaboration with scientists in the relevant fields is often necessary.

Textual Features of International Legal Instruments

With regard to treaties in the generic sense, they may be drafted in different forms. However, they generally have a characteristic textual form. In some ways, they resemble private contracts. Usually, a treaty consists of the following elements:

- a title;
- preambular recitals expressing the background, object and purpose of the treaty;
- Main text, that is, articles covering the substantive provisions, normally containing definition, rights and obligations, enforcement and dispute resolution clauses;
- final clauses;
- an attestation clause or testimonium, and signature block; and
- annexes, which may include protocols, exchanges of letters, agreed minutes, annexes or schedules. Exchanges of notes and letters, when intended to constitute a treaty, contain a paragraph usually at the end, which states that the notes and letters when exchanged will 'constitute an agreement between the two governments' or words to that effect.

Both bilateral and multilateral treaties generally follow such a similar format.

Bilateral treaties

A large number of bilateral treaties have been entered into between two states to increase the legal protection to private parties of one contracting states in the other contracting state. Generally, there are two major categories of bilateral treaties: (1) treaties of friendship, commerce and navigation (known as the FCN treaties), which cover a wide range of trade relations in addition to providing legal protection against non-commercial risks; and (2) bilateral investment treaties that focus specifically on protection of the foreign investor against specified non-commercial risks. Many of these investment treaties have their roots in the Draft Convention on the Protection of Foreign Property prepared under the auspices of the Organisation for Economic Co-operation and Development (OECD) and adopted in 1967 by the OECD Council (Henkin *et al.* 1993: 759), for instance, the Agreement Between the Government of the People's Republic of China and the Government of the Republic of France on the Reciprocal Promotion and Protection of Investments 1984, and the Agreement Between the Government of the People's Republic of China and the Government of the Republic of Italy Concerning the Encouragement and Reciprocal Protection of Investments 1985. For the latter, the treaty reads:

The Government of the People's Republic of China and the Government of the Republic of Italy (Hereinafter referred to as the 'Contracting Parties'),

DESIRING to intensify economic cooperation between both countries,

INTENDING to create favourable conditions for investments by nationals and companies of either country in the territory of the other country, and

RECOGNISING that encouragement and protection of such investments will benefit the economic prosperity of both countries.

HAVE AGREED AS FOLLOWS: *

. . . .

For the purpose of this Agreement:

The term 'investment' means . . . .

. . . .

In bilateral agreements, the authentic language may vary. For instance, it may only be in English as in the case of an agreement between the US and Israel. But often, bilateral agreements are written in the two languages of the two contracting states. In other cases, English is used as the third original language even though the two contracting states' official languages do not include English. For instance, the Agreement on Trade and Economic Cooperation between the Government of the State of Israel and the Government of the Hashemite Kingdom of Jordan 1995 has the authentic texts in Arabic, English and Hebrew. Other examples are the Agreement Between the Government of the People's Republic of China and the Government of the Republic of Italy Concerning the Encouragement and Reciprocal Protection of Investments 1985, with the authentic text in Chinese, English and Italian; and the Agreement Between the Government of the People's Republic of China and the Government of the Kingdom of Thailand for the Promotion and Protection of Investments 1984, with the authentic languages being Chinese, English and Thai.

Multilateral treaties

International conventions normally follow an established format as described earlier, consisting of the title, preamble, main text, final clauses, an attestation clause and signature block and annex. For instance:

Convention on International Trade in Endangered Species of Wild Fauna and Flora 1973

The Contracting States,

Recognising that wild fauna and flora in their many beautiful and varied forms are an irreplaceable part of the natural systems of the earth which must be protected for this and the generations to come;

Conscious of the ever-growing value of wild fauna and flora from aesthetic, scientific, cultural, recreational and economic points of view;

Recognising that peoples and States are and should be the best protectors of their own wild fauna and flora;

Recognising, in addition, that international co-operation is essential for the protection of certain species of wild fauna and flora against over-exploitation through international trade;

Convinced of the urgency of taking appropriate measures to this end;

Have agreed as follows: . . . .

The preamble is normally followed by the substantive provisions set out under such heading as: Part X, Section X or Chapter X, Article X. The substantive provisions normally start with definitions. For instance, the Convention on International Trade in Endangered Species of Wild Fauna and Flora 1973 starts with:

Article I

Definitions

For the purpose of the present Convention, unless the context otherwise requires:

(a) 'Species' means any species, subspecies, or geographically separate population thereof;
(b) 'Specimen' means:
  (i) any animal or plant, whether alive or dead;
  (ii) in the case of an animal: for species included in Appendices I and II, any readily recognisable part or derivative thereof; and for species included in Appendix III, any readily recognisable part or derivative thereof specified in Appendix III in relation to the species; and
  (iii) in the case of a plant: for species included in Appendix I, any readily recognisable part or derivative thereof; and for species included in Appendices II and III, any readily recognisable part

or derivative thereof specified in Appendices II and III in relation to the species;

(c) 'Trade' means export, re-export, import and introduction from the sea;

(d) 'Re-export' means export of any specimen that has previously been imported; . . . .

For discussions of statutory definition in municipal statutes, see Chapter 6.

Final clauses

Final clauses of a treaty refer to the final provisions typically found at the end of a treaty. For a multilateral treaty, the final clauses generally include articles on the settlement of disputes, amendment and review, the status of annexes, signature, ratification, accession, entry into force, withdrawal and termination, reservation, designation of the depository, and authentic texts. They may also include articles on the relationship of the treaty to other treaties, its duration, provisional application, territorial applicant and registration. The final clauses generally relate to procedural aspects rather than to substantive aspects of the treaty. The Treaty Section of the United Nations Office of Legal Affairs has published a handbook for the drafting of final clauses – *Final Clauses of Multilateral Treaties Handbook* (2003) as a reference tool and practical guide for those involved in multilateral treaty making (available at http://untreaty.un.org).

For the standard format and wording of the various final provisions, the UN Final Clause Handbook is a useful guide. For our purpose, most final clauses today include the authentic texts provision as most multilateral treaties are now concluded in more than one language. Authentic languages refer to the languages in which the meaning of the provisions of a treaty is to be determined, and an authentic or authenticated text is the version of the treaty that has been authenticated by the parties, that is, the procedure whereby the text of a treaty is established as authentic and definitive. Accordingly, treaties normally specify the languages of the authentic texts. Treaties concluded under the auspices of the UN normally provide in their final clauses that the texts are authentic in all the official languages of the UN, that is, in the six official languages – Arabic, Chinese, English, French, Russian and Spanish. For instance, Article 26 of the UN Framework Convention on Climate Change 1992 reads:

Authentic texts
The original of this Convention, of which the Arabic, Chinese, English, French, Russian and Spanish texts are equally authentic, shall be deposited with the Secretary-General of the United Nations.

The more common form of authentic text provision is found in the depositary clause, for instance, in Article XX of the Convention on the Conservation of Migratory Species of Wild Animals 2003:

> Depositary
> 1. The original of this Convention, in the English, French, German, Russian and Spanish languages, each version being equally authentic, shall be deposited with the Depositary. The Depositary shall transmit certified copies of each of these versions to all States and all regional economic integration organisations that have signed the Convention or deposited instruments of accession to it.

For treaties adopted by other international bodies, the authentic texts are generally in the official languages of the organisations concerned. For instance, the WTO has English, French and Spanish as its official working languages. WTO's legal documents are authentic in these languages only.

It is rare today that international treaties do not contain provisions on the authentic texts as in the case of earlier conventions, e.g. the Convention on the Privileges and Immunities of the United Nations 1946 and the Convention for the Suppression of the Traffic in Persons and of the Exploitation of the Prostitution of Others 1950.

In terms of translation of the final clauses of treaties, generally speaking, the translator must be familiar with the standard format and actual wording of final clauses in both English and other languages. The established and standard translation must be adopted.

Verifying Foreign Language Texts in Bilateral Treaty Negotiation

The verification of foreign language versions of bilateral treaty texts is an integral part of the treaty process. The process seeks to minimise the potential for future disputes over interpretation by providing impartial confirmation that the texts in additional languages are in complete accord (see *Signed, Sealed and Delivered: Treaties and Treaty Making: An Officials' Handbook*, Treaty Secretariat 2004). Even if the substance of the agreement has been settled, the requirement for verification may demand an entirely new negotiation to reconcile differences about meanings in translation. In cases where there are 'cultural' issues (regarding the proper use of language in the context of domestic legislation) it has the potential to create tensions (see Treaty Secretariat 2004).

The following is a description of the process of verifying foreign language texts of bilateral treaties used by the Australian government as a reference for bilateral treaty negotiation and formation involving two languages (one being English, which is the official language in Australia) as detailed in *Signed, Sealed and Delivered*.

Before substantive negotiations begin on a bilateral treaty, the Australian delegation normally obtains the other party's agreement that at the language verification stage, each side will provide the other with fully annotated and clearly defined texts. These texts should indicate those passages in the other side's text where change is deemed as essential (those sections, which unless changed, alter meaning) and those where change is desirable (style, semantics, grammar, felicity of expression, etc.).

If a bilateral treaty is to be signed in a language or languages additional to English, the other side should be requested to provide a full translation. Should a treaty text be negotiated in a language other than English, Australia will provide an English language translation. In that event, verification of the English text is the responsibility of the other party. For reasons of consistency and clarity, negotiations commenced in one language should not be concluded in another. Irrespective of the number of languages that the other side may require, translation into those languages should be done only after the parties have agreed on the text in the language in which the negotiations were conducted. Staff at the overseas posts may verify foreign language versions of an English text provided the office confirms to the Australian Department of Foreign Affairs and Trade Treaties Secretariat, and that the staff member's English meets the appropriate local translating qualification standards. Alternatively, the Australian overseas posts may wish to employ an appropriately qualified translator or translation agency.

In rare cases, Australia negotiates bilateral treaties where the other side requires more than one foreign language text. In such a case, the base language remains constant throughout the course of the negotiation, and to ensure consistency, it is recommended that the same person verify both foreign language texts (see Treaty Secretariat 2004).

Arrangements of Less Than Treaty Status

As stated earlier, not all agreements reached between states are legally binding. Countries use instruments in which the parties do not intend to create legal rights and obligations or a legal relationship. These instruments, whether in the name of governments or agencies, are termed 'arrangements of less than treaty status' (Treaty Secretariat 2004). The most appropriate form for an arrangement of less than treaty status is often a memorandum of understanding (MOU), although records of discussion, joint communiqués and exchanges of notes or letters recording understandings are also common.

The intention not to create legally binding rights and obligations should be reflected in a document of less than treaty status. Some guidelines have been issued by the Australian government for preparing such arrangements (see Treaty Secretariat 2004). In particular, the linguistic and textual requirements are worth noting for our purpose. In drafting such texts:

- There should be a specific reference to the fact that the arrangement embodies the understandings of the parties. In an MOU, this should occur in a recital at the commencement of the document. In an exchange of correspondence, this should be proposed in the final substantive paragraph of the initiating piece of correspondence and be confirmed in the complementary reply.
- The words 'agree', 'agreement' and 'agreed', may be considered to signify a treaty, thus should be avoided. Constructions such as 'mutually arrange', 'mutually decide', 'mutually consent' or 'jointly determine' should be used instead. It is permissible to speak of the 'agreement' of delegations in an arrangement of less than treaty status, such as a record of discussion, if it is clear that the agreement is only to refer a matter to governments.
- The mandatory 'shall' used in treaties should be avoided and 'will' should be used instead.
- Arrangements should avoid formal preambles, although informally phrased opening recitals may be appropriate.
- Any provision for the settlement of disputes should generally be in terms of amicable resolution, not formal arbitration.
- Subdivisions of the document should be referred to as paragraphs rather than articles.
- The arrangement should be expressed to 'come into effect' rather than to 'enter into force'.
- The attestation clause should read 'SIGNED at . . . on . . .'rather than 'DONE at . . . on . . .'.

Multilingual Instrument Drafting and Translation

Today, most multilingual instruments are negotiated under the auspices of international organisations such as the UN.[5] Naturally, we will use the UN and the EU as examples in the following discussion. International legal instruments produced under the auspices of the UN are written in its six official languages. In the EU, currently, there are twenty official languages.

In this connection, it is necessary to clarify the legal status of the EU and its laws. The founding treaties of the EU are international treaties that are governed by international law. However, there have been debates as to whether EU laws, in particular, whether the legislation passed by the European Parliament, are still a form of international law. EU legislation once adopted becomes the domestic law of the EU Members States and directly binding on EU citizens. It is different from UN treaties and conventions in relation to different countries. Such international treaties do not automatically become domestic law of the signatory countries. In many countries, for instance, Australia, the legislature must specifically incorporate treaty provisions into the municipal law for them to become effective domestically. In contrast, the European Parliament makes laws that are directly enforceable in the domestic jurisdictions of the Member States, and the ECJ is empowered with the task of judicial supervision in the interpretation and application of EU treaties and Community laws. Some argue that EU law now so differs from traditional international law that it should be counted a legal system. It is more municipal than international law in character, or a hybrid (see Slaughter *et al.* 1998, de Cruz 1999, Janis 2003: 307–308).

Notwithstanding, international multilingual treaties of the UN and EU laws share commonalities in terms of drafting and translation. In the EU institutions, multilingual production of legislative texts is an integral part of the legislative process. EU law related multilingual documents, the so-called *acquis communautaire*, consist of a body of EU law, made up of primary legislation (the treaties), secondary legislation derived from the treaties (regulations, directions, decisions, recommendations and opinions), and the case law of the ECJ. So, translating treaties and secondary legislation is a major activity of the translators in EU institutions. Secondary legislative instruments consist of three types of directly binding laws of regulations, directives and decisions, and to a lesser extent, the non-binding, declaratory instruments of recommendations and opinions.[6]

One important principle in multilingual law is the principle of equal authenticity. The common practice is that in the final clause of a treaty, it usually specifies the original languages of the treaty and the fact that all official language texts are equally authentic, that is, having equal legal force (see earlier discussion of final clauses in this chapter on p. 146). This practice was codified in the 1969 Vienna Convention. Article 33(1) provides that when a treaty has been authenticated in two or more languages, the text is equally authoritative in each language unless the treaty provides or the parties agree that, in case of divergence, a particular text shall prevail. Article 33(3) provides that the terms of the treaty are presumed to have the same meaning in each authentic text. As pointed out, the importance attached to the principle of equal authenticity was intended to confer undisputable authority on each of the authentic texts, de facto eliminating the inferior status of authoritative translations (Sarcevic 1997: 199).

As regards drafting, in the EU, as part of the European Community legislative process, a proposal for a particular piece of legislation first comes from the European Commission (EC). As reported by Robinson (2005), normally, the first step is that the initial draft of a legislative proposal is prepared by the technical department or technical experts for the sector concerned. Drafters must write in either English or French and their choice is determined by the language used in their department. Once the technical department has prepared its preliminary draft, as a second step, the draft is submitted to the other Commission departments as part of the internal consultation procedure. The Commission's Legal Service is consulted on all draft legislation with lawyers specialising in the sector examining the draft for compliance with the law and coherence with other legislation.[7] The legal revisers, who all have dual legal and language qualifications, will examine it for compliance with the rules on form and presentation of legislation, in particularly the *Joint Practical Guide of the European Parliament, the Council and the Commission for Persons Involved in the Drafting of Legislation within the Community Institutions* (available at http://europa.eu.int/eur-lex/lex/en/techleg/index.htm). As Robinson (2005) points out, at this early stage, the draft exists in only one language. As a third step, the text must then be translated into all the official languages by the DGT. At this stage, the legal revisers will have another opportunity to review the text. The legal revisers must also correct formal or terminological errors and ensure that the legal scope is exactly the same in the different language versions. Then, the legislative proposal is submitted to the European Parliament and the European Council where it passes through those institutions' internal pre-adoption procedures before their final deliberation and eventual adoption (see also Gordon-Smith 1989).

We can see that translation is an integral part of the legislative process in the EC. This is similar and also different from the efforts in multilingual drafting experimented at the UN as a means of improving the quality and reliability of parallel texts.

An earlier example of multilingual drafting is found in the preparation of the Convention on the Law of the Sea 1982. According to Nelson (1987, see also Tabory 1980, Rosenne 1983), the Drafting Committee of the Law of the Sea first had a single negotiating text prepared in English. It was subsequently translated into the other UN official languages. These six language versions then went through the harmonisation process in terms of the consistency in usage of terminology, grammar, syntax, spelling etc., and the concordance process. The resulting concordance text in six language versions then appeared side by side for negotiation and deliberation. The six language groups that were set up for this purpose worked closely and interacted for changes and revisions. They went through all the texts, article by article to improve their interlingual concordance and achieve juridical concordance, resolving any linguistic, legal and technical issues. The deliberation and negotiation of the Convention lasted almost ten years. The aim of the multilingual drafting process was to ensure that all the authentic texts reflect the intent of the negotiating states. If viewed this way, the final six language texts of the Convention are not mere translations (Nelson 1987: 198), but truly negotiated texts.

Despite the experiment with multilingual drafting, the general practice for international treaties at the UN has been through translation. The draft texts are first produced in English and/or French, and then translated into other languages. Parallel and simultaneous multilingual drafting is very rare at the international level.

For our purpose, as Sarcevic (1997: 226) concludes, the multilingual drafting experiment in the Convention of the Law of the Sea 1982 made considerable progress in coordinating the production of the parallel texts, and this did not have any visible effect on translation and drafting methods. In addition, it does not seem to solve the problem of disputes associated with multilateral instruments arising from terminological incongruency and the incongruency in institutions of different legal systems (Sarcevic 1997: 226).

As regards the process of multilingual instruments, there are two sub-processes during drafting: concordance and harmonisation. Harmonisation is the process of ensuring internal consistency of terminology and presentation within a given text while concordance is the process of ensuring consistency of terminology and presentation between each and all the authentic texts (Rosenne 1983: 775–776). Furthermore, as is pointed out, translators of instruments of international law are under constant pressure to achieve interlingual concordance or intertextual symmetry or correspondence (Sarcevic 1997: 202), and for many lawyers, the yardstick for measuring the reliability of the parallel texts of multilateral instruments is the degree of their interlingual concordance, more specifically, how closely the terminology and syntax of the parallel texts of the same instruments are coordinated for the purpose of promoting or achieving uniform interpretation and application of statutory provisions (Sarcevic 1997: 202).

An important factor in the multilateral instrument making process relevant to the translator is the fact that international agreements are negotiated texts to represent the diverse interests of the participating state parties (Tabory 1980; Sarcevic 1997: 204). There are no particular requirements as to the manner of negotiation or reaching agreement or the form of a treaty, and as it happens, in international diplomacy, negotiators frequently resort to a compromise that glosses over their differences with vague, obscure or ambiguous wording, sacrificing clarity for the sake of obtaining consensus in treaties and conventions (Tabory 1980; Sarcevic 1997: 204). In the EC, as EU draft legislative texts go through extensive consultation, examination and revision, EU law is often the fruit of difficult compromises (Robinson 2005: 5). As Robinson points out, often changes are made in the draft legislation to achieve policy ends. Sometimes a provision is delicately left vague (known in French as *flou artistique*) to paper over a failure to reach full agreement (Robinson 2005: 7).

As a result, an important advice to translators of international instruments is that translators should avoid attempts to clarify vague points, obscurities and ambiguities, and as pointed out, those who do run the risk of upsetting the delicately achieved balance and misrepresenting the intent of the parties (Rosenne 1983: 783, Sarcevic 1997: 204, see also the discussion of international legal instrument and their legal status in this chapter, pp. 135–138). However, there is also the difficult question of how the translator distinguishes the deliberate obscurity that is the expression of a political and often hard-won compromise from inadvertent obscurity produced when those drafting the original text use a language that is not their mother tongue (Correia 2003: 42).

How the Court Approaches Divergence in Multilingual Law

Not infrequently, cases come before the court involving disputes arising from the differences, alleged or real, in the different language versions of multilingual laws. In this regard, the case law of the ECJ is illuminating as to how translation relates to the development of law.

It is said that an EU law's effectiveness depends upon its ability to harmonise the different versions of its multilingual texts (Huntington 1991: 333). This task largely falls on the ECJ. Over the years, the ECJ has developed a number of legal principles in the interpretation of EU multilingual law.

Firstly, EU legislation is drafted and effective in all the official languages of its Member States. This reflects the general principle of linguistic equality among EU members.[8] All the language versions of EU laws are equally binding or equally authentic – the equal authenticity rule. This has been confirmed in ECJ case law (Case 283/81 *CILFIT* [1982] ECR 3415; Case C-236/97 *Skatteministeriet v Codan* [1998] ECR I-8679; and Joined Cases T-22/02 and T-23/02 *Sumitomo Chemical* [judgment delivered on 6 October 2005]).

Secondly, a well-established principle in interpreting EU law is that the different language versions must be given a uniform interpretation. In the case of divergence between the language versions, the provision in question must be interpreted by reference to the purpose and general scheme of the rules of which it forms part and Community law as a whole (Case 26/69 *Stauder v City of Ulm* [1969] ECR 419; Case 30/77 *Régina v Pierre Bouchereau* [1977] ECR 1999; *CILFIT*; Case 100/84 *Commission v United Kingdom* [1985] ECR 1169; Case C-372/88 *Milk Marketing Board v Cricket St Thomas Estate* [1990] ECR I-1345). Furthermore, it is also settled law that the interpretation of Community law involves a comparison of the different language versions; it should not be considered in isolation but, in cases of doubt, should be interpreted and applied in the light of the other official languages and in context (*CILFIT* and *Sumitomo* cases). In other words, ECJ case law seems to suggest that considerable emphasis has been given to uniform interpretation, the comparison of the different language versions and the paramount consideration of the object and purpose of the law when attempting to identify uniform meaning.

To illustrate, the case *Skatterministeriet v Codan* concerns the wording of Article 12(1)(a) of Directive 69/335 relating to the payment of tax on the transfer of shares. The court found that the wording of the Article is not identical in all the language versions. The Danish and German versions have the equivalent of the phrase 'stock exchange turnover taxes', but most of the other language versions, namely, the Greek, Spanish, French, Italian, Dutch, Portuguese and English versions, have the expression 'taxes on the transfer of securities'. The court held that the interpretation of a provision of Community law involves a comparison of the different language versions, and the need for a uniform interpretation of the language versions requires, in the case of divergence between them, that the provision in question be interpreted by reference to the purpose and general scheme of the relevant law. It thus follows both from a general principle of interpretation of Community law and from the purpose of the Directive that taxes are to be charged for the transfer of shares as indicated in the majority of the language versions.

To further illustrate, Case T-174/01 *Goulbourn v Office for Harmonisation in the Internal Market* [2003] ECR 789 involves the interpretation of the notion of 'genuine use' under Article 43(2) of Regulation No. 40/94 and Article 15(1) related to trade marks. The court stated that it is first necessary to effect a comparative analysis of the different language versions of the provisions. It found that the German (*ernsthafte Benutzung*), French (*usage sérieux*), Italian (*seriamente utilizzata*) and Portuguese (*utilizaçao séria*) versions state the requirement of 'serious use'. The English version (genuine use) has the same meaning. On the other hand, the Spanish version uses the expression 'actual use' (*uso efectivo*), which also corresponds to the wording of the recital in the preamble to Regulation No. 40/94 in the German, English, Spanish, French and Italian versions. Lastly, the Dutch version places a slightly different emphasis, namely requiring 'normal use'. Accordingly, the court found that it is not possible to contrast 'genuine use' with 'real use'. It is by contrast necessary to define 'genuine use' by taking account of the different language versions of the relevant regulation on the one hand, and of the recital in the preamble to that regulation, on the other.

Another example of the court using different language versions in comparison to clarify or define meanings of words in dispute is found in Case C-1/97 *Birden v Stadtgemeinde Bremen* [1998] ECR I-7747. The case concerns the interpretation of Article 6(1) of Decision No. 1/80 related to the Association Agreement between the European Economic Community and Turkey. The court found that from a comparison of the language versions, the Dutch, Danish and Turkish versions use the same adjective 'legal' to describe both the labour force of a Member State and the employment pursued in that State. Although the English version does not use the same word in both respects ('duly registered' and 'legal employment') they are deemed to have the same meaning. The court also stated that the French (*appartenant au marché régulier de l'emploi d'un État membre* and *emploi régulier*) and Italian (*inserito nel regolare mercato del lavoro di uno Stato membro* and *regolare impiego*) versions use the word 'regular' twice. Finally, the German version (*der dem regulären Arbeitsmarkt eines Mitgliedstaats angehört* and *ordnungsgemässer Beschäftigung*) is less clear, in so far as it uses two different expressions, the first of which corresponds to 'regular' and the second more closely to 'legal'. However, the court said that these versions are clearly open to interpretation, but the term 'regular' can undoubtedly be understood as a synonym for 'legal' for the purposes of the uniform application of Community law.

The ECJ has also over the years ruled that words in Community law have their own independent meanings in Community law and they must be given a Community definition, taking account of all the language versions.

This means that reference may be made to the various versions of the relevant law in the official languages in order to achieve a harmonious interpretation, and the term should not have attributed to it a meaning deriving from domestic law where that would lead to disparate interpretations (Case C-498/03 *Kingscrest* [judgment delivered on 26 May 2005], see also Case C-358/97 *Commission v Ireland* [2000] ECR I-6301). In *CILFIT*, it was held that legal concepts do not necessarily have the same meaning in Community law and in the law of the various Member States. Even where the different language versions are entirely in accord with one another, Community law uses terminology which is peculiar to it. The court said that every provision of Community law must be placed in its context and interpreted in the light of the provisions of Community law as a whole, regard being had to the objectives thereof and to its state of evolution at the date on which the provision in question is to be applied.

Another issue in statutory interpretation is how to determine the meaning of wording that is open to several interpretations. One method adopted is that preference is to be given to the interpretation that ensures the effectiveness of the relevant law. In Case C-174/05 *Stichting Zuid-Hollandse Milieufederatie* [judgment delivered on 9 March, 2006], it involves the interpretation of Article 2(3) of Decision No. 2003/199 concerning the non-inclusion of 'aldicarb' in a relevant Council Directive and the withdrawal of authorisations for plant protection products containing this active substance. The action in the main proceedings was essentially due to the divergence between the different language versions of that provision. According to the Dutch version, the Member States concerned may grant authorisations to place plant protection products containing the active substance 'aldicarb' on the market whereas according to the other language versions of that provision, those Member States are only able to maintain such authorisations in force.

The court held that, firstly, according to settled case law, where a provision of Community law is open to several interpretations, preference must be given to the interpretation that ensures the provision retains its effectiveness and does not detract from its validity. Secondly, the need for a uniform interpretation of Community law makes it impossible for the text of a provision to be considered, in case of doubt, in isolation; on the contrary, it requires that it be interpreted in the light of the versions existing in the other official languages. Thus, the court ruled that to interpret the decision that allows Members States to issue new authorisations is both inconsistent with the general scheme and aims of the directive, and inconsistent with the other language versions, in particular, the German, English ('may maintain in force'), Polish and Slovak versions.

Lastly, the Court has also discussed the issue of the interpretation of international treaties. For instance, Case C-268/99 *Aldona Malgorzata Jany* [2001] ECR I-8615 involves the interpretation of Article 44(4)(a)(i) of the Association Agreement between the Community and Poland and of Article 45(4)(a)(i) of the Association Agreement between the Community and the Czech Republic. The court stated that according to well-established case law, an international treaty must be interpreted not solely by reference to the terms in which it is worded but also in the light of its objectives. The court cited Article 31 of the Vienna Convention on the Law of Treaties, which stipulates that a treaty must be interpreted in good faith in accordance with the ordinary meaning to be given to its terms in their context and in the light of its object and purpose.

Separate from judicial interpretation, it may also be constructive to single out some of the ECJ cases with specific linguistic problems. They show the type and the range of the linguistic issues involved in litigation, including lexical divergence, syntactical and grammatical variance and others.

In Case C-280/04 *Jyske Finans v Skatteministeriet* [judgment delivered on 8 December 2005], one provision of an EU law has the wording that the taxable dealer is defined 'as a taxable person who, in the course of his economic activity, purchases or acquires for the purposes of his undertaking, or imports with a view to resale second-hand goods'. Many versions of the relevant directive, including the English language version, could suggest that the expression 'with a view to resale' only applies to the verb 'import', which appears immediately before it. Thus, there are two possible interpretations: 'with a view' to qualify 'imports' only, or to qualify both 'purchases or acquires for the purposes of his undertaking' and 'imports'.

In Case C-275/02 *Engin Ayaz v Land Baden-Württemberg* [2004] ECR I-08765, the issue involved the use of a pronoun and the definite article. The German and Dutch versions of a law use 'his spouse and *the* children', but the English, Italian and French versions refer to the worker, his spouse and *their* children ('their descendants', *i loro discendenti* and *leurs descendants*). Similarly, in Case C-127/00 *Hässle AB v Rationpharm GmbH* [2003] ECR I-14781, the use of the indefinite article is found in the German, French, Italian and Dutch versions of a regulation while the English version and others use the definite article. In Case C-437/97 *Evangelischer Krankenhausverein Wien and Others v Abgabenberufungskommission Wien and Others* [2000] ECR I-1157, the German, Spanish, French, Italian and Portuguese versions of the law use the word 'or' indicating an alternative while the English, Danish, Finnish, Greek, Dutch and Swedish versions use 'and' with the meaning of being accumulative rather than alternative. In Case C-265/03 *Igor Simutenkov v*

Ministerio de Educación y Cultura and Real Federación Española de Fútbol [judgment delivered on 12 April 2005], an issue was raised as to the use of 'shall ensure' and its equivalent to impose an obligation. In Case C-257/00 *Givane and Others* [2003] ECR I-345, a question was the interpretation of the phrase 'for at least two years' in English and other languages including Spanish, Danish, Greek, Dutch, Portuguese, Finnish and Swedish in contrast to the French *'depuis au moins 2 anees'*, German *'seit mindestens Jahren'* and Italian *'da almeno due anni'*. A difference was said to lie in the two-year period of a continuous duration in the latter and the vaguer and more neutral meaning in the former.

These examples from the ECJ illustrate the diverse type and range of linguistic issues arising in multilingual laws that may concern translation and the translator. It must be noted that given the large volume of translated legal texts and the large number of languages involved in the EU, it is pleasantly surprising that very few serious translation errors have been detected in litigation.

The Use of Translation Technology for Translating Multilingual Texts

With the increasing demand for the translation of multilingual texts in multilateral organisations and transnational corporations, CAT tools and technology have started to make an impact. They are able to provide certain benefits to the translation of legal and other texts in multilingual environments such as cost effectiveness, efficiency and improved quality (see McCallum 2004).

CAT today consists of a number of tools that allow the translator to access and use previously translated materials through translation memories, access various general and tailor-made terminology databases and electronic dictionaries, and access full text documentation databases. Machine translation and other translation support technologies are also available. These tools seem to be particularly helpful for the translation of LSP texts and the translation of repetitive and evolutive documents. Repetitive documents refer to those that are repetitive within themselves, containing sentences or phrases that reappear within the same text and those that are drawn up at frequent intervals and are based on standard models (Tucker 2003: 80). Evolutive texts are those that evolve over time and go through several stages of drafting and translation before a final version is produced, for instance, the legislative documents produced by the European Parliament (Tucker 2003: 80). Another important consideration for the translation of multilingual texts is the maintenance of textual and terminological consistency, both over time and among teams of translators. CAT is also useful in this regard.

Major CAT tools used at the UN and EC

The major CAT tools in use today at the UN and the EC include terminology databases and tools, translation memory technology, documentation databases and resources, machine translation systems and voice recognition technology.

Translation memories

Currently, the translation memory systems being trialled at the UN are MultiTrans and TRADOS. MultiTrans is a translation support and language management system, a second-generation CAT tool. It integrates a full text multilingual corpus and has a comprehensive terminology management infrastructure. It adopts a document repository approach. It can spot text that has been translated before and shows what it has found in context: the entire document in which any match was found in both the original and translated versions. MultiTrans allows the user to create reference pools of legacy of multilingual content, to access terminology and previous translations in their usage and style context, recycle translations of any length, not just whole sentences, to extract, create and manage terminology, and to share and manage multilingual assets across the organisation. The MultiTrans system consists of an indexed multilingual reference corpus, tools to build and search the corpus, terminology extraction technology, terminology management tools, and an integrated translation workbench.

TRADOS is another system being used at the UN. Its translation memory software can build a linguistic knowledgebase of translation and identifies reusable content. It looks for whole sentences that have been translated before and automatically proposes re-use suggestions and translation equivalents. It can view sentences in content so that it can distinguish between the different ways a word, phrase or sentence can be used.

In the translation department of the EC, – the DGT (see the resources at http://ec.europa.eu/translation/reading/articles/tools_and_workflow_en.htm#cat, see also Tucker 2003), – its CAT system consists of, among others, a translator workbench and a local translation memory that can store and retrieve documents in all the EC official languages. According to the DGT, all the EC translators have the facilities to use the system, and many regard it as a valuable working tool, since a high percentage of the preparatory texts drafted in the EC are based on previous texts or existing legislation. Re-using already translated words or passages saves considerable amounts of time and makes for consistent terminology, which is vitally important in legislative texts (see DGT 2005c).

The translation memory systems used in the EC include both central and local memories. At the central level, the Euramis Central Translation

Memory, is a huge memory to provide facilities for data sharing among DGT staff. It is a database layer that is accessed to retrieve or store data processed locally with Translator's Workbench and/or Word as a front end. At present, the Euramis central memory contains more than 88 million translation units in all official EU languages. According to the DGT, more than 1,700,000 pages were retrieved from the *Euramis* central memory in 2003.[9]

Of the local translation memory systems, TRADOS Translator's Workbench (TWB) is an integrated translation support tool used in the EC adapted to meet the European institutions' specific needs. It gives translators access to all language, terminology and phraseology resources from a local translation memory: when the user enters an original text, similar or identical segments from previously translated texts will present themselves as suggestions.

According to the DGT (2005b), TWB has defined a given set of attributes (translator, document number, year and client) to allow for labelling of segments in the translation memory. TWB is particularly useful since a high proportion of legislative and preparatory documents are based on previous texts or existing legislation. It is mainly used as a front end for the local and interactive processing of data that is retrieved from, or is to be saved in, the *Euramis* central translation memory.

Terminological tools

There are various types of terminology tools and databases used at the UN and the EC. For the UN, the United Nations Multilingual Terminology Database – UNTERM (http://unterm.un.org) provides UN nomenclature and special terms in all six official UN languages. The database is mainly intended for use by the language and editorial staff of the UN to ensure consistent translation of common terms and phrases used within the organisation. It has about 70,000 entries in six languages and daily updates.

Similarly, in the EC, the main terminology tools include Eurodicautom (*Europe dictionnaire automatisé*, http://europa.eu.int/eurodicautom), the EC's central terminology database maintained by the DGT. Eurodicautom is a multilingual dictionary that covers all areas of the EC's activities. Access is free of charge. It contains words and expressions (scientific, technical, administrative and economic), acronyms and abbreviations and definitions. Eurodicautom is believed to be the largest terminology database in the world. It operates in all the EU's official languages and Latin. The Eurodicautom system, first developed in the 1970s, covers a broad spectrum of human knowledge and is particularly rich in technical and specialised terminology related to EU policy. It processes terminological data and equivalents in EU official languages. By the beginning of 2006, there are more than 7 million entries in the base, including 400,000 abbreviations, presented in some 1.5 million files including more than 2 million definitions. The terminology in the base covers the legal, political and technical fields in which the EC works and keeps pace with technological developments.

Eurodicautom will soon be replaced by a new inter-institutional multilingual terminology database system – the Inter-Agency Terminology Exchange (IATE). IATE is to provide a single web-based infrastructure and management system for all EU terminology. When it is implemented, it will consist of a central terminology database, a web server for remote consultation, data inputting and editing, and an application server for the management of access rights, data administration, validation workflow and messaging.

The EC also has an on-line multilingual Glossary of EU Terms (http://www.europa.eu.int/scadplus/glossary/index_en.htm), which contains some 220 terms relating to European integration and the institutions and activities of the EU. It is updated regularly. The definitions in the glossary explain how the individual terms have evolved and provide references to the EU treaties.

Documentation databases and resources

One documentation database is the UN Official Document System (ODS) (http://ods.un.org). This is a multilingual database of UN documents with full text search in six UN official languages. It covers all types of official United Nations documentation, beginning in 1993. Older UN documents are being added to the system. ODS also provides access to the resolutions of the General Assembly, Security Council, Economic and Social Council and the Trusteeship Council from 1946 onwards. This is also accessible by the public via http://documents.un.org.

Another useful and law-related database is the UNTS database (http://untreaty.un.org). Apart from the printed volumes of the UNTS, the UNTS database is an on-line storage and retrieval system for the international instruments published in the UNTS. The site also contains the full text of treaties deposited with the Secretary-General but not yet published in the UNTS. The UNTS database contains the texts of over 50,000 bilateral and multilateral treaties and subsequent treaty actions in their authentic languages, along with a translation into English and French.

For the EU, CELEX (http://www.europa.eu.int/celex) is a source of complete and authoritative information in EU law, and gives access to a broad multilingual range of legal instruments: the founding treaties, binding and non-binding secondary legislation, opinions and resolutions by EU institutions and bodies, and the case law of the ECJ. But it has stopped updating and has been merged with EUR-Lex.

EUR-Lex (http://www.eur-lex.europa.eu) is a free public resource tool. It is the result of merging the EUR-Lex site with the CELEX database to provide the biggest documentary holdings existing on EU law. It contains the full texts in EU official languages of the treaties, secondary legislation and preparatory acts in all official EU languages, as well as national implementing measures and case law of the ECJ. It offers extensive search facilities.

The DGT of the EC also has a free on-line CCVista Translation Database (http://ccvista.taiex.be), which contains translations of the legal acts of the EU in all its official languages.

Machine translation and voice recognition system

Machine translation, generally speaking, is not widely used, but in the EC, machine translation has been developed and used since 1976. Systran (an acronym for 'System Translation') is the multilingual machine translation system used in the EC. It has been adapted to the EC's own needs. It uses dictionaries and linguistic programs that enable it to translate a document automatically from one language into another. Its main use is to produce an initial translation to be human edited. Eighteen EU language pairs are currently available. The total machine translation production in the EC was 696,347 pages in 2004, of which DGT requested 181,060 pages. Machine translation in the EC is used both as a genuine translation aid and as an administrative support tool.

In recent years, voice recognition technology has been developed for translation purposes. The widely used system is Dragon Naturally Speaking, used both in the Commission and the UN. It is an application that allows the user to dictate text directly onto the computer in a natural way, with a fairly high degree of accuracy and efficiency. It is available in German, Spanish, English, French, Italian, Dutch and other European language, and also in Chinese.

Notes

1   Case C-428/02 *Fonden Marselisborg Lystbådehavn v Skatteministeriet* [judgment delivered on 3 March, 2005]. All the ECJ decisions cited here can be found at http://curia.europa.eu. In the citations of some of the more recent cases, the

European Court Reports (ECR) page numbers are not yet available, and the paragraph numbers of the cases cited are omitted.

2 Article 13B(b)(2) of the Sixth Directive 77/388.

3 For discussions of the sources of international law, see Henkin *et al.* (1993), Malanczuk (1997), Janis (2003) and Schachter (1991).

4 Regarding the linguistic regime of the ECJ (the official name of the court is the Court of Justice of the European Communities, CJEC), cases may be brought before the court in any of the official languages, and all documents have to be translated into French, which is the internal working language of the court. The court's judgments and orders are translated into the language in which the case was brought and will become the sole authentic version. They are also translated into all the other languages for information. In addition, the opinions of the Advocates General, which they draft in their own language, have to be translated too (see Wagner *et al.* 2002: 54). The ECJ has its own interpreter and translation services, which are composed of lawyer-linguists and legal revisers. The judges deliberate without interpreters and in a common language, which traditionally has been French. See ECJ website at: http://curia.europa.eu.

5 For the history of multilingualism in international law, see Tabory (1980).

6 According to Article 249 of the Treaty Establishing the European Community:

> A *regulation* shall have general application. It shall be binding in its entirety and directly applicable in all Member States.
> A *directive* shall be binding, as to the result to be achieved, upon each Member State to which it is addressed, but shall leave to the national authorities the choice of form and methods.
> A *decision* shall be binding in its entirety upon those to whom it is addressed. *Recommendations* and *opinions* shall have no binding force. (Italics added)

The proposed European Constitution provides for a simpler typology of Community instruments: legislative instruments (European laws and framework laws), non-legislative instruments (regulations and decisions), non-mandatory instruments (opinions and recommendations), and *sui generis* documents of guidelines and conclusions of the European Council.

7 The Legal Service of the European Commission has a small number of lawyer-linguists who have both law and language degrees.

8 For a comparison between the EU and English Common Law approach to legislative interpretation, see McLeod (2004). For criticisms of the ECJ's approach to linguistic equality, see Petra Braselmann (1992), *Der Richter als Linguist. Linguistische Überlegungen zu Sprachproblemen in Urteilen des Europäischen Gerichtshofes* (The Judge as Linguist: Linguistic Consideration of Language Problems in Judgments from the European Court of Justice), where she attacked the idea of linguistic equality within the EU system and the role of the interpreting judge, cited in Engberg (2004).

9 For discussion of EURAMIS, see Blatt (1998) and Leick (1998).

List of Cases

Bibliography

Adler, Mark, 1990, *Clarity for Lawyers*, London, Law Society Publication.

Aitken, J.K. and Butter, Peter, 2004, *Piesse – The Elements of Drafting*, 10th edition, Sydney, Lawbook Co.

Allard, France, undated, 'The Supreme Court of Canada and its Impact on the Expression of Bijuralism', http://canada.justice.gc.ca/en/dept/pub/hfl/fasc3/fascicule_3(a)_eng.pdf

Alston, William P., 1964, *Philosophy of Language*, Englewood Cliffs, NJ, Prentice-Hall.

Aprill, E.P., 1998, 'The Law of the Word: Dictionary Shopping in the Supreme Court', *Arizona State Law Journal*, 30: 275–336.

Asprey, Michèle M., 2003, *Plain Language for Lawyers*, 3rd edition, Sydney, The Federation Press.

Athanassiou, Phoebus, 2006, 'The Application of Multilingualism in the European Union Context', *Legal Working Paper Series*, Frankfurt am Main, European Central Bank.

Austin, John L., 1832/1995, *The Province of Jurisprudence Determined*, edited by W. Rumble, Cambridge, Cambridge University Press.

Austin, John L., 1962, *How to Do Things With Words*, Cambridge, MA, Harvard University Press.

Austin, John L., 1979, *Philosophical Papers*, 3rd edition, edited by J.O. Urmson and G.J. Warnock, Oxford, Clarendon Press.

Azar, Moshe, 2006, 'Transforming Ambiguity into Vagueness in Legal Interpretation', in Anne Wagner, Wouter Weiner and Deborah Cao (eds), *Interpretation, Law and the Construction of Meaning*, Berlin/New York, Springer, 121–137.

Bach, Kent and Hamish, Robert M., 1979, *Linguistic Communication and Speech Acts*, Cambridge, MA, The MIT Press.

Bachman, Lyle, F., 1990, *Fundamental Considerations in Language Testing*, New York, Oxford University Press.

Bachman, Lyle, F. and Palmer, A.S., 1996, *Language Testing in Practice*, Oxford, Oxford University Press.

Baker, Mona, Francis, Gill and Tongnini-Bonelli, Elena (eds), 1993, *Text and Technology: In Honour of John Sinclaire*, Amsterdam, John Benjamins.

Bassnett, Susan, 1991, *Translation Studies*, London, Routledge.

Bassnett, Susan, and Lefevere, André (eds), 1990, *Translation, History and Culture*, London/New York, Pinter Publishers.

Bassnett, Susan, and Lefevere, André, 1998, *Constructing Cultures: Essays on Literary Translation*, Clevedon, Multilingual Matters.

Beaupré, Michael, 1986, *Interpreting Bilingual Legislation*, Toronto, Carswell.

Bell, John, 2001, *French Legal Cultures*, London, Butterworths.

Bell, John, Byron, Sophie and Whittaker, Simon, 1998, *Principles of French Law*, Oxford, Oxford University Press.

Bell, Roger T., 1987, 'Translation Theory: Where Are We Going?', *Meta*, 32(4): 403–415.

Bell, Roger T., 1991, *Translation and Translating: Theory and Practice*, London/New York, Longman.

Benjamin, Walter, 1923/2000, 'The Task of the Translator', in Lawrence Venuti (ed.), 2000, *The Translation Studies Reader*, London/New York, Routledge, 15–25.

Bennion, F.A.R., 2002, *Statutory Interpretation: A Code*, London, Butterworths.

Benson, R.W., 1984–1985, 'The End of Legalese: The Game is Over', *New York University Review of Law and Social Change*, 13(3): 519–573.

Beveridge, Barbara J., undated, 'Legal English – How it Developed and Why it is Not Appropriate for International Commercial Contracts', http://www.tradulex. org

Bhatia, Vijay K., 1983a, 'Simplification v. Easification: The Case of Legal Texts', *Journal of Applied Linguistics*, 4(1): 42–54.

Bhatia, Vijay K., 1983b, *Applied Discourse Analysis of English Legislative Writing*, Birmingham, University of Aston.

Bhatia, Vijay K., 1987, 'Language of the Law', *Language Teaching*, 20(3): 227–234.

Bhatia, Vijay K. 1993, *Analysing Genre: Language Use in Professional Settings*, London, Longman.

Bhatia, Vijay K., 1997, 'Translating Legal Genres', in Anna Trosborg (ed.), *Text Typology and Translation*, Amsterdam, John Benjamins, 203–216.

Bhatia, Vijay K., 2000, 'Genres in Conflict', in Anna Trosborg (ed.), *Analysing Professional Genres*, Amsterdam, John Benjamins, 147–162.

Bhatia, Vijay K., 2001, 'Legal Discourse Across Linguistic, Cultural, Socio-Political and Legal Contexts', *Proceedings of the Conference on Law and Language: Prospect and Retrospect*, Rovaniemi, The University of Lapland.

Bhartia, Vijay K., Engberg, Jan, Gotti, Maurizio and Heller, Dorothee (eds), 2005, *Vagueness in Normative Texts*, Berlin, Peter Lang.

Biggerstaff, Knight, 1961, *The Earliest Modern Government Schools in China*, Ithaca, NY, Cornell University Press.

Bix, Brian H. (ed.), 1993, *Law, Language and Legal Determinacy*, Oxford, Clarendon Press.

Bix, Brian H., 2003, 'Can Theories of Meaning and Reference Solve the Problem of Legal Determinacy?' *Ratio Juris*, 16(3): 281–295.

Black, Max, 1949/1970, *Language and Philosophy: Studies in Method*, Ithaca, NY/London, Cornell University Press.

Blatt, Achim, 1998,'EURAMIS Alignment and Translation Memory Technology', http://europa.eu.int/comm/translation/reading/articles/tools_and_workflow _en.htm

Bobbio, N., 1950, 'Scienza del diritto e analisi del linguaggio' (Legal Science and Linguistic Analysis), translated by Teresa Chataway, *Rivista trimestrale di Diritto e Procedura Civile*, 2: 342–367.

Borja Albi, A., 1999, 'Judicial Translation in Spain at the Turn of the Millennium', *Perspectives: Studies in Transtology*, 7(2): 199–208.

Bowers, Frederick, 1989, *The Linguistic Aspects of Legislative Expression*, Vancouver, University of British Columbia.

Bowker, Lynne, 2002, *Computer-Aided Translation Technology*, Ottawa, University of Ottawa Press.

Buchin, Nichole and Seymour, Edward, 2003, 'Equivalences or Divergences in Legal Translation?', in Arturo Tosi (ed.), *Crossing Barriers and Bridging Cultures: The Challenges of Multilingual Translation for the European Union*, Clevedon, Multi-lingual Matters, 111–116.

Burke, Lucy, Crowley, Tony and Girvin, Alan (eds), 2000, *The Routledge Language and Cultural Theory Reader*, London/New York, Routledge.

Campbell, Stuart, 1998, *Translating into the Second Language*, New York, Longman.

Cao, Deborah, 1996a, 'Towards A Model of Translation Proficiency', *Target*, 8(2): 325–340.

Cao, Deborah, 1996b, 'On Translational Language Competence', *Babel*, 42(4): 231–238.

Cao, Deborah, 1997, 'Consideration in Translating Chinese/English Contracts', *Meta*, 42(4): 661–669.

Cao, Deborah, 1998, 'The Illocutionary Act in Translating Chinese Legislation', *Babel*, 44(3): 244–253.

Cao, Deborah, 1999, ' "Ought to" As a Chinese Legal Performative?', *International Journal for the Semiotics of Law*, 12(2): 153–169.

Cao, Deborah, 2001, '*Fazhi* vs/and/or Rule of Law: A Semiotic Venture Into Chinese Law', *International Journal for the Semiotics of Law*, 14(3): 223–247.

Cao, Deborah, 2002, 'Finding the Elusive Equivalents in Chinese/English Legal Translation', *Babel*, 48(4): 330–341.

Cao, Deborah, 2004, *Chinese Law: A Language Perspective*, Aldershot, Ashgate.

Cao, Deborah, 2006a, 'Key Words in Chinese Law', in Anne Wagner and William Pencak (eds), *Images in Law*, Aldershot, Ashgate, 35–50.

Cao, Deborah, 2006b, 'The Right to an Interpreter and the Right Interpreter', *Translation Watch Quarterly*, 2 (4): 7–29.

Cao, Deborah, 2006c, 'Legal Speech Act as Intersubjective Communicative Action', in Anne Wagner, Wouter Weiner and Deborah Cao (eds), *Interpretation, Law and the Construction of Meaning*, Berlin/New York, Springer, 65–82.

Cao, Deborah, 2007, 'Inter-lingual Uncertainty in Bilingual and Mulitilingual Law', *Journal of Pragmatics*, 39: 69–83.

Cao, Deborah and Zhao, Xingmin, 2006, *Lianheguo wenjian fanyi (Translation at the United Nations)*, Beijing, China Translation and Publishing Corporation.

Cao, Deborah, Wagner, Anne and Weiner, Wouter (eds), 2006, *Interpretation, Law and the Construction of Meaning*, Berlin/New York, Springer.

Carballa, Pablo de Torres, 1988, 'Trends in Legal Translation: The Focusing of Legal Translation Through Comparative Studies', in *Translation – Our Future: Proceedings of the XIth World Congress of FIT*, Maastricht, Euroterm, 431–437.

Carroll, John Bissell, 1964, *Language and Thought*, Englewood Cliffs, NJ, Prentice-Hall Inc.

Carter, J.W. and Harland, D.J., 1993, *Cases and Materials on Contract Law in Australia*, Sydney, Butterworths.

Catford, J.C., 1965, *A Linguistic Theory of Translation: An Essay in Applied Linguistics*, London, Oxford University Press.

Caton, Charles (ed.), 1963, *Philosophy and Ordinary Language*, London, University of Illinois Press.

CCH Macquarie Dictionary of Law, 1993, Sydney, CCH Australia.

Certoma, G. Leroy, 1985, *The Italian Legal System*, London, Butterworths.

Chesterman, Andrew, 1997, *Memes of Translation*, Amsterdam, John Benjamins.

Child, Barbara, 1992, *Drafting Legal Documents: Principles and Practices*, St Paul, MN, West Publishing Co.

Chomsky, N., 1964, *Aspects of the Theory of Syntax*, Cambridge, MA, The MIT Press.

Christie, George C., 1963–1964, 'Vagueness and Legal Language', *Minnesota Law Review*, 48: 885–911.

Cooke, Michael, 1995, 'Understood by All Concerned?: Anglo-Aboriginal Legal Translation', in Marshall Morris (ed.), *Translation and the Law*, Amsterdam, John Benjamins, 37–66.

Correia, Renato da Costa, 2003, 'Translation of EU Legal Texts', in Arturo Tosi (ed.), *Crossing Barriers and Bridging Cultures: The Challenges of Multilingual Translation for the European Union*, Clevedon, Multilingual Matters, 21–37.

Côté, Pierre-André, 2004, 'Bilingual Interpretation of Enactments in Canada: Principles v Practice', *Brooklyn Journal of International Law*, 29(3): 1067–1084.

Cross, Rupert, Bell, John and Engle, George, 1995, *Cross – Statutory Interpretation*, London, Butterworths.

Crystal, David and Davy, D., 1969, *Investigating English Style*, London, Longman.

Cunningham, Clarke D. and Fillmore, C.J., 1995, 'Using Common Sense: A Linguistic Perspective on Judicial Interpretation of "Use of a Firearm"', *Washington University Law Quarterly*, 73: 1125–1214.

Cutts, Martin, 2001, 'Clarifying Eurolaw', paper to the European Law Conference, Stockholm, June 2001.

Cutts, Martin, 2004, *The Oxford Guide to Plain English*, Oxford, Oxford University Press.

Dadomo, Christian and Farran, Susan, 1996, *The French Legal System*, 2nd edition, London, Sweet & Maxwell.

Dale, William, 1977, *Legislative Drafting: A New Approach*, London, Butterworths.

Danet, Brenda, 1980, 'Language in the Legal Process', *Law and Society*, 14(3): 447–563.

David, René and Brierley, John, 1985, *Major Legal Systems in the World Today*, London, Stevens.

De Cruz, Peter, 1999, *Comparative Law in a Changing World*, London, Cavendish Publishing.

De Groot, G.R. 1988, 'Problems of Legal Translation From the Point of View of a Comparative Lawyer', *XIth World Congress of FIT Proceedings: Translation – Our Future*, Maastricht, Euroterm, 407–421.

Delisle, Jean, 1988, *Translation: An Interpretative Approach*, Ottawa, University of Ottawa Press.

Dessemontet, F. and Ansay, T. (eds), 1995, *Introduction to Swiss Law*, The Hague, Kluwer Law International.

De Vattel, E., 1863, *The Law of Nations*, Philadelphia, T. & J.W. Johnsen.

De Vries, Henry P., 1962, 'Choice of Language in International Contracts', in Willis L.M. Reese (ed.), *International Contracts: Choice of Law and Language*, New York, Oceana Publications, 14–22.

De Vries, Henry P., 1969, *Foreign Law and The American Lawyer: An Introduction to Civil Law Method and Language*, New York, Parker School of Foreign and Comparative Law, Columbia University.

Dick, Robert C., 1985, *Legal Drafting*, Toronto, Carswell.

Directorate-General for Translation of the European Commission, 2005a, *Translating for a Multilingual Community*, Brussels, European Commission.

Directorate-General for Translation of the European Commission, 2005b, *Translation Tools and Workflow*, Brussels, European Commission.

Directorate-General for Translation of the European Commission, 2005c, *English Style Guide: A Handbook for Authors and Translators in the European Commission*, http://europa.eu.int/comm/translation/writing/style_guides/english/style_guide_en.pdf

Dodova, L., 1989, 'A Translator Looks at English Law', *Statute Law Review*, 10: 69–78.

Domínguez, Pedro J. Chamizo and Nerlich, Brigitte, 2002, 'False Friends: Their Origin and Semantics in Some Selected Languages', *Journal of Pragmatics*, 34: 1833–1849.

Driedger, Elmer A., 1976, *The Composition of Legislation/Legislative Forms and Precedents*, Ottawa, Department of Justice.

Driedger, Elmer A., 1982, 'Legislative Drafting Style: Civil Law vs Common Law', in Jean-Claude Gémar (ed.), *Langage du droit et traduction (Language of Law and Translation)*, Montreal, Linguatech/Conseil de la langue francaise, 61–82.

Driedger, Elmer A., 1983, *Construction of Statutes*, 2nd edition, Totonto, Butterworths.

Dummett, Michael, 1993, *The Seas of Language*, Oxford, Clarendon Press.

Duranti, Alessandro and Goodwin, Charles (eds), 1992, *Rethinking Context: Language as an Interactive Phenomenon*, Cambridge, Cambridge University Press.

Duranti, Alessandro, 1997, *Linguistic Anthropology*, Cambridge, Cambridge University Press.

Eco, Umberto, 1976, *A Theory of Semiotics*, Bloomington, IN, Indiana University Press.

Eco, Umberto, 1979, *The Role of the Reader*, Bloomington, IN, Indiana University Press.

Eco, Umberto, 1984, *Semiotics and the Philosophy of Language*, London, Macmillan.

Eco, Umberto, 1992, *Interpretation and Overinterpretation*, with Umberto Eco, Richard Rorty, Jonathan Culler and Christine Brooke-Rose, edited by Stefan Collini, Cambridge, Cambridge University Press.

Eco, Umberto, 1996, *From Marco Polo to Leibniz: Stories of Intercultural Misunderstanding*, a lecture presented to the Italian Academy for Advanced Studies in America, 10 December 1996.

Eco, Umberto, 1997, *The Search for a Perfect Language*, translated by J. Fentress, London, Fontana.

Eco, Umberto, 2004, *Mouse or Rat: Translation as Negotiation*, London, Weidenfeld & Nicolson.

Edgington, Dorothy, 2001, 'The Philosophical Problem of Vagueness', *Legal Theory*, 7: 371–378.

Edwards, Alica Betsy, 1995, *The Practice of Court Interpreting*, Amsterdam/Philadelphia, John Benjamins.

Ehrmann, W., 1976, *Comparative Legal Cultures*, Englewood Cliffs, NJ, Prentice Hall.

Elliott, Catherine, Geirnaert, Carole and Houssais, Florence, 1998, *French Legal System and Legal Language: An Introduction in French*, London and New York, Longman.

Elon, Menachem, 1985, 'The Legal System of Jewish Law', *International Law and Politics*, 17: 221–243, reprinted in Martin P. Golding (ed.), 1994, *Jewish Law and Legal Theory*, Aldershot, Dartmouth, 21–44.

Empson, William, 1970, *Seven Types of Ambiguity*, 3rd edition, London, Chatto and Windus.

Endicott, Timothy, 2000, *Vagueness in Law*, Oxford, Oxford University Press.

Endicott, Timothy, 2002, 'Law and Language', *The Stanford Encyclopedia of Philosophy (Winter 2002 Edition)*, Edward N. Zalta (ed.), http://plato.stanford.edu/archives/win2002/entries/law-language.

Endicott, Timothy, 2004, 'Law is Necessarily Vague', *Legal Theory*, 7: 379–385.

Engberg, Jan, 2002, 'Legal Meaning Assumptions – What are the Consequences for Legal Interpretation and Legal Translation?' *International Journal for the Semiotics of Law*, 15(4): 375–388.

Engberg, Jan, 2004, 'Statutory Texts as Instances of Language(s): Consequences and Limitations on Interpretation', *Brooklyn Journal of International Law*, 29(3): 1135–1166.

European Communities, 2003, *Joint Practical Guide of the European Parliament, the Council and the Commission for Persons Involved in the Drafting of Legislation within the Community Institutions*, Luxembourg, Office for Official Publications of the European Communities.

Even-Zohar, I. 1997, 'The Making of Culture Repertoire and the Role of Transfer', *Target*, 9(2): 355–363.

Fassberg, Celia Wasserstein, 2003, 'Language and Style in a Mixed System', *Tulane Law Review*, 78: 151–173.

Flew, Antony (ed.), 1968, *Logic and Language*, Oxford, Basil Blackwell.

Foster, Nigel, 1993, *German Law and Legal System*, London, Blackstone Press Limited.

Frawley William (ed.), 1984, *Translation: Literary, Linguistic and Philosophical Perspectives*, Cranbury, NJ, Associated University Presses.

Freckmann, Anke and Wegerich, Thomas, 1999, *The German Legal System*, London, Sweet & Maxwell.

Freeman, Michael D.A., 1994, *Lloyd's Introduction to Jurisprudence*, 6th edition, London, Sweet & Maxwell.

Friedman, Lawrence M., 1975, *The Legal System: A Social Science Perspective*, New York, Russell Sage Foundation.

Fung, Spring Yuen-Ching, 1997, 'The Rise and Fall of the Proviso', *Statute Law Review*, 18(2): 104–112.

Gadamer, Hans-Georg, 1975, *Truth and Method*, New York, The Seabury Press, translated and edited by Garrett Barden and John Cumming, originally published in 1960 as *Wahrheit und Methode*, Tübingen.

Gadamer, Hans-Georg, 1976, *Philosophical Hermeneutics*, translated and edited by David E. Linge, Berkeley, CA, University of California Press.

Garre, Marianne, 1999, *Human Rights in Translation: Legal Concepts in Different Languages*, Copenhagen, Copenhagen Business School Press.

Garzone, G., 2000, 'Legal Translation and Functionalist Approaches: A Contradiction in Terms?' *ASTTI/ETI*, 395–414.

Geeroms, Sofie M.F., 2002, 'Comparative Law and Legal Translation: Why the Terms Cassation, Revision and Appeal Should not be Translated', *American Journal of Comparative Law*, 50(1): 210–228.

Geis, Michael L., 1995, 'The Meaning of Meaning in the Law', *Washington University Law Quarterly*, 73(3): 1125–1144.

Gémar, Jean-Claude (ed.), 1982, *Langage du droit et traduction (Language of Law and Translation)*, Montreal, Linguatech/Conseil de la langue francaise.

Gémar, Jean-Claude, 2002, 'Le *plus* et le *moins-disant* culturel du texte juridique: Langue, culture et équevalence', *Meta*, 47(2): 163–176.

Gervais, Marie-Claude and Séguin, Marie-France, undated, 'Some Thoughts on Bijuralism in Canada and the World', www.justice.gc.ca/en/dept/ pub/hfl/ fasc2/fascicule_2_eng.pdf

Getzler, Edwin, 1993, *Contemporary Translation Theories*, London, Routledge.

Gibbons, John, 1994, *Language and the Law*, London/New York, Longman.

Gifford, Donald, 1990, *Statutory Interpretation*, Sydney, The Law Book Company Ltd.

Gile, Daniel, 1995, *Basic Concepts and Models for Interpreter and Translator Training*, Amsterdam/Philadelphia, John Benjamins.

Goldstein, Tom and Lieberman, Jethro K., 2002, *The Lawyer's Guide to Writing Well*, Berkeley, CA, University of California Press.

Goodrich, Peter, 1987, *Legal Discourse: Studies in Linguistics, Rhetoric and Legal Analysis*, London, Macmillan.

Gorlée, Dinda L., 1994, *Semiotics and the Problem of Translation: With Special Reference to the Semiotics of Charles S. Peirce*, Amsterdam, Rodopi.

Gordon-Smith, D., 1989, 'The Drafting Process in the European Community', *Statute Law Review*, 10: 56–68.

Graham, Joseph F. (ed.), 1985, *Difference in Translation*, New York, Cornell University.

Greenlee, Douglas, 1973, *Peirce's Concept of Sign*, The Hague/Paris, Mouton.

Greenawalt, Kent, 2001, 'Vagueness and Judicial Responses to Legal Indeterminacy', *Legal Theory*, 7: 433–445.

Greig, D.W., 1970, *International Law*, London, Butterworths.

Guest, Stephen (ed.), 1996, *Positivism Today: Issues in Law and Society*, Aldershot, Dartmouth.

Gutt, Ernst-August, 1991, *Translation and Relevance: Cognition and Context*, London, Blackwell.

Habermas, Jürgen, 1998, *On the Pragmatics of Communication*, edited by Maeve Cooke, Cambridge, MA, The MIT Press.

Halliday, M.A.K., 1975, *Learning How to Mean: Explorations in the Development of Language*, London, Edward Arnold.

Halliday, M.A.K., 1979, *Language as Social Semiotic: The Social Interpretation of Language and Meaning*, London, Edward Arnold.

Halliday, M.A.K. and Hasan, R. 1985, *Language, Context and Text: Aspects of Language in a Social-Semiotic Perspective*, Melbourne, Deakin University.

Halliday, M. A. K., McIntosh, Angus and Strevens, Peter, 1965, *The Linguistic Sciences and Language Teaching*, London, Longmans.

Hammond, Deanna L., 1994, *Professional Issues for Translators and Interpreters*, Amsterdam, John Benjamins.

Harris, D.J., 2004, *Cases and Materials on International Law*, London, Sweet and Maxwell.

Hart, H.L.A., 1954, 'Definition and Theory in Jurisprudence', *The Law Quarterly Review*, 70: 37–60.

Hart, H.L.A., 1961/1994, *The Concept of Law*, 2nd edition, with a Postscript edited by Penelope A. Bulloch and Joseph Raz, Oxford, Clarendon Press.

Harvey, Malcolm, 2000, 'A Beginner's Course in Legal Translation: The Case of Culture-Bound Terms', *ASTTI/ETII*, 357–369.

Harvey, Malcolm, 2002, 'What's so Special About Legal Translation?' *Meta*, 47(2): 177–185.

Hatim, B. and Mason, I., 1989, *Discourse and the Translator*, London, Longman.

Henderson, Dan Fenno, 1980, 'Japanese Law in English: Reflections on Translation', *Journal of Japanese Studies*, 6(1): 117–154.

Henderson, Sandra, 1997, 'The Concept of Equivalence in Translation Studies: Much Ado About Something', *Target*, 9(2): 207–233.

Henkin, Louis, Crawford, Richard Pugh, Schachter, Oscar and Smit, Hans (eds), 1993, *International Law: Cases and Materials*, 3rd edition, St Paul, West Publishing Co.

Hill, Claire A., 2001, 'Why Contracts are Written "Legalese"', *Chicago-Kent Law Review*, 59: 75–81.

Hill, Claire A. and King, Christopher, 2004, 'How Do German Contracts do as Much with Fewer Words?', *Chicago-Kent Law Review*, 79: 889–926.

Hjort-Pedersen, Mette and Faber, Dorrit, 2001, 'Lexical Ambiguity and Legal Translation: A Discussion', *Multilingua: Journal of Cross-Cultural and Interlanguage Communication*, 20(4): 379–392.

Hoijer, Harry (ed.), 1954, *Language in Culture*, Chicago, University of Chicago Press.

Holmes, James S. (ed.), 1970, *The Nature of Translation: Essays on the Theory and Practice of Literary Translation*, The Hague, Mouton.

Holmes, O.W., 1881/1990, *The Common Law*, Boston, Little, Brown & Company.

Holmes, O.W., 1899, 'The Theory of Legal Interpretation', 12 *Harvard Law Review*, 12: 417–420.

Hönig, Hans G., 1998, 'Positions, Power and Practice: Functionalist Approaches and Translation Quality Assessment', in Christina Schäffner (ed.), *Translation and Quality*, Clevedon, Multilingual Matters, 6–34.

House, Juliane, 1977, *A Model for Translation Quality Assessment*, Tübingen, TBL Verlag Gunter Narr.

House, Juliane, and Blum-Kulka, Shoshana (eds), 1986, *Interlingual and Intercultural Communication, Discourse and Cognition in Translation and Second Language Acquisition Studies*, Tübingen, Verlag Gunter Narr.

Hunt, Brian, 2002, 'Plain Language in Legislative Drafting: Is it Really the Answer?', *Statute Law Review*, 23(1): 24–46.

Huntington, Robert, 1991, 'European Unity and the Tower of Babel', *Boston University International Law Journal*, 9: 321–346.

Hymes, Dell, 1974, *Foundations in Sociolinguistics: An Ethnographic Approach*, Philadelphia, University of Pennsylvania Press.

Ingram, David E. and Elias, G.C., 1974, 'Bilingual Education and Reading', *RECL Journal*, V(1): 64–76.

Ingram, David E. and Wylie, Elaine, 1991, 'Developing Proficiency Scales for Communicative Assessment', *Language & Language Education*, 1: 31–60.

Innis, Robert E., 1985, *Semiotics: An Introductory Anthology*, London, Hutchinson.

Jackson, Bernard S., 1985, *Semiotics and Legal Theory*, London, Routledge.

Jackson, Bernard S., 1988, *Law, Fact and Narrative Coherence*, Merseyside, Deborah Charles Publications.

Jackson, Bernard S., 1995, *Making Sense in Law: Linguistic, Psychological and Semiotic Perspectives*, Liverpool, Deborah Charles Publications.

Jackson, Bernard S., 1996, *Making Sense in Jurisprudence*, Liverpool, Deborah Charles Publications.

Jakobson, Roman, 1960, 'Closing Statement: Linguistics and Poetics', in Thomas A. Sebeok (ed.), *Style in Language*, Cambridge, MA, MIT Press, 350–377.

Jakobson, Roman, 1971, 'On Linguistic Aspects of Translation', in Roman Jakobson (ed.), *Selected Writings (Volume 2): Word and Language*, The Hague, Mouton, 260–266.

Janis, Mark W., 2003, *An Introduction to International Law*, New York, Aspen Publishers.

Jenkins, Iredell, 1980, *Social Order and the Limits of Law: A Theoretical Essay*, Princeton, NJ, Princeton University Press.

Jespersen, Otto, 1964, *Language: Its Nature, Development and Origin*, London, Allen & Unwin.

Jori, Mario, 1994, 'Legal Performative', in R.E. Asher and J.M.Y. Simpson (eds), *The Encyclopedia of Language and Linguistics, Volume 4*, Oxford, Pergamon Press, 2092–2097.

Joseph, John E., 1995, 'Indeterminacy, Translation and the Law', in Marshall Morris (ed.), *Translation and the Law*, Amsterdam, John Benjamins, 13–36.

Keith, H. and Mason, I. (eds) 1987, *Translation in the Modern Languages Degree*, London, CLT.

Kelsen, Hans, 1967, *Pure Theory of Law*, Berkeley, CA, University of California Press.

Kevelson, Roberta, 1996, *Spaces and Significations*, New York, Peter Lang.

Kjaer, Anne Lise, 2004, 'A Common Legal Language in Europe?', in Mark Van Hoecke (ed.), *Epistemology and Methodology of Comparative Law*, Oxford and Portland, Hart Publishing, 377–398.

Kögler, Hans Herbert, 1996, *The Power of Dialogue: Critical Hermeneutics after Gadamer and Foucault*, translated by Paul Hendrickson, Cambridge, MA, The MIT Press.

Koller, Werner, 1995, 'The Concept of Equivalence and the Object of Translation Studies', *Target*, 7(2): 191–222.

Komissarov, Vilen N., 1995, 'Intuition in Translation', *Target*, 7(2): 347–354.

Kooij, Jan G., 1971, *Ambiguity in Natural Language: An Investigation of Certain Problems in its Linguistic Description*, Amsterdam/London, North-Holland Publishing Company.

Kuiper, Koos, 1993, 'Dutch Loan-Words and Loan-Translations in Modern Chinese: An Example of Successful Sinification by Way of Japan', in Lloyd Haft (ed.), *Words From the West: Western Texts in Chinese Literary Context*, Leiden, CNWS Publications, 116–144.

Kurzon, Dennis, 1986, *It Is Hereby Performed . . . Explorations in Legal Speech Acts*, Amsterdam, John Benjamins.

Kurzon, Dennis, 1998, 'Language of the Law and Legal Language', in Lauren Christer and Marianne Nordman (eds), *Special Language: From Humans Thinking to Thinking Machines*, Clevedon, Multilingual Matters, 283–290.

Lackner, Michael, Amelung, Iwo and Kurtz, Joachim (eds), 2001, *New Terms for New Ideas: Western Knowledge and Lexical Change in Late Imperial China*, Leiden/Boston/Koln, Brill.

Lane, A., 1982, 'Legal and Administrative Terminology and Translation Problems', in Jean-Claude Gémar (ed.), *Langage du droit et traduction*, Montreal, Conseil de la langue française, 219–232.

Langton, Nicola M., 2001, 'Can Pragmatic and Non-Lexical Epistemic Hedges Improve Student Legal Writing', *Proceedings of the Conference on Law and Language: Prospect and Retrospect*, Rovaniemi, The University of Lapland.

Larson, Mildred L., 1984, *Meaning-Based Translation: A Guide to Cross-Language Equivalence*, London, University Press of America.

Laster, Kathy and Taylor, Veronica L., 1994, *Interpreters and the Legal System*, Sydney, The Federation Press.

Lavallée, Louise, undated, 'Bijuralism in Supreme Court of Canada Judgments Since the Enactment of the Civil Code of Quebec', http://www.canada.justice.gc.ca/en/dept/pub/hfl/table.html

Lavoie, Judith, 2002, 'Le discours sur la traduction juridique au Canada', *Meta*, 47(2): 198–210.

Lavoie, Judith, 2003, 'Should One Be a Jurist or a Translator in Order to Translate the Law?', *Meta*, 48(3): 393–401.

Law Drafting Division of the Department of Justice of Hong Kong, 1998, *A Paper Discussing Cases Where the Two Language Texts of an Enactment Are Alleged to Be Different*, http://www.justice.gov.hk/inprmain.htm, 1–9.

Law Drafting Division of the Department of Justice of Hong Kong, 1999, 'The Common Law and the Chinese Language', *Hong Kong Lawyer*, February 1999, 39–43.

Law Drafting Division of the Department of Justice of Hong Kong, 2001, *Legislative Drafting in Hong Kong: Crystallisation in Definitive Form*, 2nd edition, http://www.justice.gov.hk

Leick, Jean-Marie, 1998, 'EURAMIS: the Ultimate Multilingual Blackbox?', http://europa.eu.int/comm/translation/reading/articles/tools_and_workflow_en.htm

Lerat, P., 2002, 'Vocabulaire juridique et schemas d'arguments juridiques', *Meta*, 47(2): 155–162.

Levert, Lionel A., undated. 'Harmonisation and Dissonance: Language and Law in Canada and Europe: The Cohabitation of Bilingualism and Bijuralism in Federal Legislation in Canada: Myth or Reality?', http://www.canada.justice. gc.ca/en/dept/pub/hfl/table.html

Levi, Judith and Walker, A. (eds), 1990, *Language in the Judicial Process*, New York, Plenum Press.

Lewis, G. and Slade, C. 2000, *Critical Communication*, Frenchs Forest, Prentice Hall.

Liang, Yuen-Li, 1953a, 'Methods and Procedures of the General Assembly for Dealing with Legal and Drafting Questions', *American Journal of International Law*, 47: 70–83.

Liang, Yuen-Li, 1953b, 'The Question of Revision of a Multilingual Treaty Text', *American Journal of International Law*, 47: 263–272.

López-Rodríguez, Ana M., 2004, 'Towards a European Civil Code without a Common European Legal Culture: The Link between Law, Language and Culture', *Brooklyn Journal of International Law*, 29(3): 1195–1220.

Lörscher, Wolfgang, 1991, *Translation Performance, Translation Process and Translation Strategies: A Psychological Investigation*, Tübingen, Verlag Gunter Narr.

Loubser, Max, 2003–2004, 'Linguistic Factors into the Mix: The South African Experience of Language and Law', *Tulane Law Review*, 78: 105–149.

Lu, Wenhui (ed.), 2004, *Falü fanyi: cong shijian chufa (Legal Translation in Practice)*, Beijing, Law Press.

McCallum, Bob, 2004, 'Translation Technology at the United Nations', *Localisation Reader: 2004–2005*, http://www.localisation.ie/resources/reader 27–30

McCary, Kevin P., 2001, 'The (Not-so) Universal Language of Law: Translation, Interpretation and Confusion in the NAFTA Chapter 19 Panel Process', *Proceedings of the Conference on Law and Language: Prospect and Retrospect*, Rovaniemi, The University of Lapland.

MacCormick, D. Neil and Summers, Robert S. (eds), 1991, *Interpreting Statutes: A Comparative Study*, Aldershot, Dartmouth,

Macdonald, Roderick A. 1997, 'Legal Bilingualism', *McGill Law Journal/Revue de droit de McGill*, 42: 119–167.

Macdonald, Roderick A., undated, 'Harmonising the Concepts and Vocabulary of Federal and Provincial Law: The Unique Situation of Quebec Civil Law', http://www.bijurilex.org/

McLeod, Ian, 2004, 'Literal and Purposive Techniques of Legislative Interpretation: Some European and English Common Law Perspectives', *Brooklyn Journal of International Law*, 29(3): 1109–1134.

MacMurray, John V.A. (ed.), 1973, *Treaties and Agreements with and Concerning China: 1894–1919*, Volume 1, New York, Fertig.

Madsen, Dorte, 1997a, 'A Model for Translation of Legal Texts', in Mary Snell-Hornby, Z. Jettmarov, and K. Kaindl (eds), *Translation as Intercultural Communication*, Amsterdam, John Benjamins, 291–299.

Madsen, Dorte, 1997b, 'Towards a Description of Communication in the Legal Universe: Translation of Legal Texts and the Skopos Theory', *Fachsprache – International Journal of LSP*, 19(3): 17–27.

Malanczuk, Peter, 1997, *Akehurst's Modern Introduction to International Law*, London, Routledge.

Maley, Yon, 1994, 'The Language of the Law', in John Gibbons (ed.), *Language and the Law*, New York, Longman, 11–50.

Marks, Margaret, 1997, 'Teaching German-English Legal Translation to German Students of Translation', http://accurapid.com/journal/02wkshop.htm

Mattei, Ugo, 1997, 'Three Patterns of Law: Taxonomy and Change in the World's Legal Systems', *The American Journal of Comparative Law*, 45: 5–44.

Mellinkoff, David, 1963, *The Language of the Law*, Boston, Little, Brown and Company.

Meredith, R.C., 1979, 'Some Notes on English Legal Translation', *Meta*, 24(1): 213–217.

Merryman, John Henry, Clark, Avid S. and Haley, John O., 1994, *The Civil Law Tradition: Europe, Latin America, and East Asia*, Charlottesville, VA, The Michie Company.

Mey, Jacob L. 2003, 'Context and (Dis)ambiguity: A Pragmatic View', *Journal of Pragmatics*, 35: 331–347.

Millett, Timothy, 1989, 'Rules of Interpretation of E.E.C. Legislation', *Statute Law Review*, 10: 163–182.

Montgomery, Scott L., 2000, *Science in Translation: Movements of Knowledge Through Cultures and Time*, Chicago/London, University of Chicago Press.

Moore, Michael S., 1981, 'The Semantics of Judging', *Southern California Law Review*, 55: 151–294.

Moore, Michael S., 1985, 'A Natural Law Theory of Interpretation', *Southern California Law Review*, 58: 277–398.

Morris, Marshall (ed.), 1995, *Translation and the Law*, Amsterdam, John Benjamins.

Morrison, Mary Jane, 1989, 'Excursions into the Nature of Legal Language', *Cleveland State Law Review*, 37: 271–336.

Nelson, L.D.M., 1987, 'The Drafting Committee of the Third United Nations Conference on the Law of the Sea: The Implications of Multilingual Texts', *British Yearbook of International Law*, 57: 169–199.

Neubert, Albrecht, 1985, *Text and Translation*, Leipzig, Verlag Enzyklopädie.

Neubert, Albrecht, 1991, 'Models of Translation', in Sonja Tirkonnen-Condit (ed.), *Empirical Research in Translation and Intercultural Studies*, Tübingen, Narr, 17–26.

Neubert, Albrecht, 1994, 'Translation Competence in Translation: A Complex Skill, How to Study and How to Teach it', in Mary Snell-Hornby, Franz Pochhacker and Claus Kaindl (eds), *Translation Studies: An Interdiscipline*, Amsterdam, John Benjamins, 411–420.

Neubert, Albert, 2000, 'Competence in Language, in Languages, and in Translation', in Christina Schäffner and Beverly Adab (eds), *Developing Translation Competence*, Amsterdam, John Benjamins, 3–19.

Neubert, Albrecht and Shreve, Gregory, 1992, *Translation as Text*, Kent, OH, Kent State University Press.

Newmark, Peter, 1981, *Approaches to Translation*, Oxford, Pergamon Press.

Newmark, Peter, 1988, *A Textbook of Translation*, London, Prentice Hall International (UK) Ltd.

Newman, Aryeh, 1980, *Mapping Translation Equivalence*, Leuven, ACCO.

Nicholas, Barry, 1992, *The French Law of Contract*, Oxford, Clarendon Press.

Nida, Eugene A., 1964, *Towards a Science of Translation*, Leiden, E.J. Brill.

Nida, Eugene A., 1975, *Language Structure and Translation*, Stanford, CA, Stanford University Press.

Nida, Eugene A., 1982, *Signs, Sense and Translation*, Pretoria, University of Pretoria.

Nida, Eugene A. and Reyburn, W.D., 1981, *Meaning Across Cultures*, Maryknoll, NY, Orbis Books.

Nida, Eugene A. and Taber, Charles R., 1969, *The Theory and Practice of Translation*, Leiden, E.J. Brill.

Nielsen, Sandro, 1994, *The Bilingual LSP Dictionary: Principles and Practice for Legal Language*, Tübingen, Gunter Narr.

Nord, Christiane, 1991, *Text Analysis in Translation: Theory, Methodology, and Didactive Application of a Model for Translation-Oriented Text Analysis*, Amsterdam / Atlanta, GA, Rodopi.

Nordland, Rasmus, 2002, 'Equality and Power in EU Language Work', *Perspectives: Studies in Translatology*, 10(1): 31–54.

Northcott, Jill, Brown, Gillian and Maclean, Joan, 2001, 'When Is a Potato Not an Agricultural Product?: EC Law Language and the Legislative Translator', *Proceedings of the Conference on Law and Language: Prospect and Retrospect*, Rovaniemi, The University of Lapland.

Noth, W., 1990, *Handbook of Semiotics*, Bloomington, IN/Indianapolis, IN, Indiana University Press.

Obenaus, Gerhard, 1995, 'The Legal Translator as Information Broker', in Marshall Morris (ed.), *Translation and the Law*, Amsterdam, John Benjamins, 247–262.

Ogden, C.K. and Richards, I.A., 1949, *The Meaning of Meaning: A Study of the Influence of Language upon Thought and of the Science of Symbolism*, London, Routledge & Kegan Paul Ltd.

O'Hagan, Minako and Ashworth, David, 2002, *Translation-Mediated Communication in a Digital World: Facing the Challenges of Globalisation and Localisation*, Clevedon, Multilingual Matters.

Olivecrona, Karl, 1971, *Law as Fact*, London, Stevens & Sons.

Osborn's Concise Law Dictionary, 1993, 8th edition, London, Sweet & Maxwell.

Palmer, R., 1969, *Hermeneutics: Interpretation Theory in Schleiermacher, Dilthey, Heidegger, and Gadamer*, Evanston, IL, Northwestern University Press.

Pearce, D.C. and Geddes, R.S. 2001, *Statutory Interpretation in Australia*, Sydney, Butterworths.

Peters, Ellen A., 1981, 'Reality and the Language of the Law', *The Yale Law Journal*, 90: 1193–1197.

Peirce, Charles Sanders, 1934/1979, *Collected Papers of Charles Sanders Peirce*, edited by Charles Hartshorne and Paul Weiss, 4th printing, Cambridge, MA, The Belknap Press of Harvard University Press.

Perrin, Geoffrey, 1988, '*Rechtsverordnung* and the Terminology of Legal Translation', *Lebende Sprachen*, 1: 17–18.

Perrin, Geoffrey, 1989, 'A Short German-English Glossary of the Juvenile Criminal Law', *Lebende Sprachen*, 2: 67–72.

Phillips, Alfred, 2003, *Lawyers' Language: How and Why Legal Language is Different*, London, Routledge.

Platts, Mark de Bretton, 1997, *Ways of Meaning: An Introduction to a Philosophy of Language*, Cambridge, MA, The MIT Press.

Poon, Emily Wai-Yee, 2002a, 'The Pitfalls of Linguistic Equivalence: The Challenge for Legal Translation', *Target*, 14(1): 75–106.

Poon, Emily Wai-Yee, 2002b, 'The Right of Abode Issues: Its Implication on Translation', *Meta*, 47(2): 211–224.

Posner, Richard, 2005, *The Problems of Jurisprudence*, Cambridge, MA, Harvard University Press.

Presas, Marisa, 2000, 'Bilingual Competence and Translation Competence', in Christina Schäffner and Beverly Adab (eds), *Developing Translation Competence*, Amsterdam, John Benjamins, 19–32.

Pym, Anthony, 1991, 'Definition of Translational Competence Applied to the Training of Translators', *Proceedings of the 12th World Congress of FIT*, Belgrade, 541–546.

Pym, Anthony, 1992, *Translation and Text Transfer: An Essay on the Principles of Intercultural Communication*, Frankfurt am Main, Peter Lang.

Pym, Anthony, 2000, 'The European Union and Its Future Languages: Questions for Language Policies and Translation Theories', *Across Languages and Cultures*, 1(1): 1–17.

Ramsfield, Jill J., 2005, *Culture to Culture: A Guide to U.S. Legal Writing*, Durham, Carolina Academic Press.

Rayar, Louise, 1988, 'Problems of Legal Translation From the Point of View of a Translator', *XIth World Congress of FIT Proceedings: Translation – Our Future*, Maastricht, Euroterm, 451–454.

Rayar, Louise, 1990, 'Law and Language: Postgraduate Training of Legal Translators', *Proceedings of the 12th World Congress of FIT*, Belgrade, 643–646.

Reed, David, 1993, 'Some Terminological Problems of Translating Common Law Concepts from English to French', in H. Sonneveld and K. Loening (eds), *Terminology, Applications in Interdisciplinary Communication*, Amsterdam, John Benjamins, 79–86.

Reese, Willis L.M. (ed.), 1962, *International Contracts: Choice of Law and Language*, New York, Oceana Publications.

Renis, Chiara, 2001, 'Periphrasis: The Most Suitable Translation Approach in Multilingual Legal Communication', *Proceedings of the Conference on Law and Language: Prospect and Retrospect*, Rovaniemi, The University of Lapland.

Revell, Donald L., 2004, 'Authoring Bilingual Laws: The Importance of Process', *Brooklyn Journal of International Law*, 29(3): 1085–1105.

Richards, I.A., 1953, 'Toward a Theory of Translating', in Arthur F. Wright (ed.), *Studies in Chinese Thought*, Chicago, University of Chicago Press, 247–262.

Risser, James, 1997, *Hermeneutics and the Voice of the Other: Re-Reading Gadamer's Philosophical Hermeneutics*, Albany, NY, State University of New York Press.

Roberts, David (ed.), 1995, *Reconstructing Theory: Gadamer, Habermas, Luhmann*, Melbourne, Melbourne University Press.

Roberts, Roda, 1987, 'Legal Translator and Legal Interpreter Training in Canada', *L'Actualite Terminologique/Terminology Update*, 20(6): 8–10.

Roberts, Roda, 1992, 'The Concept of Function of Translation and its Application to Literary Texts', *Target*, 41: 1–16.

Robinson, Douglas, 1997, *Western Translation Theory: from Herodotus to Nietzsche*, Manchester, St Jerome Publishing.

Robinson, Douglas, 2003, *Performative Linguistics: Speaking and Translating as Doing Things with Words*, New York/London, Routledge.

Robinson, William, 2005, 'How the European Commission Drafts Legislation in 20 Languages', *Clarity*, 53: 4–10.

Roebuck, Derek and Sin, King-Kui, 1993, 'The Ego and I and Ngo: Theoretical Problems in the Translation of the Common Law into Chinese', in R. Wacks (ed.), *China, Hong Kong and 1997: Essays in Legal Theory*, Hong Kong, Hong Kong University Press, 185–210.

Rosenne, Shabtai, 1971, 'On Multi-Lingual Interpretation', *Israel Law Review*, 6(3): 360–366.

Rosenne, Shabtai, 1983, 'The Meaning of "Authentic Text" in Modern Treaty Law', in R. Bernhardt, W.K.Geck, G. Jaenicke and H. Steinberger (eds), *Festschrift für Herrmann Mosler*, Berlin/New York, Springer, 759–784.

Sager, Juan C., 1990a, 'Professional Examinations for Professional Translators', *Babel*, 36(1): 58–61.

Sager, Juan C., 1990b, *A Practical Course in Terminology Processing*, Amsterdam/Philadelphia, John Benjamins Publishing Company.

Sager, Juan C., 1993, *Language Engineering and Translation: Consequences of Automation*, Amsterdam/Philadelphia, John Benjamins Publishing Company.

Sager, Juan C. and Kageura, Kyo, 1994–1995, 'Concept Classes and Conceptual Structures: Their Role and Necessity in Terminology', *Actes de langue francaises et de linguistique*, 7(8): 191–216.

Sager, Juan C. and Ndi-Kimbi, Augustin, 1995, 'The Conceptual Structure of Terminological Definitions and Their Linguistic Realisations: A Report on Research in Progress', *Terminology*, 2(1): 61–81.

Salmi-Tolonen, Tarja, 1994, 'The Linguistic Manifestations of Primary and Secondary Functions of Law in the National and Supranational Contexts', *International Journal for the Semiotics of Law*, 7(1): 13–39.

Salmi-Tolonen, Tarja, 2004, 'Legal Linguistic Knowledge and Creating and Interpreting Law in Multilingual Environments', *Brooklyn Journal of International Law*, 29(3): 1167–1191.

Samuelsson-Brown, Geoffrey, 2004, *A Practical Guide for Translators*, Clevedon, Multilingual Matters Ltd.

Sandrini, Peter, 1996, 'Comparative Analysis of Legal Terms: Equivalence Revisited', in C. Galinski and K.D. Schimitz (eds), *Terminology and Knowledge Engineering '96*, Frankfurt, Indeks, 342–351.

Sarcevic, Susan, 1985, 'Translation of Culture-bound Terms in Laws', *Multilingua*, 4(3): 127–133.

Sarcevic, Susan, 1989, 'Conceptual Dictionaries for Translation in the Field of Law', *International Journal of Lexicography*, 2(4): 277–293.

Sarcevic, Susan, 1991, 'Bilingual and Multilingual Legal Dictionaries: New Standards for the Future', *Meta*, 36(4): 615–626.

Sarcevic, Susan, 1994, 'Translation and the Law: An Interdisciplinary Approach', in M. Snell-Hornby, Fraz Bochlech and K. Kindle (eds), *Translation Studies: An Interdiscipline*, Amsterdam, John Benjamins, 301–307.

Sarcevic, Susan, 1997, *New Approach to Legal Translation*, The Hague, Kluwer Law International.

Sarcevic, Susan, 2000, 'Legal Translation and Translation Theory: A Receiver-oriented Approach', in *La Traduction juridique: Histoire, theorie(s) et pratique*, Geneve, Universite de Geneve, Ecole de Traduction et d'Interpretation /ASTTI, 329–347.

Scalia, A. 1997, *A Matter of Interpretation*, Princeton, NJ, Princeton University Press.

Schachter, Oscar, 1991, *International Law in Theory and Practice*, Dordrecht, M. Nijhoff Publishers.

Schäffner, Christina, 1989, 'An Account of Knowledge Use in Text Comprehension as a Basis for Frame-based Interference', in Heide Schmidt (ed.), *Interferenz in der Translation*, Leipzig, Verlag Enzyklopädie, 65–72.

Schäffner, Christina, 1991, 'World Knowledge in the Process of Translation', *Target*, 3(1): 1–16.

Schäffner, Christina (ed.), 1998a, *Translation and Norms*, Clevedon, Multilingual Matters.

Schäffner, Christina (ed.), 1998b, *Translation and Quality*, Clevedon, Multilingual Matters.

Schäffner, Christina (ed.), 2000, *Translation in the Global Village*, Clevedon, Multilingual Matters.

Schäffner, Christina and Adab, Beverley (eds), 2000, *Developing Translation Competence*, Amsterdam, John Benjamins.

Schäffner, Christina and Kelly-Holmes, Helen (eds), 1995, *Cultural Functions of Translation*, Clevedon, Multilingual Matters.

Schauer, Federick, 1987, 'Precedent', *Stanford Law Review*, 39: 571.

Schauer, Federick (ed.), 1993, *Law and Language*, Aldershot, Dartmouth.

Scheffler, Israel, 1979, *Beyond the Letter: A Philosophical Inquiry into Ambiguity, Vagueness and Metaphor in Language*, London, Routledge & Kegan Paul.

Schroth, Peter W., 1986, 'Legal Translation', *American Journal of Comparative Law*, 34: 47–65.

Schulte, R. and Biguenet, John (eds), 1992, *Theories of Translation: An Anthology of Essays from Dryden to Derrida*, Chicago, University of Chicago Press.

Schwab, Wallace, 2002, 'A Quebec-Canada Constitutional Law Lexicon (French to English)', *Meta*, 47(2): 279–288.

Searle, John R., 1969, *Speech Acts: An Essay in the Philosophy of Language*, Cambridge, Cambridge University Press.

Searle, John R., 1976, 'A Taxonomy of Illocutionary Acts', *Language in Society*, 5: 1–25.

Searle, John R., 1979, *Expression and Meaning: Essays in the Theory of Speech Acts*, Cambridge, Cambridge University Press.

Searle, John R., 1998, *Mind, Language and Society: Philosophy in the Real World*, New York, Basic Books.

Searle, John R. and Vanderveken, Daniel, 1985, *Foundations of Illocutionary Logic*, Cambridge, Cambridge University Press.

Searle, John R., Kiefer, Ferenc and Bierwisch, Mandred (eds), 1980, *Speech Act Theory and Pragmatics*, Dordrecht/London/Boston, D. Reidel Publishing Company.

Sebeok, Thomas A. (ed.), 1978, *Sight, Sound, and Sense*, Bloomington, IN, Indiana University Press.

Seymour, Edward, 2002, 'A Common EU Language', *Perspectives: Studies in Translatology*, 10(1): 7–14.

Sin, King-Kui, 1989, 'Meaning, Translation and Bilingual Legislation', in P. Pupier and J. Woehrling (eds), *Proceedings of the 1st International on Language and Law*, Montreal, Wilson and Lafleur, 509–515.

Sin, King-Kui and Roebuck, D., 1996, 'Language Engineering for Legal Transplantation: Conceptual Problems in Creating Common Law Chinese', *Language & Communication*, 16(3): 235–254.

Sin, King-Kui and Kit, Chunyu, 2004, 'Clause Alignment for Hong Kong Legal Texts: A Lexical-based Approach', *International Journal of Corpus Linguistics*, 9(1): 29–51.

Slaughter, A.M., Sweet, A.S. and Weiler, J.H.H. (eds), 1998, *The European Court and National Courts – Doctrine and Jurisprudence: Legal Change in its Social Context*, Oxford, Hart Publishing.

Smith, Sylvia A. 1995, 'Cultural Clash: Anglo-American Case Law and German Civil Law in Translation', in Marshall Morris (ed.), *Translation and the Law*, Amsterdam, John Benjamins, 179–200.

Snell-Hornby, Mary, 1988, *Translation Studies: An Integrated Approach*, Amsterdam, John Benjamins.

Snell-Hornby, Mary, Jettmarová, Z. and Kaindl, K. (eds), 1997, *Translation as Intercultural Communication: Selected Papers from the EST Congress – Prague 1995*, Amsterdam, John Benjamins.

Snell-Hornby, Mary, Pohl, Esther and Bennani, Benjamin (eds), 1988, *Translation and Lexicography*, Amsterdam, John Benjamins.

Snow, Gérard, 2002, 'Le *use* de la *common law*: étude terminologique', *Meta*, 47(2): 186–197.

Solan, Lawrence, 1993, *The Language of Judges*, Chicago, The University of Chicago Press.

Solan, Lawrence, 2001a, 'Ordinary Meaning in Legal Interpretation', *Proceedings of the Conference on Law and Language: Prospect and Retrospect*, Rovaniemi, The University of Lapland.

Solan, Lawrence, 2001b, 'Why Laws Work Pretty Well, but not Great: Words and Rules in Legal Interpretation', *Law & Social Inquiry*, 26: 243–270.

Solan, Lawrence, 2004, 'Pernicious Ambiguity in Contracts and Statutes', *Chicago-Kent Law Review*, 79: 859–888.

Solan, Lawrence and Tiersma, Peter, 2005, *Speaking of Crime: Language of Criminal Justice*, Chicago, University of Chicago Press.

Somers, Harold (ed.), 1996, *Terminology, LSP and Translation: Studies in Language Engineering in Honour of Juan C. Sager*, Amsterdam, John Benjamins.

Sparer, Michel, 2002, 'Peut-on faire de la traduction juridique? Comment doit-on l'enseigner?' *Meta*, 47(2): 265–278.

Sprung, Robert C. and Jaroniec, Simone (eds), 2000, *Translating into Success: Cutting-edge Strategies for Going Multilingual in a Global Age*, Amsterdam, John Benjamins.

Steiner, George, 1998, *After Babel: Aspects of Language and Translation*, 3rd edition, London, Oxford University Press.

Stolze, Radegundis, 2001, 'Translating Legal Texts in the European Union', *Perspectives: Studies in Translatology*, 9(4): 301–311.

Stone, Christopher D. 1981, 'From a Language Perspective', *The Yale Law Journal*, 90: 1149–1192.

Sullivan, Ruth, 2002, *Sullivan and Driedger on the Construction of Statutes*, 4th edition, Toronto, Butterworths.

Sullivan, Ruth, 2004, 'The Challenges of Interpreting Multilingual, Multijural Legislation', *Brooklyn Journal of International Law*, 29(3): 985–1066.

Tabory, Mala, 1980, *Multilingualism in International Law and Institutions*, New York, Sijthoff & Noordhoff.

Taes, Andreas, 2001, 'Introducing CAT in the European Commission's Translation Service', http://ec.europa.eu/translation/reading/articles/tools_and_workflow _en.htm#cat

Tetley, William, 2000, 'Mixed Jurisdictions: Common Law vs Civil Law (Codified and Uncodified)', *Louisana Law Review*, 60: 677–738.

Tetley, William, 2003–2004, 'Nationalism in a Mixed Jurisdiction and the Importance of Language (South Africa, Israel, and Quebec/Canada)', *Tulane Law Review*, 78: 175–218.

Tiersma, Peter Meijes, 1986, 'The Language of Offer and Acceptance: Speech Acts and the Question of Intent', *California Law Review*, 74(1): 189–232.

Tiersma, Peter Meijes, 1999, *Legal Language*, Chicago, Chicago University Press.

Tosi, Arturo (ed.), 2003, *Crossing Barriers and Bridging Cultures: The Challenges of Multilingual Translation for the European Union*, Clevedon, Multilingual Matters.

Toury, Gideon, 1978, 'The Nature and Role of Norms in Literary Translation', in J. Holmes, J. Lambert and R. van den Broeck (eds), *Literature and Translation: New Perspectives in Literary Studies*, Leuven, Acco, 83–100.

Toury, Gideon, 1980, *In Search of a Theory of Translation*, Tel Aviv, The Porter Institute for Poetics and Semiotics.

Toury, Gideon, 1986, 'Translation: A Cultural-semiotic Perspective', in Thomas A. Sebeok (ed.), *Encyclopaedic Dictionary of Semiotics*, Berlin, Mouton de Gruyter, 2: 1111–1124.

Toury, Gideon, 1995, *Descriptive Translation Studies and Beyond*, Amsterdam, John Benjamins.

Translation Centre for the Bodies of the European Union, 2003, *Écrire pour être traduit/Writing for Translation*, Luxembourg, Centre de traduction des organes de l'Union européenne/Translation Centre for the Bodies of the European Union.

Treaty Secretariat, Department of Foreign Affairs and Trade, 2004, *Signed, Sealed and Delivered: Treaties and Treaty Making: An Officials' Handbook*, Canberra, Department of Foreign Affairs and Trade.

Trosborg, Anna, 1994, 'Acts in Contracts: Some Guidelines for Translation', in Mary Snell-Hornby, Franz Pochhacker and Claus Kaindle (eds), *Translation Studies: An Interdiscipline*, Amsterdam, John Benjamins, 309–318.

Trosborg, Anna (ed.), 1997, *Text Typology and Translation*, Amsterdam, John Benjamins.

Trosborg, Anna (ed.), 2000, *Analysing Professional Genres*, Amsterdam, John Benjamins.

Tucker, Anne, 2003, 'Translation and Computerisation at the EU Parliament', in Arturo Tosi (ed.), *Crossing Barriers and Bridging Cultures: The Challenges of Multilingual Translation for the European Union*, Clevedon, Multilingual Matters, 73–87.

Turnbull, I., 1997, 'Legislative Drafting in Plain Language and Statements of General Principle', *Statute Law Review*, 18(1): 21–31.

Tymoczko, Maria and Gentzler, Edwin (ed.), 2002, *Translation and Power*, Amherst, MA, University of Massachusetts Press.

United Nations, 1999, *United Nations Treaty Collection: Treaty Reference Guide*, New York, United Nations Publication.

United Nations, 2003, *Final Clauses of Multilateral Treaties Handbook*, New York, United Nations Publication.

Urban, Nikolaus, 2000, 'One Legal Language and the Maintenance of Cultural and Linguistic Diversity?', *European Review of Private Law*, 8(1): 51–57.

Vanderveken, Daniel, Kubo, Susumu (eds), 2001, *Essays in Speech Act Theory*, Amsterdam, John Benjamins.

Van Hecke, Georges A., 1962, 'A Civilian Looks at the Common-Law Lawyer', in Willis L.M. Reese (ed.), *International Contracts: Choice of Law and Language*, New York, Oceana Publications.

Van Leuven-Zwart, Kitty M., 1989, 'Translation and Original: Similarities and Dissimilarities', Part One, *Target*, 1(2): 151–181.

Van Leuven-Zwart, Kitty M., 1990, 'Translation and Original: Similarities and Dissimilarities', Part Two, *Target*, 2 (1): 69–95.

Varó, Enrique Alcaraz and Hughes, Brian, 2002, *Legal Translation Explained*, Manchester, St Jerome Publishing.

Venuti, Lawrence, 1995, *The Translator's Invisibility: A History of Translation*, London/New York, Routledge.

Venuti, Lawrence, 1998, *The Scandals of Translation: Towards an Ethics of Difference*, London/New York, Routledge.

Venuti, Lawrence (ed.), 2005, *The Translation Studies Reader*, London/New York, Routledge.

Vermeer, Hans, 1996, *A Skopos Theory of Translation*, Heidelberg, TEXTconTEXT.

Vermeer, Hans, 1998, 'Starting to Unask What Translatology is About', *Target*, 10(1): 41–68.

Vranken, Martin, 1997, *Fundamentals of European Civil Law*, Sydney, The Federation Press.

Wagner, Anne, 2002, *La langue de la Common Law*, Paris, L'Harmattan.

Wagner, Anne, 2003, 'Translation of the Language of the Common Law into Legal French: Myth or Reality', *International Journal for the Semiotics of Law*, 16(2): 177–193.

Wagner, Emma, 2005, 'Producing Multilingual Legislation in Switzerland', *Clarity*, 53: 18–20.

Wagner, Emma, undated, *Fight the FOG: Write Clearly*, http://europa.eu.int/comm/translation/en/ftfog/

Wagner, Emma, Bech, Svend, and Martinez, Jesus M. (eds), 2002, *Translating for the European Union Institutions*, Manchester, St Jerome Publishing.

Waismann, Friedrich, 1968, 'Verifiability', in Antony Flew (ed.), *Logic and Language*, Oxford, Basil Blackwell, 117–144.

Waldron, Jeremy, 1994, 'Vagueness in Law and Language: Some Philosophical Issues', *California Law Review*, 82(3): 509–540.

Watson, Alan, 1974, *Legal Transplant, An Approach to Comparative Law*, Edinburgh, Scottish Academic Press.

Watson-Brown, A., 1997, 'The Classification and Arrangement of the Elements of Legislation', *Statute Law Review*, 18(1): 32–45.

Weisflog, W.E., 1987, 'Problems of Legal Translation', Swiss Reports presented at the *XIIth International Congress of Comparative Law*, Zürich, Schulthess, 179–218.

Wellington, Louise Maguire, undated, 'Bijuralism in Canada: Harmonisation Methodology and Terminology', http://www.canada.justice.gc.ca/en/dept/pub/hfl/

Weston, Martin, 1983, 'Problems and Principles in Legal Translation', *The Incorporate Linguist*, 22(4): 207–211.

Weston, Martin, 1991, *An English Reader's Guide to the French Legal System*, Oxford, Berg.

Wheaton, Henry, 1836/1878, edited by A.C. Boyd, *Elements of International Law*, London, Stevens and Sons.

White, James Boyd, 1982, 'Law as Language: Reading Law and Reading Literature', *Texas Law Review*, 60: 415–445.

Whorf, Benjamin Lee, 1956, *Language, Thought and Reality: Selected Writings of Benjamin Lee Whorf*, edited by John B. Carroll, Cambridge, MA, The MIT Press.

Williams, Glanville, 1946, 'Language and the Law', *Law Quarterly Review*, 61: 71–86, 179–195, 293–303, 384–406, and 62: 387–406.

Williams, Raymond, 1976, *Keywords: A Vocabulary of Culture and Society*, London, Fontana.

Wilson, Barry, 2003, 'The Multilingual Translation Service in the EU Parliament', in Arturo Tosi (ed.), *Crossing Barriers and Bridging Cultures: The Challenges of Multilingual Translation for the European Union*, Clevedon, Multilingual Matters, 1–7.

Wilss, Wolfram, 1989, 'Towards a Multi-facet Concept of Translation Behaviour', *Target*, 1(2): 129–149.

Wilss, Wolfram, 1982, *Science of Translation: Problems and Methods*, Tübingen, Verlag Gunter Narr.

Wilss, Wolfram (ed.), 1984, *Translation Theory and its Implication*, Tübingen, Gunter Narr.

Wilss, Wolfram, 1990, 'Cognitive Aspects of the Translation Process', *Language & Communication*, 10(1): 19–36.

Wilss, Wolfram, 1996a, *Knowledge and Skills in Translator Behaviour*, Amsterdam, John Benjamins.

Wilss, Wolfram, 1996b, 'Translation as Intelligent Behaviour', in Harold Somers (ed.), *Terminology, LSP and Translation: Studies in Language Engineering in Honour of Juan C. Sager*, Amsterdam, John Benjamins, 161–168.

Wilss, Wolfram and Gisela, Thome (eds), 1984, *Translation Theory and Its Implementation in the Teaching of Translating and Interpreting*, Tübingen, Verlag Gunter Narr.

Wittgenstein, Ludwig, 1961, *Tractatus Logico-Philosophicus*, translated by D.F. Pears and B.F. McGuinnes, London, Routledge & Kegan Paul.

Wittgenstein, Ludwig, 1997, *Philosophical Investigations*, 2nd edition, translated by G.E.M. Anscombe , Oxford, Blackwell Publishers.

Wright, David, 2001, 'Yan Fu and the Tasks of the Translator', in Michael Lackner, Iwo Amelung and Joachim Kurtz (eds), *New Terms for New Ideas: Western Knowledge and Lexical Change in Late Imperial China*, Leiden/Boston/Koln, Brill, 235–256.

Wright, Sue Ellen and Wright, Leland D. Jr (eds), 1993, *Scientific and Technical Translation*, Amsterdam, John Benjamins.

Wydick, Richard, 1998, *Plain English for Lawyers*, Durham, NC, Carolina Academic Press.

Yan, Fu, 1913/1981, *Fayi (De l'esprit de lois by Montesquieu)*, Beijing, Commercial Press.

Zethsen, Karen Korning, 2004, 'Latin-based Terms: True or False Friends?' *Target*, 16(1): 125–142.

Zweigert, Konrad and Kötz, Hein, 1992, *An Introduction to Comparative Law*, translated from the German by Tony Weir, Oxford, Clarendon Press.

Index